Get the eBook FREE!

(PDF, ePub, Kindle, and liveBook all included)

We believe that once you buy a book from us, you should be able to read it in any format we have available. To get electronic versions of this book at no additional cost to you, purchase and then register this book at the Manning website.

Go to https://www.manning.com/freebook and follow the instructions to complete your pBook registration.

That's it!
Thanks from Manning!

Praise for the first edition

The best microservices in .Net reference I have read so far.

—Julien Pohie, Senior Software Developer, Thoughtworks

This book lays out all the necessary details to design new solutions with microservices; it has material to transform your existing monolithic, tiered, service-oriented architectures.

—Karthikeyarajan Rajendran, Architect, McAfee

Detailed analysis on how to use microservices in the .Net world with a good set of real-world examples.

—Raushan Jha, SDE 2, Microsoft IDC

Microservices in .Net *provides the knowledge to start working in a professional environment to develop real industry microservices, with the perfect tuning to be cost effective.*

—Daniel Vasquez, Senior Developer, Tokiota

If you're building SaaS products, you will eventually realize that agility in product delivery is important. This book provides a detailed understanding of how microservices can enable your .Net applications to be resilient in production.

—Adhir Ramjiawan, Software Developer, Dotdigital

A well-written, concise, and comprehensive book covering important topics surrounding microservices. I could not put it down and would definitely recommend it.

—Tanya Wilke, Web Application Developer, Sanlam

Microservices in .NET

SECOND EDITION

CHRISTIAN HORSDAL GAMMELGAARD

MANNING
SHELTER ISLAND

For online information and ordering of this and other Manning books, please visit www.manning.com. The publisher offers discounts on this book when ordered in quantity. For more information, please contact

    Special Sales Department
    Manning Publications Co.
    20 Baldwin Road
    PO Box 761
    Shelter Island, NY 11964
    Email: orders@manning.com

Manning Publications Co.
20 Baldwin Road
PO Box 761
Shelter Island, NY 11964

Development editor:	Helen Stergius
Technical development editor:	Michael Lund
Review editor:	Mihaela Batinić
Production editor:	Deirdre S. Hiam
Copy editor:	Michele Mitchell
Proofreader:	Keri Hales
Technical proofreader:	Karsten Strøbæk
Typesetter and cover designer:	Marija Tudor

ISBN 9781617297922
Printed in the United States of America

brief contents

contents

        What belongs in middleware?   256

11.6 Writing middleware   257
        Middleware as lambdas   257 ▪ Middleware classes   258

11.7 Testing middleware and pipelines   259

PART 4   BUILDING APPLICATIONS 263

12 Creating applications over microservices   265

12.1 End user applications for microservice systems:
        One or many applications?   266
        *General-purpose applications   266 ▪ Specialized
        applications   267*

12.2 Patterns for building applications over microservices   268
        *Composite applications: Integrating at the frontend   268 ▪ API
        Gateway   271 ▪ Backend for frontend (BFF) pattern   273
        When to use each pattern   274 ▪ Client-side or server-side
        rendering?   275*

12.3 Example: A shopping cart and a product list   276
        *Creating an API Gateway   279 ▪ Creating the product list
        GUI   281 ▪ Creating the shopping cart GUI   286 ▪ Letting users
        add products to the shopping cart   289 ▪ Letting users remove
        products from the shopping cart   290*

appendix   *Development environment setup   293*

        further reading   299

        index   301

preface

When I first talked to Manning about writing a book, we discussed a book about Nancy. Part of me was excited to write about Nancy again, because it was an awesome web framework, but my first book was also about Nancy, and a different part of me wanted this book to be something more. After some contemplation and some back and forth with Manning, it became clear that I wanted to write about *microservices*; I wanted to write a book that was more about designing and implementing microservices than about any specific technology, while at the same time showcasing some great, lightweight .NET technologies. That became the first edition of this book.

Since then, the technology landscape has moved on: development of Nancy has stopped and .NET Core (which was nascent when the first edition was written) has incorporated many useful ideas from community projects and changed its name to .NET. At the same time, microservices have become even more widespread, and most of the design and architecture advice from the first edition still holds up. I felt the first edition still has a lot to offer, but I also felt it needed a technology update. That's the book you're about to read, and I hope you'll not only learn how to be successful with microservices, but also learn the value of simplicity.

acknowledgments

Writing a book takes time—a lot of time. So the first thank you is to my wife, Jane Horsdal Gammelgaard, for supporting me all the way through. You're awesome, Jane.

I would like to thank my editor on the second edition, Helen Stergius, whose patience through many missed deadlines, advice, and guidance made this edition possible. I'd also like to thank the editor on the first edition, Dan Maharry, who pushed me to write a much better book than I thought I could at the time. A big thank you also goes to my technical editor, Michael Lund, for his thorough code reviews and suggestions for improvements, and for ripping apart my line of reasoning whenever it wasn't clear. A special thanks to Karsten Strøbæk for his in-depth technical proofreading.

I can't thank enough the amazing group of technical peer reviewers: Adhir Ramjiawan, Allan Makura, Alper Silistre, Daniel Vasquez, David Paccoud, Dennis Hayes, Edin Kapic, Emanuele Origgi, Ernesto Cardenas Cangahuala, George Onofrei, Jeff Smith, Johnathan Sewell, Juan Luis Barreda, Julien Pohie, Justin Coulston, Kalyan Chanumolu, Karthikeyarajan Rajendran, Matt Ferderer, Mike Burgess, Mike Manuel, Oliver Korten, Raushan Jha, Raymond Cheung, Ricardo Peres, Richard B. Ward, Sau Fai Fong, Simon Seyag, Stefan Turalsk, Sumit K Singh, Tanya Wilke, Thomas Overby Hansen, Unnikrishnan Kumar, Viorel-Marian Moisei, and Wayne Mather. They suggested topics and other ways of presenting topics and caught typos and mistakes in code and terminology. Each pass through the review process and each piece of feedback provided through the forum discussions helped shape the book.

Finally, I want to thank the people at Manning who made this book possible: publisher Marjan Bace, acquisitions editor Eleonor Gardner, production editor Deirdre Hiam, copyeditor Michele Mitchell, page proofer Keri Hales, and everyone else on the editorial and production teams.

about this book

Microservices in .NET is a practical introduction to writing microservices in .NET using powerful yet easy-to-use technologies, like the simple MVC controllers and middleware. I've tried to present the material in a way that will enable you to use what you learn right away. To that end, I've tried to tell you why I build things the way I do, as well as show you exactly how to build them.

Who should read this book

Microservices in .NET has 12 chapters spread across four parts.

Part 1 gives a quick introduction to microservices, answering what they are and why they're interesting. This part also introduces ASP.NET, MVC, middleware, and Kubernetes, the main technologies used throughout the book.

- Chapter 1 introduces microservices—what they are and why they matter. It introduces the six characteristics of microservices that I use to guide the design and implementation of them. At the end of the chapter, we say hello to ASP.NET and MVC.
- Chapter 2 is a comprehensive example of coding a microservice using ASP.NET, along with the Polly library. At the end of the chapter, we have a complete, albeit simple, microservice.
- Chapter 3 gives a quick introduction to containerizing ASP.NET microservices and deploying them to Kubernetes—both locally and in the Azure cloud.

Part 2 covers how to split a system into microservices and how to implement functionality in a system of microservices.

- Chapter 4 covers how to identify microservices and decide what to put into each. This chapter is about the design of a system of microservices as a whole.

- Chapter 5 shows how to design and implement the collaboration between microservices. This chapter discusses the different ways microservices can collaborate and shows how to implement those collaborations.
- Chapter 6 discusses where data should be stored in a system of microservices and how some of the data may be replicated across several microservices.
- Chapter 7 explains and demonstrates the implementation of some important techniques for making microservice systems robust.
- Chapter 8 takes a thorough look at testing a microservice system, including testing the complete system, testing each microservice, and testing the code inside the microservices.

Part 3 shows how to speed up development of new microservices by building a solid microservice platform leveraging features of ASP.NET and Kubernetes, tailored toward the needs of your particular system. Such a platform provides implementation of many important concerns that cut across the entire system of microservices, such as logging, monitoring, and security. In this part, you'll build such a platform and see how it's used to create new microservices quickly.

- Chapter 9 explains the importance of monitoring and logging in a microservice system and shows how to leverage ASP.NET and Kubernetes to implement consistent logging, tracing, and monitoring across all your microservices.
- Chapter 10 discusses the highly distributed nature of a microservice system, which poses some security concerns. As an example, I'll also walk you through using Kubernetes to secure the collaboration between microservices.
- Chapter 11 builds on top of chapters 9 and 10 to create a microservice platform by taking code from the previous chapters and packaging it in NuGet packages ready to be shared across microservices. The chapter includes an introduction to middleware, as well as an example of creating a new microservice using the platform.

Part 4 consists of chapter 12, which rounds off the book with some approaches to creating end-user applications for a microservices system. The chapter also shows how to build a small application on top of some of the microservices from earlier chapters.

Together, the 12 chapters will teach you how to design and code microservices using a lightweight, no-nonsense, .NET-based technology stack.

About the code

Most chapters in this book have sample code. All of this can be found in the download for this book on Manning's site at https://www.manning.com/books/microservices -in-net-second-edition, or in the Git repository at https://github.com/horsdal/micro services-in-dotnet-book-second-edition. The code is based on .NET 5, so you need to install .NET, the dotnet command-line tool, and a suitable IDE. You can find information on how to set these up in the appendix.

In the GitHub repository (https://github.com/horsdal/microservices-in-dotnet
-book-second-edition), the main branch contains the code as it appears in the book. I
may add additional branches that show updated or alternative implementations of the
examples, but the main branch will remain the same.

This book contains many examples of source code both in numbered listings and
in line with normal text. In both cases, source code is formatted in a `fixed-width`
`font like this` to separate it from ordinary text. Sometimes code is also **in bold** to
highlight code that has changed from previous steps in the chapter, such as when a
new feature adds to an existing line of code.

In many cases, the original source code has been reformatted; we've added line
breaks and reworked indentation to accommodate the available page space in the
book. In rare cases, even this was not enough, and listings include line-continuation
markers (➥). Additionally, comments in the source code have often been removed
from the listings when the code is described in the text. Code annotations accompany
many of the listings, highlighting important concepts.

liveBook discussion forum

Purchase of *Microservices in .NET* includes free access to a private web forum run by
Manning Publications where you can make comments about the book, ask technical
questions, and receive help from the author and from other users. To access the
forum, go to https://livebook.manning.com/#!/book/microservices-in-net-second-
edition/discussion. You can also learn more about Manning's forums and the rules of
conduct at https://livebook.manning.com/#!/discussion.

Manning's commitment to our readers is to provide a venue where a meaningful
dialogue between individual readers and between readers and the author can take
place. It is not a commitment to any specific amount of participation on the part of
the author, whose contribution to the forum remains voluntary (and unpaid). We sug-
gest you try asking the author some challenging questions lest his interest stray! The
forum and the archives of previous discussions will be accessible from the publisher's
website as long as the book is in print.

about the author

CHRISTIAN HORSDAL GAMMELGAARD is an independent consultant and trainer with many years of experience building web and distributed systems on .NET as well as other platforms. He is an experienced solution architect and domain-driven design practitioner. Christian is always trying to learn more about building software systems well and tries to share what he learns in blogs, on Twitter, speaking at conferences, and occasionally contributing to open source.

about the cover illustration

The figure on the cover of *Microservices in .NET* is captioned "Emperor of China in his Robes, in 1700." The illustration is taken from publisher Thomas Jefferys' *A Collection of the Dresses of Different Nations, Ancient and Modern* (four volumes), London, published between 1757 and 1772. The title page states that these are hand-colored copperplate engravings, heightened with gum Arabic. Thomas Jefferys (1719–1771) was called "Geographer to King George III." He was an English cartographer who was the leading map supplier of his day. He engraved and printed maps for government and other official bodies and produced a wide range of commercial maps and atlases, especially of North America. His work as a mapmaker sparked an interest in local dress customs of the lands he surveyed and mapped, which are brilliantly displayed in this collection.

Fascination with faraway lands and travel for pleasure were relatively new phenomena in the late 18th century, and collections such as this one were popular, introducing both the tourist as well as the armchair traveler to the inhabitants of other countries. The diversity of the drawings in Jefferys' volumes speaks vividly of the uniqueness and individuality of the world's nations some 200 years ago. Dress codes have changed since then and the diversity by region and country, so rich at the time, has faded away. It is now often hard to tell the inhabitant of one continent from another. Perhaps, trying to view it optimistically, we have traded a cultural and visual diversity for a more varied personal life—or a more varied and interesting intellectual and technical life.

At a time when it is hard to tell one computer book from another, Manning celebrates the inventiveness and initiative of the computer business with book covers based on the rich diversity of regional life of two centuries ago, brought back to life by Jeffreys' pictures.

Part 1

Getting started with microservices

This first part explains what microservices are and why you should care. I'll begin by discussing six characteristics you can use to recognize and guide your design of microservices. Along the way, we'll look at the benefits and costs of microservices.

Toward the end of chapter 1, I'll give you a whirlwind tour of the technology stack used throughout the book; the stack consists of .NET, ASP.NET, and the ASP.NET MVC web framework. Chapter 2 moves on to an example of building your first microservice. You'll see how little is needed to get started, and begin to see ASP.NETs strength. Chapter 3 shows how to containerize the microservice from chapter 2 and how to deploy it to Kubernetes in Azure.

By the end of part 1, you will have your first microservice running in the cloud.

Microservices at a glance

1

In this chapter, I'll explain what microservices are and demonstrate why they're interesting. We'll also look at the six characteristics of a microservice. Finally, I'll introduce you to the most important technologies we'll use in this book: ASP.NET and ASP.NET MVC.

1.1 What is a microservice?

A *microservice* is a service with one, and only one, very narrowly focused capability that a remote API exposes to the rest of the system. For example, think of a system for managing a warehouse. If you broke down its capabilities, you might come up with the following list:

- Receive stock arriving at the warehouse.
- Determine where new stock should be stored.
- Calculate placement routes inside the warehouse for putting stock into the right storage units.
- Assign placement routes to warehouse employees.
- Receive orders.
- Calculate pick routes in the warehouse for a set of orders.
- Assign pick routes to warehouse employees.

Let's consider how the first of these capabilities—receive stock arriving at the warehouse—would be implemented as a microservice. We'll call it the *Receive Stock microservice.*

1 A request to receive and log new stock arrives over HTTP. This might come from another microservice or perhaps from a web page that a foreman uses to register stock arrivals. The responsibility of Receive Stock microservice is to handle such requests by validating the request and correctly registering the new stock in a data store.

2 A response is sent back from the Receive Stock microservice to acknowledge that the stock has been received.

Figure 1.1 shows the Receive Stock microservice receiving a request from another collaborating microservice.

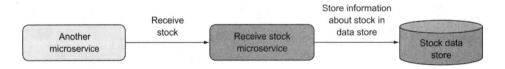

Figure 1.1   The Receive Stock microservice exposes an API for use when new stock arrives. Other microservices can call that API, as indicated by the arrow. The Receive Stock microservice is responsible for registering all received stock in a data store.

Each capability in the system, no matter how small, is implemented as an individual microservice. Every microservice in a system

- Runs in its own separate process
- Can be deployed on its own, independently of the other microservices
- Has its own dedicated data store
- Collaborates with other microservices to complete its own action

It's also important to note that a microservice doesn't need to be written in the same programming language (C#, Java, Erlang, Javascript, etc.) as the one it collaborates with. They just need to know how to communicate with each other. Some may communicate via queues, a service bus, gRPC, or GraphQL, for instance, depending on system requirements; but often, microservices do communicate over HTTP.

NOTE This book focuses on implementing microservices in .NET using C# and ASP.NET. The microservices I'll show you are small, tightly focused ASP.NET applications that collaborate over HTTP.

NOTE This book focuses on collaboration over HTTP, but the principles guiding how the collaboration is designed are not specific to HTTP. I choose to use HTTP because it is ubiquitous and familiar to many developers and I want to focus more on the design principles than the technology. These principles also apply with different technology, notably gRPC, which is gaining in popularity in the .NET space and is also a good choice.

1.2 What is a microservices architecture?

This book focuses on designing and implementing individual microservices, but it's worth noting that the term *microservices* can also be used to describe an *architectural style* for an entire system consisting of many microservices. Microservices as an architectural style is a lightweight form of service-oriented architecture (SOA) where the services are each tightly focused on doing one thing and doing it well. A system with a microservices architecture is a distributed system with a (probably large) number of collaborating microservices.

The microservices architectural style has been quickly gaining in popularity for building and maintaining complex server-side software systems. And understandably so: microservices offer a number of potential benefits over both more traditional service-oriented approaches and monolithic architectures. Microservices, when done well, are malleable, scalable, and robust, and they allow for systems that do well on all four of the key metrics identified by Nicole Forsgren et al., Accelerate[1] and the DORA state of DevOps reports,[2] namely

1. Deployment frequency
2. Lead time for changes
3. Time to restore service
4. Change failure rate

This combination often proves elusive for complex software systems. Furthermore, it is, as documented by Forsgren et al., a reliable predictor of software delivery performance.

In this book you will learn how to design and implement malleable, scalable, and robust microservices that form systems that deliver on all four of these key metrics.

---

[1] Nicole Forsgren, Gene Kim, and Jez Humble. *Accelerate*. IT Revolution Press: 2018.
[2] Nicole Forsgren, Dustin Smith, Jez Humble, and Jessie Frazelle, "Accelerate: State of DevOps 2018," https://inthecloud.withgoogle.com/state-of-devops-18/dl-cd.html.

1.2.1   *Microservice characteristics*

I've said that a microservice is "a service with a very narrowly focused capability," but what exactly does that mean? Well, there's not a broadly accepted definition in the industry of precisely what a microservice is.[3] We can, however, look at what generally characterizes a microservice. I've found there to be six core microservice characteristics:

- A microservice is responsible for a single capability.
- A microservice is individually deployable.
- A microservice consists of one or more processes.
- A microservice owns its own data store.
- A small team can maintain a few handfuls of microservices.
- A microservice is replaceable.

This list of characteristics should help you recognize a well-formed microservice when you see one, and it will also help you scope and implement your own microservices. By incorporating these characteristics, you'll be on your way to getting the best from your microservices and producing a malleable, scalable, and robust system as a result. Throughout this book, I'll show how these characteristics should drive the design of your microservices and how to write the code that a microservice needs to fulfill them. Now, let's look briefly at each characteristic in turn.

RESPONSIBLE FOR A SINGLE CAPABILITY

A microservice is responsible for one and only one capability in the overall system. We can break this statement into two parts:

- A microservice has a single responsibility.
- That responsibility is for a capability.

The single responsibility principle has been stated in several ways. One traditional form is, "A class should have only one reason to change."[4] Although this way of putting it specifically mentions a *class*, the principle turns out to apply beyond the context of a class in an object-oriented language. With microservices, we apply the single responsibility principle at the service level.

Another, newer, way of stating the single responsibility principle, also from Robert C. Martin, is as follows: "Gather together the things that change for the same reasons. Separate those things that change for different reasons."[5] This way of stating the principle applies to microservices: a microservice should implement exactly one capability. That way, it will have to change only when there's a change to that capability. Furthermore, you should strive to have the microservice fully implement the capability so that only one microservice has to change when the capability is changed.

---

[3] For further discussion of what characterizes microservices, I recommend this article on the subject: Martin Fowler and James Lewis, "Microservices: A Definition of This New Architectural Term," March 25, 2014, http://martinfowler.com/articles/microservices.html.

[4] Robert C. Martin, "SRP: The Single Responsibility Principle," http://mng.bz/zQyz.

[5] Robert C. Martin, "The Single Responsibility Principle," May 8, 2014, http://mng.bz/RZgU.

There are two types of capabilities in a microservice system:

- A *business capability* is something the system does that contributes to the purpose of the system, like keeping track of users' shopping carts or calculating prices. A good way to tease apart a system's separate business capabilities is to use domain-driven design.
- A *technical capability* is one that several other microservices need to use—integration to some third-party system, for instance. Technical capabilities aren't the main drivers for breaking down a system to microservices; they're only identified when you find several business-capability microservices that need the same technical capability.

NOTE Defining the scope and responsibility of a microservice will be covered in chapter 4.

INDIVIDUALLY DEPLOYABLE

A microservice should be *individually deployable.* When you change a particular microservice, you should be able to deploy it to the production environment without deploying (or touching) any other part of your system. The other microservices in the system should continue running and working during the deployment of the changed microservice and continue running once the new version is deployed.

Consider an e-commerce site. Whenever a change is made to the shopping cart microservice, you should be able to deploy just that microservice, as illustrated in figure 1.2. Meanwhile, the price calculation, recommendation, and product catalog microservices, and others, should continue working and serving user requests.

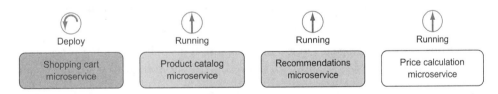

Figure 1.2   Other microservices continue to run while the shopping cart microservice is being deployed.

Being able to deploy each microservice individually is important because in a microservice system there are many microservices, and each may collaborate with several others. At the same time, development work is done on some or all of the microservices in parallel. If you had to deploy all or groups of them in lockstep, managing the deployments would quickly become unwieldy, typically resulting in infrequent and big, risky deployments. This is something you should avoid. Instead, you want to be able to deploy small changes to each microservice frequently, resulting in small, low-risk deployments.

To be able to deploy a single microservice while the rest of the system continues to function, the build process should be set up with the following in mind:

- Each microservice should be built into separate artifacts (e.g., separate Docker containers).
- The deployment process should also be set up to support deploying microservices individually while other microservices continue running. For instance, you might use a rolling deployment process where the microservice is deployed to one server at a time in order to reduce downtime. Kubernetes—as well as other orchestration technologies—supports this and other useful deployment patterns.

The fact that you want to deploy microservices individually affects the way they interact. Changes to a microservice's interface usually must be backward compatible so that other existing microservices can continue to collaborate with the new version the same way they did with the old. Furthermore, the way microservices interact must be robust in the sense that each must expect other services to fail once in a while and continue working as best it can. One microservice failing—for instance, due to downtime during deployment—must not result in other microservices failing, only in reduced functionality or slightly longer processing time.

> **NOTE**   Microservice collaboration and robustness will be covered in chapters 4, 5, and 7.

CONSISTS OF ONE OR MORE PROCESSES

A microservice must run in a separate process, or in separate processes, if it's to remain as independent as possible of other microservices in the same system. The same is true if a microservice is to remain individually deployable. This can be summarized in two points:

- Each microservice must run in separate processes from other microservices.
- Each microservice can have more than one process.

Consider a shopping cart microservice again. If it ran in the same process as a product catalog microservice, as shown in figure 1.3, the shopping cart code might cause a side

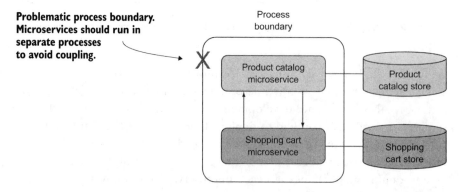

Figure 1.3   Running more than one microservice within a process leads to high coupling between the two: they cannot be deployed individually, and one might cause downtime in the other.

effect in the product catalog. That would mean a tight, undesirable coupling between the shopping cart and product catalog microservices: one might cause downtime or bugs in the other.

Now consider deploying a new version of the shopping cart microservice. You'd either have to redeploy the product catalog microservice or need some sort of dynamic code-loading capable of switching out the shopping cart code in the running process. The first option goes directly against microservices being individually deployable. The second is complex and at a minimum puts the product catalog microservice at risk of going down due to a deployment to the shopping cart microservice.

Speaking of complexity, why should a microservice consist of more than one process? You are, after all, trying to make each microservice as simple as possible to handle.

Let's consider a recommendation microservice. It implements and runs the algorithms that drive recommendations for your e-commerce site. It also has a database that stores the data needed to provide recommendations. The algorithms run in one process, and the database runs in another. Often, a microservice needs two or more processes so that it can implement everything (such as data storage and background processing) it needs in order to provide a capability to the system.

OWNS ITS OWN DATA STORE

A microservice owns the data store where it stores the data it needs. This is another consequence of a microservice's scope being a complete capability. Most business capabilities require some data storage. For instance, a product catalog microservice needs some information about each product to be stored. To keep the product catalog loosely coupled with other microservices, the data store containing the product information is completely owned by the microservice. The product catalog microservice decides how and when the product information is stored. As illustrated in figure 1.4, other

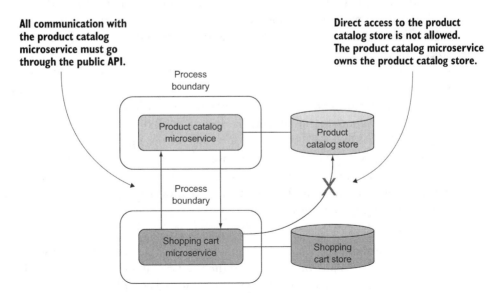

All communication with the product catalog microservice must go through the public API.

Direct access to the product catalog store is not allowed. The product catalog microservice owns the product catalog store.

Process boundary

Product catalog microservice

Product catalog store

Process boundary

Shopping cart microservice

Shopping cart store

Figure 1.4 One microservice can't access another's data store.

microservices, such as a shopping cart, can only access product information through the interface to the product catalog and never directly from the product catalog data store.

The fact that each microservice owns its own data store makes it possible to use different database technologies for different microservices depending on the needs of each microservice. The product catalog microservice, for example, might use an SQL server to store product information; the shopping cart microservice might store each user's shopping cart in Redis; and the recommendations microservice might use an Elasticsearch index to provide recommendations. The database technology chosen for a microservice is part of the implementation and is hidden from the view of other microservices.

This approach allows each microservice to use whichever database is best suited for the job, which can also lead to benefits in terms of development time, performance, and scalability. The obvious downside is the need to administer, maintain, and work with more than one database, if that's how you choose to architect your system. Databases tend to be complicated pieces of technology, and learning to use and run one reliably in production isn't free. When choosing a database for a microservice, you need to consider this tradeoff. But one benefit of a microservice owning its own data store is that you can swap out one database for another later.

NOTE Data ownership, access, and storage will be covered in chapter 5.

MAINTAINED BY A SMALL TEAM

So far, I haven't talked much about the size of a microservice, even though the "micro" part of the term indicates that microservices are small. I don't think it makes sense to discuss the number of lines of code that a microservice should have, or the number of requirements, use cases, or function points it should implement. All that depends on the complexity of the capability provided by the microservice.

What does make sense, though, is considering the amount of work involved in maintaining a microservice. The following rule of thumb can guide you regarding the size of microservices: a small team of people—five, perhaps—should be able to maintain a few handfuls of microservices. Here, "maintaining a microservice" means dealing with all aspects of keeping it healthy and fit for purpose: developing new functionality, factoring out new microservices from ones that have grown too big, running it in production, monitoring it, testing it, fixing bugs, and everything else required. Depending on the volume of change in the microservices "a few handfuls" can mean anything from 10 to 30 microservices, or even more when the system, the tooling, and the automation is mature and effective. A team should usually own a cohesive set of business and technical capabilities leading to it owning the microservices that implement these capabilities.

REPLACEABLE

For a microservice to be *replaceable*, it must be able to be rewritten from scratch within a reasonable time frame. In other words, the team maintaining the microservice should be able to replace the current implementation with a completely new implementation and do so within the normal pace of their work. This characteristic is another constraint on the size of a microservice: if it grows too large, it will be expensive to replace; but if it's kept small, rewriting it is realistic.

Why would a team decide to rewrite a microservice? Perhaps the code is a big jumble and no longer easily maintainable. Perhaps it doesn't perform well enough in production. Neither is a desirable situation, but changes in requirements over time can result in a codebase that it makes sense to replace rather than maintain. If the microservice is small enough to be rewritten within a reasonable time frame, it's okay to end up with one of these situations from time to time. The team does the rewrite based on all the knowledge obtained from writing the existing implementation and keeping any new requirements in mind.

Now that you know the characteristics of microservices, let's look at their benefits, costs, and other considerations.

1.3 Why microservices?

Building a system from microservices that adhere to the characteristics outlined in the previous section has some appealing benefits: they're malleable, scalable, and robust, and they allow a short lead time from start of implementation to deployment to production. This adds up to doing well on all of the four key metrics outlined in Accelerate.[6] These benefits are realized because, when done well, microservices

- Enable continuous delivery
- Allow for an efficient developer workflow because they're highly maintainable
- Are robust by design
- Can scale up or down independently of each other

Let's talk more about these points.

1.3.1 Enabling continuous delivery

The microservices architectural style takes continuous delivery into account. It does so by focusing on services that

- Can be developed and modified quickly
- Can be comprehensively tested by automated tests
- Can be deployed independently
- Can be operated efficiently

These properties enable continuous delivery, but this doesn't mean continuous delivery follows from adopting a microservices architecture. The relationship is more complex: practicing continuous delivery becomes easier with microservices than it typically is with more traditional SOA. On the other hand, fully adopting microservices is possible only if you're able to deploy services efficiently and reliably. Continuous delivery and microservices complement each other.

---

[6] Nicole Forsgren, Gene Kim, and Jez Humble. *Accelerate*. IT Revolution Press: 2018.

The benefits of continuous delivery are well known. They include increased agility on the business level, reliable releases, risk reduction, and improved product quality.

What is continuous delivery?

Continuous delivery is a development practice where the team ensures that the software can always be deployed to production quickly at any time. Releasing to market remains a business decision, but teams that practice continuous delivery tend to deploy to production often and to deploy newly developed software shortly after it hits source control.

There are two main requirements for continuous delivery. First, the software must always be in a fully functional state. To achieve that, the team needs a keen focus on quality. This leads to a high degree of test automation and to developing in very small increments. Second, the deployment process must be repeatable, reliable, and fast in order to enable frequent production deployments. This part is achieved through full automation of the deployment process and a high degree of insight into the health of the production environment.

Although continuous delivery takes a good deal of technical skill, it's much more a question of process and culture. This level of quality, automation, and insight requires a culture of close collaboration among all parties involved in developing and operating the software, including businesspeople, developers, information security experts, and system administrators. In other words, it requires a DevOps culture where development, operations, and other groups collaborate and learn from each other.

Continuous delivery goes hand-in-hand with microservices. Without the ability to deploy individual microservices quickly and cheaply, implementing a system of them will fast become expensive. If microservice deployment isn't automated, the amount of manual work involved in deploying a full system of microservices will be overwhelming.

Along with continuous delivery comes a DevOps culture, which is also a prerequisite for microservices. To succeed with microservices, everybody must be invested in making the services run smoothly in production and in creating a high level of transparency into the health of the production system. This requires the collaboration of people with operations, development, and security skills, as well as people with insight into the business domain, among others.

This book won't focus on continuous delivery or DevOps, but it will take for granted that the environment in which you develop microservices uses continuous delivery. The services built in this book can be deployed to any cloud or to on-premise servers using any number of deployment-automation technologies capable of handling .NET. This book does cover the implications of continuous delivery and DevOps for individual microservices. In part 3, we'll go into detail about how to build a platform that handles a number of the operational concerns that all microservices must address.

As an example of deployment, we will create a Kubernetes environment in Microsoft's Azure cloud in chapter 3 and deploy a microservice to it. In the chapters that follow, we will continue to use that Kubernetes environment as an example and deploy microservices to it.

1.3.2 *High level of maintainability*

Well-factored and well-implemented microservices are highly maintainable from a couple of perspectives. From a developer perspective, several factors play a part in making microservices maintainable:

- Each well-factored microservice provides *a single capability*. Not two—just one.
- A microservice owns its own data store. No other services can interfere with a microservice's data store. This, combined with the typical size of the codebase for a microservice, means you can understand a complete service all at once.
- Well-written microservices can (and should) be comprehensively covered by automated tests.

From an operations perspective, a couple of factors play a role in the maintainability of microservices:

- A small team can maintain a few handfuls of microservices that must be built to be operated efficiently, which implies you should be able to easily determine the current health of any microservice.
- Each microservice is individually deployable.

It should follow that issues in production can be discovered in a timely manner and be addressed quickly, such as by scaling out the microservice in question or deploying a new version of it. The fact that a microservice owns its own data store also adds to its operational maintainability, because the scope of maintenance on the data store is limited to the owning microservice.

> **Favor lightweight**
>
> Because every microservice handles a single capability, microservices are by nature fairly small, both in their scope and in the size of their codebase. The simplicity that follows from this limited scope is a major benefit.
>
> When developing microservices, it's important to avoid complicating their codebase by using large, complicated frameworks, libraries, or products because you think you may need their functionality in the future. Chances are this won't be the case, so you should prefer smaller, lightweight technologies that address the microservice's current needs. Remember, a microservice is replaceable: you can completely rewrite it within a reasonable budget, if at some point, the technologies you used originally no longer meet your needs.

1.3.3   *Robust and scalable*

A microservices-based distributed architecture allows you to scale out each microservice individually, based on where bottlenecks occur. Furthermore, microservices favor asynchronous event-based collaboration and stress the importance of fault tolerance wherever synchronous communication is needed. When implemented well, these properties result in highly available, highly scalable systems. We will return to these topics in more detail in chapters 5, 6, and 7.

1.4   *Costs and downsides of microservices*

Significant costs are associated with choosing a microservices architecture, and these costs shouldn't be ignored:

- Microservice systems are distributed systems. The costs associated with distributed systems are well known: they can be harder to reason about and harder to test than monolithic systems, and communication across process boundaries or across networks is orders of magnitude slower than in-process method calls.
- Microservice systems are made up of many microservices, each of which has to be developed, deployed, and managed in production. This means you'll have many deployments and a complex production setup.
- Each microservice is a separate codebase. Consequently, refactorings that move code from one microservice to another are painful. You need to invest in getting the scope of each microservice just right.

Before jumping head-first into building a system of microservices, you should consider whether the system you're implementing is sufficiently complex to justify the associated overhead.

Do microservices perform?

One question that always seems to pop up in discussions of whether to use microservices is whether a system built with microservices will be as performant as a system that's not. The argument against is that if the system is built from many collaborating microservices, every user request will involve several microservices, and the collaboration between them will involve remote calls. What happens when a user request comes in? Do you chain together a long series of remote calls going from one microservice to the next? Considering that remote calls are orders of magnitude slower than calls inside a process, this sounds slow.

The problem with this argument is the idea that you'd be making roughly the same calls between different parts of the system as you would if everything were in one process. First, as we'll learn in chapters 5 and 7, the interaction between microservices should be much less fine-grained than calls within a process tend to be. Second, as we'll discuss in chapters 5 and 6, you'll prefer event-based asynchronous collaboration over making synchronous remote calls, and you'll store copies of the same data in several microservices to make sure it's available where it's needed. All in all, these techniques drastically reduce the need to make remote calls while a user

> is waiting. Moreover, the fine-grained nature of microservices enables you to scale out the specific parts of the system that get congested.
>
> There isn't a simple yes-or-no answer as to whether microservices perform well. What I can say is that a well-designed microservice system can easily meet the performance requirements of many, if not most, systems.

1.5 Greenfield vs. brownfield

Should you introduce microservices from the get-go on a new project, or are they only relevant for large, existing systems? This question tends to come up in discussions about microservices.

The microservices architectural style has grown out of the fact that many organizations' systems started out small but have grown big over time. Many of these systems consist of a single large application—a monolith that often exposes the well-known disadvantages of big, monolithic systems:

- Coupling is high throughout the codebase.
- There's hidden coupling between subcomponents: coupling that is now obvious at first glance can string from knowledge implicit in the code about how certain strings are formatted, how certain columns in a databases are used, and so on.
- Deploying the application is a lengthy process that may involve several people and system downtime.
- The system has a one-size-fits-all architecture intended to handle the most complex components. If you insist on architectural consistency across the monolith, the least complex parts of the system will be over-engineered. This is true of layering, technology choices, chosen patterns, and so on.

The microservices architectural style arose as a result of solving these problems in existing monolithic systems. If you repeatedly split subcomponents of a monolith into ever smaller and more manageable parts, microservices are eventually created.[7]

On the other hand, new projects are started all the time. Are microservices irrelevant for these greenfield projects? That depends. Here are some questions you need to ask yourself:

- Is the system's scope large enough to justify the complexity of a distributed architecture?
- Is the system's scope large enough to justify the cost of building the deployment automation?
- Would this system benefit from the ability to deploy subsystems separately?

---

[7] Some microservices advocates argue that the correct way to arrive at microservices is to apply the Strangler pattern repeatedly to different subcomponents of the monolith. See Martin Fowler, "MonolithFirst," June 3, 2015, http://martinfowler.com/bliki/MonolithFirst.html.

- Can you build sufficient deployment automation?
- Are you sufficiently knowledgeable about the domain to properly identify and separate the system's various independent business capabilities?
- Will the project survive long enough to recover the up-front investment in automation and distribution?

Some greenfield projects meet these criteria and may benefit from adopting a microservices architecture from the outset.

1.6   Code reuse

Adopting a microservices architecture leads to having many services, each of which has a separate codebase that you'll have to maintain. It's tempting to look for code reuse across services in the hope that you can reduce the maintenance effort. And although there's an obvious potential benefit to code reuse, pulling code out of a service and into a reusable library incurs a number of costs that may not be immediately apparent and that might mean the code reuse isn't worth it:

- The service now has one more dependency that you must understand in order to understand the complete service. This isn't to say that there's more code to comprehend, but by moving code out of the service and into a library you move the code further away, making simple code navigation slower and refactoring more difficult.
- The code in the new library must be developed and maintained with multiple use cases in mind. This tends to take more effort than developing for just one use case.
- The shared library introduces a form of coupling between the services using it. Updates to the library driven by the needs of service A may not be needed in service B. Should service B update to the new version of the library even though it's not strictly necessary? If you upgrade B, it will have code it doesn't need—and worse, B will run the risk of errors caused by that code. If you don't upgrade, you'll have several versions of the library in production, further complicating the library's maintenance. Both cases incur some complexity, either in service B or in the combined service landscape.

These points apply particularly to business code, which should almost never be reused across microservices. That type of reuse leads to harmful coupling between microservices and identifying a new business capability. Implementing it in a new microservice is usually a better option.

With these points in mind, you should be wary of code reuse and only judiciously attempt it. There is, however, a case to be made for reusing infrastructure code that implements technical concerns.

To keep a service small and focused on providing one capability well, you'll often prefer to write a new service from scratch rather than add functionality to an existing service. It's important to do this quickly and painlessly, and this is where code reuse across services is relevant. As we'll explore in detail in part 3, there are a number of technical concerns that all services need to implement in order to fit well into the overall service landscape. You don't need to write this code for every service; you can put it into a reusable platform and reuse it across services to gain consistency in how these technical aspects are handled and to reduce the effort needed to create a new service.

1.7 Serving a user request: An example of how microservices work in concert

To get a feel for how a microservices architecture works, let's look at an example: a user of an e-commerce website adding an item to their shopping cart. From the viewpoint of the client-side code, a request is fired to the backend system via an API Gateway, and an updated shopping cart along with some price information is returned. This is as simple as the interaction shown in figure 1.5. We'll return to the topic of API Gateways in chapter 13.

Figure 1.5   When frontend code makes a request to add an item to the shopping cart, it only communicates with the API Gateway microservice. What goes on behind the gateway isn't visible.

This is neither surprising nor exciting. The interesting part is the interactions taking place behind the API Gateway microservice to fulfill the request. To add the new item to the user's shopping cart, the API Gateway uses a few other microservices. Each microservice is a separate process, and in this example they communicate via HTTP requests.

1.7.1 Main handling of the user request

All the microservices and their interactions for fulfilling a user request to add an item to their shopping cart are shown in figure 1.6. The request to add an item to the shopping cart is divided into smaller tasks, each of which is handled by a separate microservice:

- The API Gateway microservice is responsible only for a cursory validation of the incoming request. Once it's validated, the work is delegated first to the shopping cart microservice and then to the price calculation microservice.
- The shopping cart microservice uses another microservice—the product catalog—to look up the necessary information about the item being added to

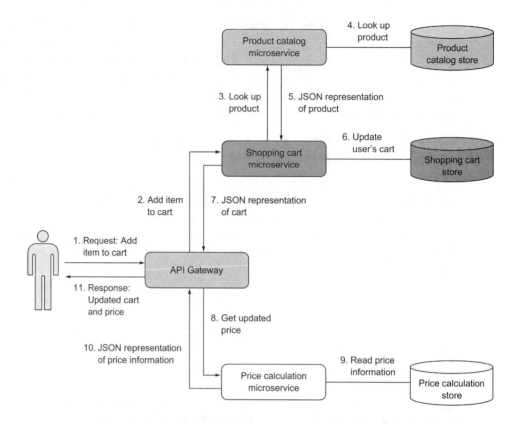

Figure 1.6   The API Gateway is all the client sees, but it's a thin layer in front of a system of microservices. The arrows indicate calls between different parts of the system, and the numbers on the arrows show the sequence of calls.

the cart. The shopping cart then stores the user's shopping cart information in its own data store and returns a representation of the updated shopping cart to the API Gateway. For performance and robustness reasons, the shopping cart will likely cache the responses from the product catalog microservice.

- The price calculation microservice uses the current business rules of the e-commerce website to calculate the total price of the items in the user's shopping cart, taking into account any applicable discounts.

Each of the microservices collaborating to fulfill the user's request has a single, narrowly focused capability and knows as little as possible about the other microservices. For example, the shopping cart microservice knows nothing about pricing or the price calculation microservice, and it knows nothing about how products are stored in the product catalog microservice. This is at the core of microservices: each has a single responsibility.

1.7.2 Side effects of the user request

At this particular e-commerce website, when a user adds an item to their shopping cart, a couple of actions happen in addition to adding the item to the cart:

1. The recommendation engine updates its internal model to reflect the fact that the user has shown a high degree of interest in that particular product.
2. The tracking service records that the user added the item to their cart in the tracking database. This information may be used later for reporting or other business intelligence purposes.

Neither of these actions needs to happen in the context of the user's request; they may as well happen after the request has ended, when the user has received a response and is no longer waiting for the backend system.

You can think of these types of actions as side effects of the user's request. During the request the fact that the user added an item to the shopping is recorded as an *event*. The side effects aren't direct effects of the request to update the user's shopping cart; they're secondary effects that happen as reactions to the event that recorded that the item was added to the cart. Figure 1.7 zooms in on the side effects of adding an item to the cart.

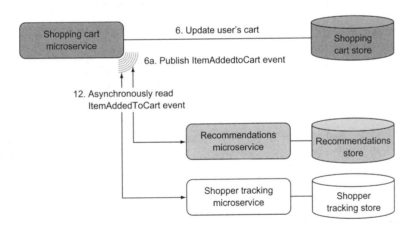

Figure 1.7   The shopping cart microservice publishes events, and other subscribing microservices react.

The trigger for these side effects is an `ItemAddedToCart` event published by the Shopping Cart microservice. Two other microservices subscribe to events from shopping cart and take the necessary actions as events (such as `ItemAddedToCart` events) occur. These two subscribers react to the events asynchronously—outside the context of the original request—so the side effects may happen in parallel with the main handling of the request or after the main handling has completed.

NOTE   Implementing this type of event-driven architecture using event feeds will be covered in chapter 5.

1.7.3   *The complete picture*

In total, six different microservices are involved in handling the request to add an item to a shopping cart, as shown in figure 1.8. None of these microservices knows anything about the internals of the others. Five have their own private data stores dedicated to serving only their purposes. Some of the handling happens synchronously in the context of the user request, and some happens asynchronously.

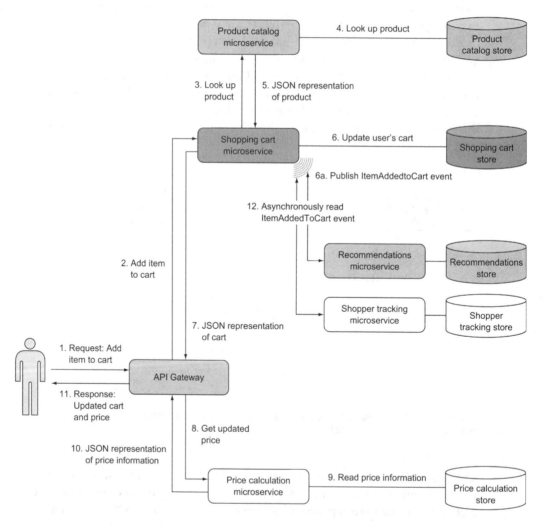

Figure 1.8   **When a user adds an item to their shopping cart, the frontend makes a request to the API Gateway microservice, which collaborates with other microservices to fulfill the request. During processing, microservices may raise events that other microservices can subscribe to and handle asynchronously.**

This is a typical microservice system. Requests are handled through the collaboration of several microservices, each with a single responsibility and as independent of the others as possible.

Now that we've taken a high-level look at a concrete example of how a microservices system can handle a user request, it's time to take a brief look at a .NET-based technology stack for microservices.

1.8 A .NET microservices technology stack

It's time to say hello to the technologies used most in this book: ASP.NET, ASP.NET MVC, and Kubernetes.

1.8.1 ASP.NET and MVC

ASP.NET is Microsoft's web platform that has a number of benefits relevant to the microservices we will create throughout this book:

- *Cross-platform*—ASP.NET is based on .NET 5, which works across Linux, Windows, and more. This allows for some nice flexibility when it comes to deciding where to run our microservices. We will be running them in Linux container on a Kubernetes cluster, but our microservice could also run on a different container orchestrator, in Windows containers, or on Windows or Linux servers.
- *Fast*—ASP.NET is fast, and so is the underlying .NET 5 platform.[8] This gives a good foundation to build fast microservices.
- *Microservices are first-class citizens*—One of the primary targets for ASP.NET is microservices, which means that the platform already implements some of the important plumbing that we would otherwise have to implement ourselves, such as request logging and monitoring support.
- *The middleware pipeline*—Middleware is a lightweight, composable, and flexible way to build a pipeline for handling incoming HTTP requests. Our microservices will have ASP.NET MVC at the end of their middleware pipelines.
- *Testable*—We will be taking advantage of the *TestHost* test helper for ASP.NET to test our microservices thoroughly in a style that lends itself to outside-in test-driven development.

On top of the ASP.NET platform we will use Microsoft's ASP.NET MVC[9] web framework, which provides us with an extra level of convenience when it comes to implementing handlers for HTTP endpoints.

1.8.2 Kubernetes

Kubernetes is a container orchestrator we will use to run our microservices. It allows us to automate deployment and to a certain degree the management of our microservices. In chapter 3, we will create a Kubernetes cluster in Azure and see how we can

---

[8] According to the Techempower benchmarks: https://www.techempower.com/benchmarks/.
[9] Throughout the book, I will often refer to ASP.NET MVC as simply MVC.

deploy our microservices to the Kubernetes cluster. Then we will continue to deploy microservices to Kubernetes.

1.8.3   Setting up a development environment

Before you can start coding your first microservice, you need to have the right tools. To follow along with the examples in this book, you'll need four primary tools: an IDE, the .NET command line, an HTTP tool, and Docker.

First, you need a development environment for creating ASP.NET applications. The three most common options are as follows:

- *Visual Studio*—Visual Studio is a fully fledged IDE with great support for writing and debugging ASP.NET application. It is Windows-only and is probably the most widely used IDE for ASP.NET development.
- *Visual Studio Code*—Visual Studio Code is a glorified editor that comes with a C# plug-in that makes a very capable editor for writing ASP.NET applications. It is lightweight and works across Windows, Linux, and Mac.
- *JetBrains Rider*—Rider is another fully fledged IDE with strong support for writing and debugging ASP.NET applications. Rider works on Windows, Linux, and Mac alike.

All these support developing, running, and debugging ASP.NET applications. They all give you a nice C# editor with IntelliSense and refactoring support. They're all aware of ASP.NET, and they can all launch and debug ASP.NET applications.

Second, you need to have a version of the .NET command-line tool. If you did not get it bundled with the IDE, follow the instructions for installing .NET at http://dot.net. This gives you a command-line tool called `dotnet` that you'll use to perform a number of different tasks involved with microservices, including restoring, building, and creating NuGet packages and running microservices. Throughout the book I will use the dotnet command line for these tasks, but if you prefer, you can also do most of them in your IDE.

Third, you'll need a tool for making HTTP requests. I recommend the REST client plug-in for Visual Studio Code, but Fiddler, Postman, and cURL are also good and popular tools. You can use any of these to follow along with the examples in this book.

Fourth, you need Docker installed, and you need to have Kubernetes turned on in your Docker settings.

> **NOTE**   In appendix A, you'll find download, installation, and quick usage information for Visual Studio, Visual Studio Code, JetBrains Rider, and Docker. Now is the time to set up the tools of your choice—you'll need them throughout the rest of the book.

1.9   A simple microservices example

Once you have a development environment up and running, it's time for a "Hello World"-style microservices example. You'll use ASP.NET to create a microservice that has only a single API endpoint. Typically, a microservice has more than one endpoint, but one is enough for this example. The endpoint responds with the current UTC date and time. This is illustrated in figure 1.9.

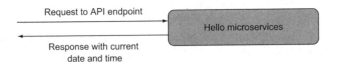

Figure 1.9   A "Hello World"-style microservice that responds with the current date and time

> **NOTE**   When I talk about an *API endpoint*, an *HTTP endpoint*, or just an *endpoint*, I mean a URL where one of your microservices reacts to HTTP requests.

To implement this example, you'll follow these three steps:

1 Create an empty ASP.NET application.
2 Add ASP.NET MVC to the application.
3 Add an MVC controller with an implementation of the endpoint.

The following sections will go through each step in detail.

1.9.1   *Creating an empty ASP.NET application*

The first thing you need to do is create an empty ASP.NET application called `Hello-Microservices` using the .NET command-line tool. If you prefer, you can create the project using your IDE—the result is the same. To use the .NET command-line tool, open a shell and issue the command `dotnet new web -n HelloMicroservices`.

Once you've created your empty ASP.NET application and named it `Hello-Microservices`, you should have a folder called HelloMicroservices that contains these files:

- appsettings.Development.json
- appsettings.json
- HelloMicroservices.csproj
- Program.cs
- Startup.cs

There are other files in the project, but these are the one you'll be concerned with right now.

This is a complete application, ready to run. It will respond to HTTP GET requests to the path "/" with the string `Hello World`. You can start the application from the command line by going to the HelloMicroservices folder and typing the command `dotnet run`.

The application runs on localhost port 5000. (Note that if you choose to run it from inside Visual Studio, you may get another port.) If you go to http://localhost:5000 in a browser, you'll get the "Hello World" response.

1.9.2   *Adding ASP.NET MVC to the project*

To add ASP.NET MVC to the project, we will replace the code in the `Startup` class. There are two parts to adding MVC to our microservice:

1   Adding the necessary types to the *service collection*. ASP.NET is designed to use *dependency injection*[10] and all types that ASP.NET should be able to instantiate must be added to the service collection.

2   Adding all the endpoints we will write in our microservices to ASP.NET's *routing table*. The routing table is used by ASP.NET every time an HTTP request comes in to try to find an endpoint that matches the request.

The code in the Startup.cs file is replaced with the following listing.

Listing 1.1   Startup with MVC

```
namespace HelloMicroservices
{
  using Microsoft.AspNetCore.Builder;
  using Microsoft.AspNetCore.Hosting;
  using Microsoft.Extensions.DependencyInjection;

  public class Startup
  {
    public void ConfigureServices(IServiceCollection services)
      => services.AddControllers();          ◁── Adds MVC controller and helper
                                                   services to the service collection
    public void Configure(
      IApplicationBuilder app,
      IWebHostEnvironment env)
    {
      app.UseHttpsRedirection();             ◁── Redirects all HTTP
      app.UseRouting();                           requests to HTTPS
      app.UseEndpoints(endpoints =>
        endpoints.MapControllers());         ◁── Adds all endpoints in all
    }                                             controllers to MVC's route table
  }
}
```

Apart from adding controller and helpers to the services collection and adding our endpoints to routing table, we also added a line that redirects all HTTP requests to HTTPS. Our application will handle HTTPS requests on port 5001. For example, a request to http://localhost:5000/ will be redirected to https://localhost:5001/. The first time you attempt to make a request to https://localhost:5001/, you will probably be warned about an unknown certificate. This is a development certificate your microservices will use and you can safely accept the certificate.

At this point, you have an ASP.NET application with MVC added, but the application can't handle any requests because you haven't set up any endpoints. If you restart the application and again go to https://localhost:5001 in a browser or in a Visual Studio Codes REST client plug-in, you'll get a "404 Page Not Found" response. Let's fix that.

---

[10]   Martin Fowler, "Inversion of Control Containers and the Dependency Injection pattern," January 23, 2004, https://martinfowler.com/articles/injection.html.

1.9.3 Adding an MVC controller with an implementation of the endpoint

Now you'll add an MVC controller with an implementation of the single API endpoint. We will implement controllers as classes that inherit from `ControllerBase` and we will use them to declare endpoints and to implement the behavior for each endpoint. Because we added the `endpoints.MapControllers` line to `Startup` in the previous section, ASP.NET will discover the endpoints we declare in our controllers. We add a controller by creating a file called CurrentDateTimeController.cs and adding the following code to it.

> **Listing 1.2   MVC Controller**

```
namespace HelloMicroservices
{
  using System;
  using Microsoft.AspNetCore.Mvc;                          Declares an
                                                           MVC controller
  public class CurrentDateTimeController : ControllerBase
  {
    [HttpGet("/")]                                         Declares an HTTP GET
    public object Get() => DateTime.UtcNow;                endpoint to the path /
  }                                            Returns the current date and
}                                              time as response to requests
```

In this controller, you declare a route for the path / with the attribute `HttpGet("/")`. This tells MVC that any HTTP GET request to / should be handled by the method following the attribute, the method `Get()` in this case. The `Get()` method returns the current UTC date and time, so that is the response to every HTTP GET request to /.

You can now rerun the application and again point your browser to https://localhost:5001. Your browser will hit the route on your MVC controller and show the current UTC date and time as a string. We can do the same with the REST client plug-in in Visual Studio Code, which looks like figure 1.10.

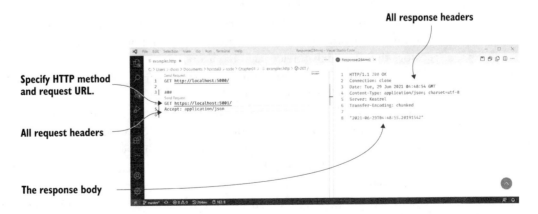

Figure 1.10   REST client in VS Code makes it easy to send HTTP requests and control the request details, such as the headers and HTTP method.

On the wire, this is the request:

```
GET / HTTP/1.1
Host: localhost:5001
Accept: application/json
```

HTTP method (GET), path (/), and protocol (HTTP/1.1) used in the request

List of request headers. In this case, there's only an Accept header with the value application/json.

Host to which the request is made

The response from this request is the current UTC data and time in a JSON string:

```
HTTP/1.1 200 OK
Connection: close
Date: Thu, 21 Nov 2019 12:28:01 GMT
Content-Type: application/json; charset=utf-8
Server: Kestrel
Transfer-Encoding: chunked

"2019-11-21T12:28:02.5561423Z"
```

NOTE   Remember you can create HTTP request and see the responses using tools like REST client for VS Code, Postman, or Fiddler.

You've now implemented your first HTTP endpoint with ASP.NET MVC.

Summary

- *Microservices* is an overloaded term used both for the microservices architectural style and for individual microservices in a system of microservices.
- The microservices architectural style is a special form of SOA, where each service is small and provides one and only one business capability.
- A microservice is a service with a single narrowly focused capability.
- I'll refer to six characteristics of a microservice in this book:
  - Provides a single capability.
  - Individually deployable. You must be able to deploy every microservice on its own without touching any other part of the system.
  - Runs in one or more processes, separate from other microservices.
  - Owns and stores the data belonging to the capability it provides in a data store that the microservice itself has access to.
  - Is small enough that a small team of around five people can develop and maintain a few handfuls or more of them.
  - Replaceable. The team should be able to rewrite a microservice from scratch in a short period of time if, for instance, the codebase has become a mess.
- Microservices go hand-in-hand with continuous delivery:
  - Having small, individually deployable microservices makes continuous delivery easier.
  - Being able to deploy automatically, quickly, and reliably simplifies deploying and maintaining a system of microservices.

- A system built with microservices allows for scalability and resilience.
- A system built with microservices is malleable: it can be easily changed according to your business needs. Each microservice by itself is highly maintainable, and even creating new microservices to provide new capabilities can be done quickly.
- Microservices collaborate to provide functionality to the end user.
- A microservice exposes a remote public API that other microservices may use.
- A microservice can expose a feed of events that other microservices can subscribe to. Events are handled asynchronously in the subscribers but still allow subscribers to react to events quickly.
- ASP.NET is well suited for implementing microservices.
- Kubernetes is the container orchestrator we will use throughout the book.
- Most microservices don't serve HTML from their endpoints, but rather data in the form of JSON, for instance. Tools like REST client, Postman, and Fiddler are good for testing such endpoints.

A basic shopping cart microservice

2

This chapter covers

- A first iteration of an implementation of the shopping cart microservice
- Creating HTTP endpoints with ASP.NET MVC
- Implementing a request from one microservice to another
- Implementing a simple event feed for a microservice

In chapter, 1 we looked at how microservices work and how they can be characterized. You also set up a simple technology stack—C#, ASP.NET, and the ASP.NET MVC framework—that lets you create microservices easily, and you saw a basic shopping cart microservice. In this chapter, you'll implement the four main parts of this microservice using the same technology stack:

1 A basic HTTP-based API allowing clients to retrieve a cart, delete it, and add items to it. Each of these methods will be visible as an HTTP endpoint, such as http://myservice/add/{item_number}.

2 A call from one service to another for more information. In this case, the shopping cart microservice will ask the product catalog microservice for product information based on the item_number of the item being added to the cart.

3 An event feed that the service will use to publish events to the rest of the system. By creating an event feed for the shopping cart, you'll make it possible for other services (such as a recommendation engine) to update their own data and improve their capabilities.

4 The domain logic for implementing the behavior of the shopping cart.

To keep things simple, you won't do a complete implementation of this microservice in this chapter. We'll look at the following topics and complete the microservice during the course of the book:

- The shopping cart microservice should have its own data store, but you won't implement it or the data access code to get data in and out of it. Chapter 6 covers this in full.

- Any production-ready microservice should include support for monitoring and logging. If a microservice doesn't provide regular insight into its health, it becomes difficult to keep the overall system running steadily. But these functions don't directly provide a business capability, so I've left logging and monitoring capabilities to be discussed in chapter 10.

Let's get to it.

> **NOTE** Be sure you've set up your development environment. In appendix A, you'll find download, installation, and quick usage information about IDEs you can use to follow along with the code throughout this book. This chapter has lots of code, so if you haven't already set up a development environment, now is the time to do it.

2.1 Overview of the Shopping Cart microservice

In chapter 1, we looked at how an e-commerce site built with microservices might handle a user's request to add an item to their shopping cart. The complete overview of how the request is handled is repeated in figure 2.1.

The shopping cart microservice plays a central role when a user wants to add an item to their shopping cart. But it's not the only process in which the shopping cart plays a role. It's equally important to let the user see their shopping cart and delete an item from it. The shopping cart microservice must support those processes through its HTTP API, just as it supports adding an item to a shopping cart. Figure 2.2 shows the interactions between the shopping cart microservice and the other microservices in the system.

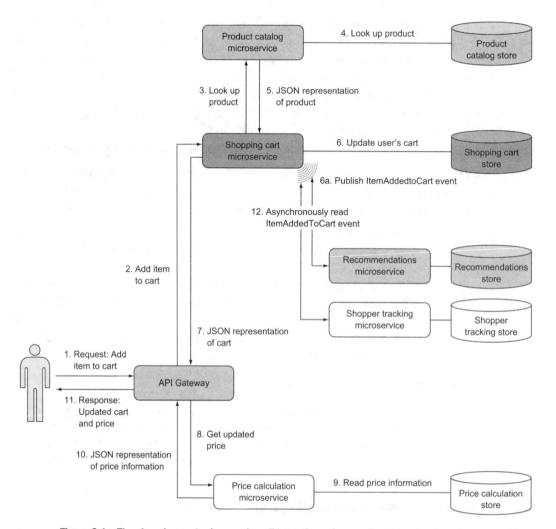

Figure 2.1   The shopping cart microservice allows other microservices to get a shopping cart, add items to and delete items from a shopping cart, and subscribe to events from the shopping cart.

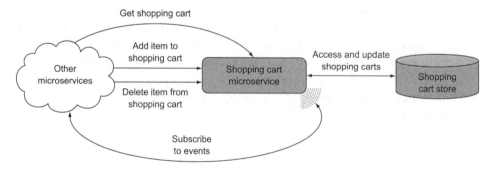

Figure 2.2   Overview of how an e-commerce site built with microservices can handle adding an item to a user's shopping cart

The shopping cart microservice supports three types of synchronous requests:

- Getting a shopping cart
- Adding an item to a shopping cart
- Deleting an item from a shopping cart

On top of that, it exposes an event feed that other microservices can subscribe to. Now that you've seen an overview of the shopping cart microservice's complete functionality, you can start drilling into its implementation.

2.1.1 Components of the Shopping Cart microservice

Let's zoom in and see what this microservice looks like at closer range. As shown in figure 2.3, the shopping cart microservice consists of these components:

- A small component called shopping cart domain model responsible for implementing any business rules related to shopping carts.
- An HTTP API component that's responsible for handling all incoming HTTP requests. The HTTP API component is divided into two parts: one handles requests from other microservices to do something, and the other exposes an event feed.

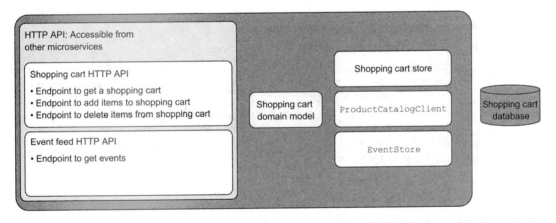

Figure 2.3 The shopping cart microservice is a small codebase with a few components that provide one focused business capability.

There are two data store components: `EventStore` and `ShoppingCartStore`. These data store components are responsible for talking to the data store (`Shopping Cart Database`):

- `EventStore` handles saving events to and reading them from the data store.
- `ShoppingCartStore` handles reading and updating shopping carts in the data store. Note that shopping carts and events may be stored in different databases; we'll return to this in chapter 6.

The `ProductCatalogClient` component is responsible for communicating with the product catalog microservice shown in figure 2.1. Placing that communication in `ProductCatalogClient` serves several purposes:

- It encapsulates knowledge of the other microservice's API in one place.
- It encapsulates the details of making an HTTP request.
- It encapsulates caching results from the other microservice.
- It encapsulates handling errors from the other microservice.

This chapter includes the code for the domain model, the HTTP API, and a basic implementation of `ProductCatalogClient`, but skips `EventStore` and `ShoppingCartStore` and the data store. In addition, for the sake of brevity, this chapter omits error-handling code. Chapter 5 will go further into detail about how to implement micro-service APIs easily with ASP.NET; chapter 6 will also return to the subject of storing data in a microservice. Chapter 7 will dive deeper into how to design robustness and error handling into clients such as `ProductCatalogClient`.

2.2 Implementing the Shopping Cart microservice

Now that you understand the shopping cart microservice's components, it's time to get into the code.

> ### New technologies used in this chapter
>
> In this chapter, you'll begin using two new technologies:
>
> - `System.Net.Http.HttpClient` is a .NET type for making HTTP requests. It provides an API for creating and sending HTTP requests as well as reading the responses that come back.
> - Polly is a library that makes it easy to implement the more common policies for handling remote-call failures. Out of the box, Polly has support for various retry and circuit breaker policies. I'll discuss circuit breakers in chapter 7.
> - Scrutor is a library that add a number of convenient extensions to ASP.NET's built-in dependency injection container

2.2.1 Creating an empty project

The first thing you need to do is set up an ASP.NET project, just as in chapter 1. First, create an empty ASP.NET application called `ShoppingCart`—on the command line, you can use the command `dotnet new web -n ShoppingCart`. Second, add ASP.NET MVC to the application in the `Startup` class, as shown in the following listing.

Listing 2.1   Startup class with MVC

```
namespace ShoppingCart
{
  using Microsoft.AspNetCore.Builder;
  using Microsoft.Extensions.DependencyInjection;
```

```
public class Startup
{
  public void ConfigureServices(IServiceCollection services)
  {
    services.AddControllers();                    ◁─┐ Adds MVC controller and helper
  }                                                  │ services to the service collection

  public void Configure(IApplicationBuilder app)
  {
    app.UseHttpsRedirection();                    ◁─┐ Redirects all HTTP
    app.UseRouting();                                │ requests to HTTPS
    app.UseEndpoints(endpoints =>
      endpoints.MapControllers());                ◁─┐ Adds all endpoints in all
  }                                                  │ controllers to MVCs route table
}
}
```

You now have an empty application that's ready to go.

2.2.2 The Shopping Cart microservice's API for other services

In this section, you'll implement the shopping cart microservice's HTTP API, which is highlighted in figure 2.4. This API has three parts, each of which is implemented as an HTTP endpoint:

- An HTTP GET endpoint where other microservices can fetch a user's shopping cart as a JSON document by providing a user ID.
- An HTTP POST endpoint where other microservices can add items to a user's shopping cart. The items to be added are passed to the endpoint as a JSON array of product IDs.
- An HTTP DELETE endpoint where other microservices can remove items from a user's shopping cart. The items to be deleted are passed in the body of the request as a JSON array of product IDs.

Figure 2.4   Implementing the HTTP API component

The following three sections each implement one of the endpoints.

> **NOTE**   I will not show implementations of `EventStore` or `ShoppingCartStore`. Chapter 6 will cover those, but for now a simple hardcoded implementation is sufficient. You can get an implementation of `EventStore` and `ShoppingCart-Store` from the book's code package or you can create one yourself.

GETTING A SHOPPING CART

The first part of the HTTP API you'll implement is the endpoint that lets other microservices fetch a user's shopping cart. Figure 2.5 shows how other microservices can use an endpoint to get a shopping cart.

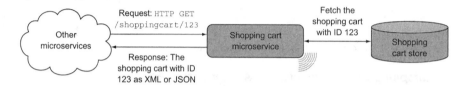

Figure 2.5   Other microservices can use an endpoint on shopping cart to get a shopping cart as a JSON document.

The endpoint accepts `HTTP GET` requests. Its URL includes the ID of the user whose shopping cart the other microservice wants, and the body of the response is a JSON serialization of that shopping cart.

For example, the API Gateway in figure 2.1 may need the shopping cart for a user with ID 123. To get that, it sends this HTTP request:

```
HTTP GET /shoppingcart/123 HTTP/1.1
Host: shoppingcart.my.company.com
Accept: application/json
```

This is a request to `shoppingcart/123` on the shopping cart microservice, and the `123` part of the URL is the user ID.

To handle such requests, you need to add a controller to the `ShoppingCart` project called `ShoppingCartController` as well `ShoppingCart` domain model. I prefer a folder structure that follows the domain and gathers closely-related things and separates less-related things. Therefore, I create the `ShoppingCartController` and the `ShoppingCart` in a new folder in the `ShoppingCart` project called `ShoppingCart`. The next listing shows the folder structure. The folder structure follows the domain and gathers closely-related things in folders named after the domain. For instance, the `ShoppingCart` domain type and controller are in the same folder.

Listing 2.2   ShoppingCart folder structure

```
ShoppingCart
    appsettings.Development.json
    appsettings.json
```

```
Program.cs
ShoppingCart.csproj
Startup.cs

ShoppingCart
    ShoppingCart.cs
    ShoppingCartController.cs
    ShoppingCartStore.cs
```

The shopping cart domain model

Implements shopping cart HTTP endpoint

Contains the data access code (not shown in this chapter but available in the code download)

The ShoppingCart domain model is simple and looks like this:

```csharp
namespace ShoppingCart.ShoppingCart
{
  using System.Collections.Generic;
  using System.Linq;

  public class ShoppingCart
  {
    private readonly HashSet<ShoppingCartItem> items = new();

    public int UserId { get; }
    public IEnumerable<ShoppingCartItem> Items => this.items;

    public ShoppingCart(int userId) => this.UserId = userId;

    public void AddItems(IEnumerable<ShoppingCartItem> shoppingCartItems)
    {
      foreach (var item in shoppingCartItems)
        this.items.Add(item);
    }

    public void RemoveItems(int[] productCatalogueIds) =>
      this.items.RemoveWhere(i => productCatalogueIds.Contains(
          i.ProductCatalogueId));
  }

  public record ShoppingCartItem(
    int ProductCatalogueId,
    string ProductName,
    string Description,
    Money Price)
  {
    public virtual bool Equals(ShoppingCartItem? obj) =>
      obj != null && this.ProductCatalogueId.Equals(obj.ProductCatalogueId);

    public override int GetHashCode() =>
      this.ProductCatalogueId.GetHashCode();
  }

  public record Money(string Currency, decimal Amount);
}
```

With the domain model in place we are ready to write the ShoppingCartController. As mentioned in chapter 1, we will implement controllers by inheriting from

Controller, and we will use controllers to implement HTTP endpoints. Put the following code in a file called ShoppingCartController.cs.

Listing 2.3   Endpoint to access a shopping cart by user ID

```
namespace ShoppingCart.Shoppingcart
{
  using Microsoft.AspNetCore.Mvc;
  using ShoppingCart;

  [Route("/shoppingcart")]                          ⟵  Tells MVC that all routes in this
  public class ShoppingCartController : ControllerBase   ⟵  controller start with /shoppingcart
  {                                                         Declares ShoppingCart-
    private readonly IShoppingCartStore shoppingCartStore;  Controller as a controller

    public ShoppingCartController(IShoppingCartStore shoppingCartStore)
    {
      this.shoppingCartStore = shoppingCartStore;
    }                                                Declares the endpoint for handling
                                                     requests to /shoppingcart/{userid},
    [HttpGet("{userId:int}")]              ⟵        such as /shoppingcart/123
    public ShoppingCart Get(int userId) =>    ⟵      Assigns the {userId} from
      this.shoppingCartStore.Get(userId);   ⟵        the URL to the userId variable
  }
}                                            Returns the user's shopping cart. MVC
                                             serializes it before sending it to the client.
```

Let's break down this code.

The attribute `[HttpGet("{userId:int}")]` declares that you want to handle HTTP GET requests to endpoints matching the pattern inside the parenthesis. The pattern can be a literal string, like `"/shoppingcart";`, or it can contain segments that match and capture parts of the request URL, like `{userid:int}`, or it can combine literal strings and segments, like `"/shoppingcart/{userId:int}"`. The `{userId:int}` is called userId and is constrained to only match integers.

The HttpGet attribute is followed by a method:

```
public ShoppingCart Get(int userId) =>
    this.shoppingCartStore.Get(userId);
```

This is the action method, and it's the piece of code that's executed every time the shopping cart microservice receives a request to a URL that matches the route declaration. For instance, when the API Gateway requests a shopping cart via the URL path /shoppingcart/123, this is the method that handles the request.

The action method can take arguments that match segments of the URL. For instance, the int userId is matched to the {userId} segment based on the names of the argument and the segment.

The action method uses a shoppingCartStore object that the ShoppingCart-Controller constructor takes as an argument and assigns to an instance variable:

```
public ShoppingCartController(IShoppingCartStore shoppingCartStore)
{
  this.shoppingCartStore = shoppingCartStore;
}
```

The constructor argument has the type IShoppingCartStore, which is an interface. If an implementation of IShoppingCartStore is registered in ASP.NET's service collection, an instance will be given to the ShoppingCartController constructor each time the framework creates an instance of the controller. We will add code to the Startup class that registers an implementation of IShoppingCartStore. Instead of explicitly registering the ShoppingCartStore class as the implementation IShoppingCartStore, we will add code that scans the shopping cart project and adds all classes that implement interfaces to the service collection. To that end, we will use the NuGet package Scrutor, which is a collection of convenient extensions to the IServiceCollection. First, we add Scrutor to the shopping cart project by running this dotnet command:

```
PS> dotnet add package scrutor
```

This installs the Scrutor NuGet package, which we can see in the shopping cart project file—ShoppingCart.csproj—where there now is a package reference to Scrutor:

```
<Project Sdk="Microsoft.NET.Sdk.Web">

  <PropertyGroup>
    <TargetFramework>netcoreapp3.0</TargetFramework>
  </PropertyGroup>

  <ItemGroup>
    <PackageReference Include="Scrutor" Version="3.1.0" />
  </ItemGroup>

</Project>
```

With Scrutor installed, we can add code to the ConfigureServices method in the Startup class, so it becomes

```
public void ConfigureServices(IServiceCollection services)
    {
      services.AddControllers();
      services.Scan(selector =>          ◁─┐ Use Scrutor to scan the
        selector                            │ ShoppingCart assembly.
          .FromAssemblyOf<Startup>()
          .AddClasses()
          .AsImplementedInterfaces());
    }
```

If there is a class implementing the IShoppingCartStore interface, this code will register it in the service collection and ASP.NET will be able to inject it into the ShoppingCartController constructor. I'm leaving out the real data-storage code in this chapter, but for now this dummy implementation of the IShoppingCart interface will suffice:

```
public interface IShoppingCartStore        ◁─┐ Simple data
  {                                           │ access interface
    ShoppingCart Get(int userId);
    void Save(ShoppingCart shoppingCart);
  }
```

```
public class ShoppingCartStore : IShoppingCartStore
{
  private static readonly Dictionary<int, ShoppingCart>          ◁─┐ Use an in-memory
    Database = new Dictionary<int, ShoppingCart>();                 │ dictionary instead of
                                                                    │ a database for now.
  public ShoppingCart Get(int userId) =>
    Database.ContainsKey(userId)
    ? Database[userId]
    : new ShoppingCart(userId);

  public void Save(ShoppingCart shoppingCart) =>
    Database[shoppingCart.UserId] = shoppingCart;
}
```

Returning attention to the `ShoppingCartController`, the action method `Get` returns a `ShoppingCart` object that it gets back from `shoppingCartStore`:

```
this.shoppingCartStore.Get(userId);
```

The `ShoppingCart` type is specific to the shopping cart microservice, so MVC has no way of knowing about this particular type. But you can return any object you want, and MVC will serialize it and return the data to the caller.

The following listing shows an example of the response to a request to /shopping-cart/123.

Listing 2.4   Example response from the shopping cart microservice

```
HTTP/1.1 200 OK
Content-Type: application/json; charset=utf-8          ◁─┐ The response
                                                          │ body is in JSON.
539                                          ◁─┐ Length of the
{                                               │ response body
    "userId": 42,            ◁─┐ Shopping cart
    "items": [                  │ serialized as JSON
        {
            "productcatalogId": 1,
            "productName": "Basic t-shirt",
            "description": "a quiet t-shirt",
            "price": {
                "currency": "eur",
                "amount": 40
            }
        },
        {
            "productcatalogId": 2,
            "productName": "Fancy shirt",
            "description": "a loud t-shirt",
            "price": {
                "currency": "eur",
                "amount": 50
            }
        }
    ]
}
```

As you can see, you can get a lot of functionality up and running with a small amount of code.

ADDING ITEMS TO A SHOPPING CART

The second endpoint you need to add to the shopping cart microservice lets you add items to a user's shopping cart. Figure 2.6 shows how other microservices can use this endpoint.

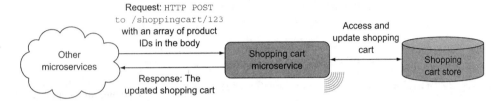

Figure 2.6 Other microservices can add items to a shopping cart with an HTTP POST request that includes an array of product IDs in the request body.

Like the HTTP GET endpoint in the previous section, this new endpoint receives a user ID in the URL. This time, the endpoint accepts HTTP POST requests instead of HTTP GET, and the request should provide a list of items in the body of the request. For example, the following request adds two items to user 123's shopping cart.

Listing 2.5 Adding two items to a shopping cart

```
POST /shoppingcart/123/items HTTP/1.1          The URL includes the ID
  Host: shoppingcart.my.company.com            of the shopping cart: 123.
  Accept: application/json                                The response should
  Content-Type: application/json               The data in the request   be in JSON format.
                                               body is in JSON.
  [1, 2]          The request body is a
                  JSON array of product IDs.
```

To handle such requests, you need to add another action method to ShoppingCart-Controller. The new action method reads the items from the body of the request, looks up the product information for each one, adds them to the correct shopping cart, and returns the updated shopping cart. (The code to fetch product information is shown in section 2.2.3.)

   The new action method is shown in the next listing. Add it to the ShoppingCart-Controller.

Listing 2.6 Handler for a route to add items to a shopping cart

```
[Route("/shoppingcart")]
public class ShoppingCartController : Controller
{
```

```
private readonly IShoppingCartStore shoppingCartStore;
private readonly IProductCatalogClient productCatalogClient;
private readonly IEventStore eventStore;

public ShoppingCartController(
  IShoppingCartStore shoppingCartStore,
  IProductCatalogClient productCatalogClient,
  IEventStore eventStore)
{
  this.shoppingCartStore = shoppingCartStore;
  this.productCatalogClient = productCatalogClient;
  this.eventStore = eventStore;
}

[HttpGet("{userId:int}")]
public ShoppingCart Get(int userId) =>
  this.shoppingCartStore.Get(userId);

[HttpPost("{userId:int}/items")]                   ⟵ Declares an HTTP POST
public async Task<ShoppingCart> Post(                 endpoint for /shoppingcart/
  int userId,                                         {userid}/item
  [FromBody] int[] productIds)      ⟵ Reads and deserializes
{                                      the array of product IDs
  var shoppingCart = shoppingCartStore.Get(userId);  in the HTTP request body
  var shoppingCartItems =
    await this.productcatalogClient                ⟵ Fetches the product
      .GetShoppingCartItems(productIds);              information from the Product
  shoppingCart.AddItems(shoppingCartItems, eventStore);  Catalog microservice
  shoppingCartStore.Save(shoppingCart);     ⟵          ⟵ Adds items
  return shoppingCart;    ⟵          Saves the updated      to the cart
}                     Returns the   cart to the data store
}                     updated cart
```

Two new MVC capabilities are at play here. First, the new action method is asynchronous because it makes a remote call to the product catalog microservice. Performing that external call asynchronously saves resources in shopping cart. ASP.NET can run fully asynchronously, which allows application code to make good use of C#'s async/await feature. When we move beyond the dummy implementation of the IShopping-CartStore and start using a real database the same principle will apply, and the Get and Save methods on the IShoppingCartStore will become async too, which in turn will make the action method Get async.

Second, the body of the request contains a JSON array of product IDs. These are the items that should be added to the shopping cart. The action uses MVC model binding to read these into a C# array:

```
[FromBody] int[] productIds
```

Model binding supports any serializable C# object. You'd often use a more structured object than a flat JSON array to send data into an endpoint, and reading that would be just as easy as in this case. The type of the parameter int[] productIds would just need to be changed to a type other than int[].

The new action handler uses two objects that aren't already present in `Shopping-CartController`. You once again rely on ASP.NET to provide them through constructor arguments.

```
public ShoppingCartController(
    IShoppingCartStore shoppingCartStore,
    IProductCatalogClient productCatalogClient,
    IEventStore eventStore)
```

Only used to pass into the AddItems call, where it will be used later

Other microservices can now add items to shopping carts. They should similarly be allowed to remove items from shopping carts.

---

async/await at a glance

C# 5 introduced two new keywords, *async* and *await*, to allow methods to run asynchronously easily. A basic async method looks like this:

```
public async Task<int> WaitForANumber()
{
    await Task.Delay(1000)
    return 10;
}
```

Declares method as async

Yields the current thread until the task completes

Because the method is async, the return value is automatically wrapped in a Task.

When you call this method, the thread of execution continues as usual until `await`. The `await` keyword works in conjunction with *awaitables*—the most common awaitable is `System.Threading.Tasks.Task<T>`—and asynchronously waits until the awaitable completes. This means that two things happen when execution reaches `await`:

- The remainder of the method is queued up for execution when the awaitable—in this case, the `Task` returned from `Task.Delay(1000)`—completes. When the awaitable completes, the rest of the method is executed, possibly on a new thread but with same state as before the `await` re-established.
- The current thread of execution returns from the async method and continues in the caller.

This mental model of async/await papers over many details of the implementation but works for understanding code that uses async/await methods.

> **NOTE**   Every time we call an async method we must await the result.

In server-side code, like microservices, many requests require some I/O, such as calling a data store or another microservice. If you can execute the I/O asynchronously instead of blocking a thread while waiting for the I/O to complete, you save resources on your servers. In some situations, you may also gain some performance, but that isn't the general case. I use async/await and `Task` a lot in this book to save resources on the server and to gain scalability.

REMOVING ITEMS FROM A SHOPPING CART

The third and last endpoint is an HTTP DELETE endpoint that, as shown in figure 2.7, lets other microservices remove items from shopping carts. You should now have the hang of adding endpoints to controllers. You need to implement an HTTP DELETE endpoint that takes an array of product IDs and removes those products from the cart. Add the following code to the ShoppingCartController.

Figure 2.7   Other microservices can remove items from a shopping cart with an HTTP DELETE request by providing an array of product IDs in the request body.

Listing 2.8   Endpoint for removing items from a shopping cart

```
[HttpDelete("{userid:int}/items")]        ◁─┐  Using the same route template for
public ShoppingCart Delete(                   │  two route declarations is fine if
    int userId,                               │  they use different HTTP methods.
    [FromBody] int[] productIds)
{
    var shoppingCart =
        this.shoppingCartStore.Get(userId);
    shoppingCart.RemoveItems(                     The eventStore will be used later
        productIds,                         ◁─┘  in the RemoveItems method.
        this.eventStore);
    this.shoppingCartStore.Save(shoppingCart);
    return shoppingCart;
}
```

This completes ShoppingCartController, which ends up at about 50 lines of code.

2.2.3   *Fetching product information*

Now that the API exposed by the shopping cart microservice is implemented, let's switch gears and look at how the product information is fetched from the product catalog microservice. Figure 2.8 highlights ProductCatalogClient, which you'll implement in this section.

The product catalog microservice and the shopping cart microservice are separate microservices running in separate processes, perhaps even on separate servers. The product catalog exposes an HTTP API that the shopping cart uses. Product catalog information is fetched in HTTP GET requests to an endpoint on the product catalog microservice.

Figure 2.8 `ProductCatalogClient`

You need to follow these three steps to implement the HTTP request to the product catalog microservice:

1 Implement the HTTP GET request.
2 Parse the response from the endpoint at the product catalog microservice and translate it to the domain of the shopping cart microservice.
3 Implement a policy for handling failed requests to the product catalog microservice.

The subsequent sections walk you through these steps.

IMPLEMENTING THE **HTTP GET**

The product catalog microservice exposes an endpoint at the path /products. The endpoint accepts an array of product IDs as a query string parameter and returns the product information for each of those products. For example, the following request fetches the information for product IDs 1 and 2:

```
HTTP GET /products?productIds=[1,2] HTTP/1.1
Host: productcatalog.my.company.com
Accept: application/json
```

You'll use the HttpClient type to perform the HTTP request. Instead of a real product catalog microservice, the implementation makes a call to a hardcoded JSON file on GitHub, which serves as a fake version of the product catalog endpoint. Using that fake endpoint, the following code makes the HTTP GET request to the product catalog microservice.

Listing 2.9   HTTP GET request to the Product Catalog microservice

```
public class ProductCatalogClient : IProductCatalogClient
    {
        private readonly HttpClient client;
        private static string productCatalogBaseUrl =
```
⟵ **URL of the fake product catalog microservice**

```
                @"https://git.io/JeHiE";
        private static string getProductPathTemplate = "?productIds=[{0}]";

        public ProductCatalogClient(HttpClient client)          ⊲──┐  ASP.NET injects
        {                                                              an HttpClient.
            client.BaseAddress =
                new Uri(productCatalogBaseUrl);          ⊲──┐  Configure the HttpClient to use the
            client                                              base address of the product catalog.
              .DefaultRequestHeaders
              .Accept                                                                    ⊲──┐
                .Add(new MediaTypeWithQualityHeaderValue("application/json"));
            this.client = client;                               Configure the HttpClient to
        }                                                          accept JSON responses
        public async Task<IEnumerable<ShoppingCartItem>>        from the product catalog.
          GetShoppingCartItems(int[] productCatalogIds)
        {
            ....          ⊲──┐  Will be implemented
        }                       in a little while
        private async Task<HttpResponseMessage>
          RequestProductFromProductCatalog(int[] productCatalogIds)
        {
            var productsResource =
              string.Format(getProductPathTemplate,
                string.Join(",", productCatalogIds));
            return await
              this.client.GetAsync(productsResource);          ⊲──┐  Tells HttpClient to perform the
        }                                                            HTTP GET asynchronously
    }
```

This is pretty straightforward. The only thing to note is that by executing the HTTP GET request asynchronously, the current thread is freed up to handle other things in the shopping cart while the request is processed in the product catalog. This is good practice because it preserves resources in the shopping cart microservice, making it a bit less resource intensive and more scalable.

For ASP.NET to be able to inject the HttpClient in ProductCatalogClient we need to register ProductCatalogClient as *typed http client*, which we do by adding this to the ConfigureServices method in Startup:

```
services.AddHttpClient<IProductCatalogClient, ProductCatalogClient>();
```

Now ASP.NET can resolve ProductCatalogClient, which can in turn be injected into other types—the ShoppingCartController, for instance.

2.2.4 Parsing the product response

The product catalog microservice returns product information as a JSON array. The array includes an entry for each requested product, as shown next.

Listing 2.10 Returning a JSON list of products

```
HTTP/1.1 200 OK
Content-Type: application/json; charset=utf-8
```

```
543
[
  {
    "productId": "1",
    "productName": "Basic t-shirt",
    "productDescription": "a quiet t-shirt",
    "price": { "amount" : 40, "currency": "eur" },
    "attributes" : [
    {
      "sizes": [ "s", "m", "l"],
      "colors": ["red", "blue", "green"]
    }]
  },
  {
    "productId": "2",
    "productName": "Fancy shirt",
    "productDescription": "a loud t-shirt",
    "price": { "amount" : 50, "currency": "eur" },
    "attributes" : [
    {
      "sizes": [ "s", "m", "l", "xl"],
      "colors": ["ALL", "Batique"]
    }]
  }
]
```

This JSON must be deserialized, and the information required to create a list of
`ShoppingCart` items needs to be read from it. The array returned from product catalog is formatted by the microservice's API. To avoid tight coupling between microservices, only the `ProductCatalogClient` class knows anything about the API of the
product catalog microservice. That means the `ProductCatalogClient` is responsible
for translating the data received from the microservice into types for the `Shopping-
Cart` project. In this case, you need a list of `ShoppingCartItem` objects. The following
listing shows the code for deserializing and translating the response data.

Listing 2.11 Extracting data from the response

```
private static async Task<IEnumerable<ShoppingCartItem>>
    ConvertToShoppingCartItems(HttpResponseMessage response)
  {
    response.EnsureSuccessStatusCode();
    var products = await
      JsonSerializer.DeserializeAsync<List<ProductCatalogProduct>>(      ◁──┐  Uses System.Text.Json
        await response.Content.ReadAsStreamAsync(),                            to deserialize the JSON
        new JsonSerializerOptions                                             from the product
        {                                                                     catalog microservice
          PropertyNameCaseInsensitive = true
        }) ?? new();
    return products
      .Select(p =>
        new ShoppingCartItem(        ◁──┐  Creates a ShoppingCartItem for
          p.ProductId,                      each product in the response
          p.ProductName,
```

```
            p.ProductDescription,
            p.Price
    ));
}

private record ProductCatalogProduct(          Uses a private record to
    int ProductId,                             represent the product data
    string ProductName,
    string ProductDescription,
    Money Price);
```

If you compare listings 2.10 and 2.11, you may notice that there are more properties in the response than in the `ProductCatalogProduct` class. This is because the Shopping Cart microservice doesn't need all the information, so there's no reason to read the remaining properties. Doing so would only introduce unnecessary coupling. I'll return to this topic in chapters 5, 6, and 8.

The following listing combines the code that requests the product information and the code that parses the response. This method makes the HTTP GET request and translates the response to the domain of the shopping cart.

Listing 2.12   Fetching products and converting them to shopping cart items

```
public async Task<IEnumerable<ShoppingCartItem>>
  GetShoppingCartItems(int[] productCatalogIds)
{
  using var response =
    await RequestProductFromProductCatalogue(productCatalogIds);
  return await ConvertToShoppingCartItems(response);
}
```

The `ProductCatalogClient` is almost finished. The only part missing is the code that handles an HTTP request failure.

2.2.5   *Adding a failure-handling policy*

Remote calls can fail. Not only can they fail, but when running a distributed system at scale, remote calls often do fail. You may not expect the call from shopping cart to product catalog to fail often, but in an entire system of microservices there will often be a failing remote call somewhere in the system.

Remote calls fail for many reasons: the network can fail, the call could be malformed, the remote microservice might have a bug, the server where the call is handled may fail during processing, or the remote microservice might be in the middle of a redeploy. In a system of microservices, you must expect failures and design a level of resilience around every place remote calls are made. This is an important topic, and I'll go into more detail in chapter 7.

The level of resilience needed around a particular remote call depends on the business requirements for the microservice making the call. The call to the product catalog microservice from the shopping cart microservice is important; without the product information, the user can't add items to their shopping cart, which means the e-commerce site can't sell the items to the user. On the other hand, product information doesn't change often, so you could store a copy of it in the shopping cart and only request it from the product catalog when the copy doesn't already contain the information. One way to populate such a copy is by caching responses from the product catalog. Caching product information has some significant advantages:

- It makes the shopping cart more resilient to failures in product catalog.
- The shopping cart microservice will perform better when the product information is present in the cache.
- Fewer calls made from the shopping cart microservice mean less stress is put on the product catalog microservice.

For now, you won't implement caching; we'll return to the subject of caching for the sake of robustness in chapter 7.

Even with caching in place, some calls from the shopping cart to the product catalog are still made. For these calls, you may decide that the best strategy for handling failed calls is to retry the call a couple of times and then give up and fail to add any items to the shopping cart. For this chapter, you'll implement a simple retry policy for handling failing requests. You'll use the Polly library and the Microsoft.Extensions .Http.Polly extension to Polly, both of which you'll install in the ShoppingCart project as a NuGet package.

> **NOTE** Failure-handling strategies and Polly are described in much more detail in chapter 7.

Using a Polly policy involves these two steps:

1. Declaring the policy.
2. Using the policy to execute the remote call.

As you can see in the following listing, Polly's API and integration with ASP.NET makes both these steps easy. Replace the current registration of ProductCatalogClient in Startup with this:

Listing 2.13 Microservice error-handling policy

```
services.AddHttpClient<IProductCatalogClient, ProductCatalogClient>()
    .AddTransientHttpErrorPolicy(p =>           ◁──┐  Wraps http calls made in
        p.WaitAndRetryAsync(                        │  ProductCatalogClient in a Polly policy
            3,
            attempt => TimeSpan.FromMilliseconds(100*Math.Pow(2, attempt)))));
```
**Uses Polly's fluent API to set up a retry
policy with an exponential back-off**

The HttpClient injected in ProductCatalogClient will use this policy around the call to the product catalog microservice: in case of failure, retry the call at most three times. And for each failure, double the amount of waiting time before making the next attempt.

This completes the implementation of `ProductCatalogClient`. Even though it has fewer than 70 lines of code, it does a lot: it builds up the HTTP GET request and executes it. It parses the response from product catalog and translates it into the shopping cart domain. And it uses the retry policy used for these calls. Next, let's tackle the event feed.

2.2.6   *Implementing a basic event feed*

The shopping cart microservice can now store shopping carts and add items to them. The items include product information from the product catalog microservice. The shopping cart also has an API for other microservices that allows them to add or delete items from shopping carts and read the contents of a shopping cart.

The piece missing is the event feed. The shopping cart needs to publish events about changes to shopping carts, and other microservices can subscribe to these events and react to them as required. In the case of items being added to a shopping cart, figure 2.9 (repeated from chapter 1) illustrates how the recommendations microservice and the shopper tracking microservice base part of their functionality on events from the shopping cart microservice.

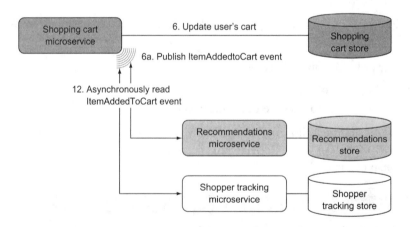

Figure 2.9   The shopping cart microservice publishes events about changes to shopping carts to an event feed. The recommendations and shopper tracking microservices subscribe to these events and react as events arrive.

In this section, you'll implement the `EventFeed` and shopping cart domain model components highlighted in figure 2.10. (Chapter 5 returns to the implementation of event feeds and event subscribers.) The domain model is responsible for raising events, and `EventFeed` allows other microservices to read the events that the shopping cart microservice has published.

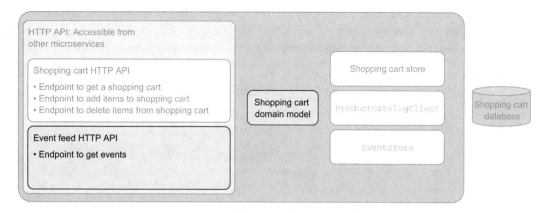

Figure 2.10   The shopping cart microservice event feed publishes events to the rest of the e-commerce system.

Implementing the event feed involves these steps:

- *Raise events.* The code in the shopping cart domain model raises events when something significant (according to the business rules) happens. Significant events are when items are added to or removed from a shopping cart.
- *Store events.* The events raised by the shopping cart domain model are stored in the microservice's data store.
- *Publish events.* Implementing an event feed allows other microservices to subscribe by polling.

We'll work through each of these in turn.

RAISING AN EVENT

In order to be published, events must first be raised. It's usually the domain code in a microservice that raises events, and that's the case in the shopping cart microservice. When items are added to a shopping cart, the `ShoppingCart` domain object raises an event by calling the `Raise` method on `IEventStore` and providing the data for the event.

Remember that I prefer to gather related things in folders, so I add a new folder called EventFeed and add two files to it: Event.cs and EventStore.cs. The first file contains the model type for events, shown in the following listing.

Listing 2.14   Simple event type

```
namespace ShoppingCart.EventFeed
{
  using System;

  public record Event(
    long SequenceNumber,
    DateTimeOffset OccuredAt,
    string Name,
    object Content);
}
```

As mentioned earlier, I am skipping the implementation of the EventStore in this chapter, but this is how the IEventStore interface in the EventStore.cs file looks as an interface for raising and reading events:

```
public interface IEventStore
  {
    IEnumerable<Event> GetEvents(
      long firstEventSequenceNumber, long lastEventSequenceNumber);
    void Raise(string eventName, object content);
  }

  public class EventStore : IEventStore
  {
    // omitted in this chapter
  }
```

Using this interface, the ShoppingCart domain object can raise events, as shown next.

Listing 2.15 Raising events

```
public void AddItems(
      IEnumerable<ShoppingCartItem> shoppingCartItems,
      IEventStore eventStore)
{
  foreach (var item in shoppingCartItems)
    if (this.items.Add(item))
      eventStore.Raise(                          ⟵── Raises an event through the
        "ShoppingCartItemAdded",                      eventStore for each item
        new { UserId, item });
}
```

From the point of view of the domain code, raising an event is just a matter of calling the Raise method on an object that implements the IEventStore interface. The ShoppingCart domain object also raises an event when an item is deleted. The code for raising that event is almost identical, and I'll leave it to you to implement it.

STORING AN EVENT

The events raised by the domain code aren't published to other microservices directly. Instead, they're stored and then published asynchronously. In other words, all Event-Store does when an event is raised is store the event in a database, as shown in the next listing. As with other database code in this chapter, I'll leave it to your imagination. The important thing to understand is that every event is stored as a separate entry in the event store database, and each event gets a monotonically increasing sequence number.

Listing 2.16 Storing event data in a database

```
public void Raise(string eventName, object content)
{                                                          Gets a sequence
  var seqNumber = database.NextSequenceNumber();    ⟵── number for the event
  database.Add(
    new Event(
```

```
          seqNumber,
          DateTimeOffset.UtcNow,
          eventName,
          content));
}
```

`EventStore` stores every incoming event and keeps track of the order in which they arrive. We'll return to the subject of event stores in chapter 6, where we'll look more at implementing them.

A SIMPLE EVENT FEED

Once events are stored, they're ready to be published—in a sense, they *are* published. Even though one microservice *subscribes* to events from another microservice, an event feed works by having subscribers ask for new events periodically (e.g., once every 30 seconds). Because subscribers are responsible for asking for new events, all you need to do in the shopping cart microservice is add an HTTP endpoint that allows subscribers to request events. A subscriber can, for example, issue the following request to get all events newer than event number 100:

```
GET /events?start=100 HTTP/1.1
Host: shoppingcart.my.company.com
Accept: application/json
```

Or, if the subscriber wants to limit the number of incoming events per call, it can add an end argument to the request:

```
GET /events?start=100&end=200 HTTP/1.1
Host: shoppingcart.my.company.com
Accept: application/json
```

Place the implementation of this /events endpoint, as shown in the following listing, in a new controller inside the EventFeed folder. The endpoint takes an optional starting point and an optional ending point, allowing other microservices to request ranges of events.

Listing 2.17   Exposing events to other microservices

```
namespace ShoppingCart.EventFeed
{
  using System.Linq;
  using Microsoft.AspNetCore.Mvc;

  [Route("/events")]
  public class EventFeedController : Controller
  {
    private readonly IEventStore eventStore;

    public EventFeedController(IEventStore eventStore) =>
      this.eventStore = eventStore;

    [HttpGet("")]
    public Event[] Get(
```

```
      [FromQuery] long start,
      [FromQuery] long end = long.MaxValue)
    =>
      this.eventStore
        .GetEvents(start, end)
        .ToArray();
  }
}
```

Reads the start and end values from a query string parameter

Returns the raw list of events. MVC takes care of serializing the events into the response body.

`EventFeedController` mostly uses MVC features that you've already encountered. The only new bit is that the `start` and `end` values are read from query string parameters. The `FromQuery` parameter in front of the method arguments tells MVC that these are query string parameters.

`EventFeedController` uses the event store to filter events between the `start` and `end` values from the client. Although filtering is probably best done at the database level, the following simple implementation illustrates it well.

> **Listing 2.18   Filtering events based on the start and end points**

```
public IEnumerable<Event> GetEvents(
  long firstEventSequenceNumber,
  long lastEventSequenceNumber)  =>
    database
      .Where(e =>
        e.SequenceNumber >= firstEventSequenceNumber &&
        e.SequenceNumber <= lastEventSequenceNumber)
      .OrderBy(e => e.SequenceNumber);
```

With the /events endpoint in place, microservices that want to subscribe to events from the shopping cart microservice can do so by polling the endpoint. Subscribers can—and should—use the `start` and `end` query string parameters to make sure they only get new events. If the shopping cart is down when a subscriber polls, the subscriber can ask for the same events again later. Likewise, if a subscriber goes down for a while, it can catch up with events from the shopping cart by asking for events starting from the last event it saw. As mentioned, this isn't a full-fledged implementation of an event feed, but it gets you to the point that microservices can subscribe to events, and the code is simple.

You've now completed the version 1 implementation of your first microservice. As you can see, a microservice is small and has a narrow focus: it provides just one business capability. You can also see that microservice code tends to be simple and easy to understand. This is why you can expect to create new microservices and replace existing ones quickly.

2.3   *Running the code*

Now that all the code for the shopping cart microservice is in place, you can run it the same way you ran the example in chapter 1: from within Visual Studio, or from the command line with `dotnet`. You can test all the endpoints with RestClient or a similar tool.

When you first try to fetch a shopping cart with an HTTP GET to /shoppingcart/ 123, the cart will be empty. Try adding some items to it with an HTTP POST to /shoppingcart/123/items and then fetching it again; the response should contain the added items. You can also look at the event feed at /events, and you should see events for each added item.

> **WARNING** I haven't shown implementations of EventStore or Shopping-CartStore. If you haven't created your own implementations of these, your microservice won't work.

Summary

- Implementing a complete microservice doesn't take much code. The shopping cart microservice has only the following:
  - Two short controllers
  - A simple ShoppingCart domain class
  - A client class for calling the product catalog microservice
  - Two straightforward data access classes: ShoppingCartDataStore and Event-Store (not shown in this chapter)
- MVC makes it simple to implement HTTP APIs. The routing attributes MVC provides make it easy to add endpoints to a microservice. Just add an action method and put a routing attribute like [HttpGet("")] or [HttpPost("")] on it.
- You should always expect that other microservices may be down. To prevent errors from propagating, each remote call should be wrapped in a policy for handling failure.
- The Polly library is useful for implementing failure-handling policies and wrapping them around remote calls.
- Implementing a basic event feed is simple and enables other microservices to react to events. The poor man's event feed implemented in this chapter is just a short controller.
- Domain model code is usually responsible for raising events, which are then stored in an event store and published through an event feed.

Deploying a microservice to Kubernetes

This chapter covers

- Packaging a microservice in a Docker container
- Deploying a microservice container to Kubernetes on localhost
- Creating a basic Kubernetes cluster on Azure's AKS (Azure Kubernetes Service)
- Deploying a microservice container to a Kubernetes cluster on AKS

In chapter 2, we developed a simple shopping cart microservice, but we only ran it on localhost directly with the `dotnet run` command. In this chapter, we take that microservice and deploy it to a production-like environment in a public cloud. Our microservices can run in many different environments, but we are going to pick just one as an example. We are going to focus on how to take the shopping cart microservice and run it in a Kubernetes cluster in Microsoft Azure. To reach that goal, in this chapter we will:

- Put the shopping cart into a Docker container
- Set up Kubernetes on localhost, so we have a testing ground

- Set up Kubernetes in Azure, so we have a production-like environment
- Run the same shopping cart container in the localhost Kubernetes cluster and the Azure Kubernetes cluster

---

Docker containers

Containers are a way of wrapping an application—or in our case, a microservice—in a portable image that brings along everything it needs to run from operating system to application code to library dependencies. A container image can be built once, moved to different environments, and still be expected to work—as long as the application code in the container does not make assumptions about the environment. In this sense, containers are similar to virtual machines. But where virtual machines virtualize the hardware, containers virtualize the operating systems, which allow containers to be much smaller. This is important in a microservice context where we are going to have many, many microservices. With containers, we are able to run many microservices on the same server while maintaining a good level of isolation between them.

We will get to the implementation of these steps soon, but first we will discuss why this is a solid approach, and touch on some alternatives.

3.1 *Choosing a production environment*

Simply running our microservices on localhost isn't very interesting. We need them to run somewhere our end users can get to them and use them. There are a number of options for doing that:

- Running the microservices on your own Windows or Linux servers on-premise. The microservices we write are .NET applications, which mean they readily run on both Windows and Linux. The HTTP APIs we create are ASP.NET apps and use ASP.NET's web server, Kestrel, which can be put behind a proxy like Nginx or IIS. So, if you or your organization prefers an on-premise solution, the microservices we create can be hosted in a fairly traditional on-premise environment.
- Using a Platform as a Service (PaaS) cloud option that supports .NET like Azure Web Apps or Azure Service Fabric. Using a PaaS option means that you are no longer maintaining the underlying infrastructure yourself. You only have to maintain your microservices. This does not mean that you have no operations work, but the operations you have to do are focused on your microservices, not the underlying infrastructure (e.g., you do not need to keep an operating system patched or worry about renewing hard drives as they age). You only have to deal with what the code in the microservices does.
- Putting microservices into containers and deploying them to a cloud-specific container service like Azure's ACS or Amazon's ECS. As we will see in this chapter, our microservices can easily be put into containers. Both ACS and ECS can run these containers and offer tooling to manage the containers. Like a PaaS

option, this frees you from maintaining the underlying infrastructure, but since containers come with an OS, you will have to keep that up-to-date and patched.
- Using cloud-agnostic container orchestrators like Kubernetes, Apache Mesos, or RedHat OpenShift. Again containerizing our microservices is easy, and once they are in containers, any container orchestrator can run them. There is wide variability in this space, and lumping Kubernetes, Mesos, and OpenShift together might not be completely fair, but they can all run and manage our microservices and are not tied to any particular cloud provider.

Throughout the book, we take care to keep these options open. On the other hand, I also want to show you how to get the microservices running in a production-like environment. That means choosing one of the options listed to use as the example of a production environment in this chapter and in the remainder of the book. This does not mean that the other options are not viable; they are.

For the purpose of this book, I choose to use containers and run them in Kubernetes (figure 3.1) because it gives us a number of benefits that dovetail nicely with the flexibility and scalability we are aiming for with microservices:

- By choosing to put our microservices in containers, we keep several of the options listed open, which gives us flexibility.
- By choosing Kubernetes, we get a mature and widely used container orchestrator, which is supported by all the major clouds and which can also run on your own servers. Kubernetes has a mature and large ecosystem that is highly scalable and built for systems that consist of many small containers that are often updated and redeployed, just like the microservices system we are talking about.

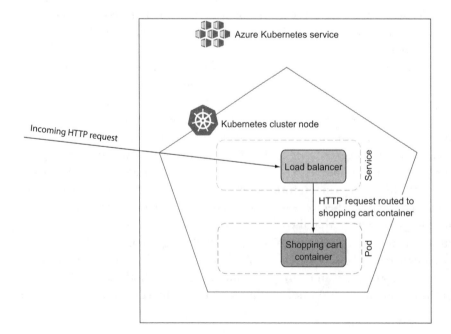

Figure 3.1 We will create a single node Kubernetes cluster in AKS and deploy a load balancer and a shopping cart container to it.

> **NOTE** Make sure you've set up Docker on your development environment. In appendix A, you'll find instructions to install Docker.

The setup we are going to build is illustrated in figure 3.1. We create a Kubernetes cluster in AKS with a single node. In that cluster, we will deploy a load balancer and an instance of the shopping cart container. The load balancer will have a public endpoint that will take traffic from the outside and route that traffic to the shopping cart container.

Now that we have settled on using Kubernetes, let's get the shopping cart running in Kubernetes—first on localhost, then on Azure.

3.2 Putting the Shopping Cart microservice in a container

The first step toward running the shopping cart microservice in Kubernetes is to put it into a container and run that container. We continue using the shopping cart microservice that we developed in chapter 2.

3.2.1 Adding a Dockerfile to the Shopping Cart microservice

To put the shopping cart microservice in a container, we first need to add a *Dockerfile* to the root folder of the shopping cart project next to the solution file. The Dockerfile is a description of the container we want to build and should look like the following code.

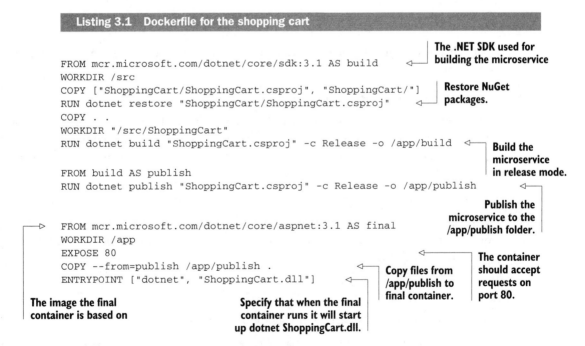

Listing 3.1 Dockerfile for the shopping cart

```
FROM mcr.microsoft.com/dotnet/core/sdk:3.1 AS build        ⟵  The .NET SDK used for
WORKDIR /src                                                   building the microservice
COPY ["ShoppingCart/ShoppingCart.csproj", "ShoppingCart/"]  ⟵  Restore NuGet
RUN dotnet restore "ShoppingCart/ShoppingCart.csproj"          packages.
COPY . .
WORKDIR "/src/ShoppingCart"
RUN dotnet build "ShoppingCart.csproj" -c Release -o /app/build  ⟵  Build the
                                                                    microservice
                                                                    in release mode.
FROM build AS publish
RUN dotnet publish "ShoppingCart.csproj" -c Release -o /app/publish  ⟵

                                                             Publish the
                                                             microservice to the
                                                             /app/publish folder.
FROM mcr.microsoft.com/dotnet/core/aspnet:3.1 AS final
WORKDIR /app
EXPOSE 80                                                    ⟵
COPY --from=publish /app/publish .        ⟵  Copy files from       The container
ENTRYPOINT ["dotnet", "ShoppingCart.dll"] ⟵  /app/publish to       should accept
                                              final container.     requests on
The image the final          Specify that when the final           port 80.
container is based on        container runs it will start
                             up dotnet ShoppingCart.dll.
```

There is a lot going on in that Dockerfile, so let's unpack it piece by piece. The first thing to understand is that the Dockerfile describes a *multistage build*, which means that there are multiple discrete steps in the file. The end result is a ready-to-run container image with the compiled shopping cart microservice. The steps in the Dockerfile are as follows:

- *Build the shopping cart code*—The first part of the Dockerfile builds the shopping cart code using a Docker image that contains the .NET SDK and calls first `dotnet restore` and then `dotnet build`. This is just like we did in chapter 2 to build the shopping cart locally, except we use a couple of extra options to indicate that we want a release build and to specify output folders.
- *Publish the shopping cart microservice*—The second part of the Dockerfile uses the `dotnet publish` command to copy the files needed at runtime from the build output folder (/app/build) to a new folder called /app/publish.
- *Create a container image based on ASP.NET*—The third and final step in the Dockerfile creates the final container image, which is the result of the multi-stage build described in the Dockerfile. The step is based on an ASP.NET Docker image from Microsoft. That image comes with the ASP.NET runtime. We add the files from the /app/publish folder and specify that the entry point to the container image is `dotnet ShoppingCart.dll`, which is a command that runs the compiled ASP.NET application in the `ShoppingCart.dll`.

To make sure the Dockerfile runs a clean build, we add a `.dockerignore` with these lines that make sure any `bin` and `obj` folders are not copied into the container:

```
[B|b]in/
[O|o]bj/
```

With this Dockerfile in place, we are ready to build a shopping cart container image and to run it.

3.2.2 *Building and running the shopping cart container*

The next step is to build a shopping cart container image from the Dockerfile we just added. First, make sure you have Docker running and then open a command line and go to the root of shopping cart—where the Dockerfile is. Then issue this Docker command:

```
> docker build . -t shopping-cart
```

This can take a while the fist time. Be patient. Subsequent builds will be faster. The output of the `docker build` is rather long. When it is successful the last few lines of the output are similar to

```
Successfully built 8d448ba53088
Successfully tagged shopping-cart:latest
```

possibly followed by this warning if you are on Windows:

```
SECURITY WARNING: You are building a Docker image from Windows against a
non-Windows Docker host. All files and directories added to build context
will have '-rwxr-xr-x' permissions. It is recommended to double-check and
reset permissions for sensitive files and directories.
```

This warning comes because you are working with Linux containers on Windows, which is fine for a development environment. The production-like environment we will set up on Azure will be based on Linux servers, so we can safely ignore the warning.

You are now ready to run the newly built container image with this command:

```
> docker run --name shopping-cart --rm -p 5000:80 shopping-cart
```

This starts the shopping cart container and maps port 80 inside the container to port 5000 outside the container, as shown in figure 3.2. This means that you can access the shopping cart on http://localhost:5000 and use the endpoints the same way we did in chapter 2.

The details of the command above are that

- `--name` gives the container a name; in this case, `shopping-cart`.
- `--rm` means that the container is automatically removed when the container exits. This is nice during development to avoid cluttering your localhost machine with too many old containers.
- `-p 5000:80` means that the container exposes port 5000 and listens to traffic on that port. Any incoming traffic to port 5000 is forwarded to port 80 inside the container.
- `shopping-cart` at the end of the command is the name of the container image to run.

To stop the shopping cart container, you can use the `docker stop` command:

```
> docker stop shopping-cart
```

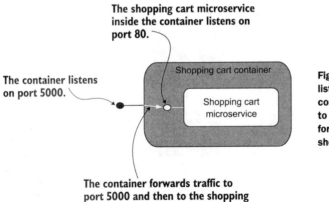

The shopping cart microservice inside the container listens on port 80.

The container listens on port 5000.

Shopping cart container

Shopping cart microservice

The container forwards traffic to port 5000 and then to the shopping cart microservice on port 80.

Figure 3.2 The shopping cart listens to port 80 inside the container. The container listens to traffic on port 5000 and forwards that traffic to the shopping cart microservice.

This confirms that we have successfully built a container with the shopping cart. All we had to do was create a Dockerfile that describes how to build the container and then use Docker to build it. From that, we got a portable container image. This is quite nice because it enables us to run the same container image in all the environments we want, including both localhost and production. Since we can run the same image across different environments, we can be reasonably confident that it will work the same across environments.

Looking at the Dockerfile, we notice that there is nothing about it that makes it specific to the shopping cart, except the names of the `.csproj` file and the `.dll` file. So not only have we built a shopping cart container that we can run in a variety of environments, we have learned how to do the same for all the other .NET-based microservices we will build.

The next thing we need to do is to run the shopping cart container in Kubernetes.

3.3 *Running the shopping cart container in Kubernetes*

Now that the shopping cart is in a container, it is ready to run in Kubernetes. We will create a Kubernetes manifest file and use it to run the shopping cart on Kubernetes—first on localhost and then on Azure. Running the shopping cart container in Kubernetes looks like figure 3.3, which is almost exactly like the diagram at the beginning of the chapter except Kubernetes is running on localhost instead of on Azure. This is no accident, since we are going run the shopping cart in the same way in localhost as we will on Azure.

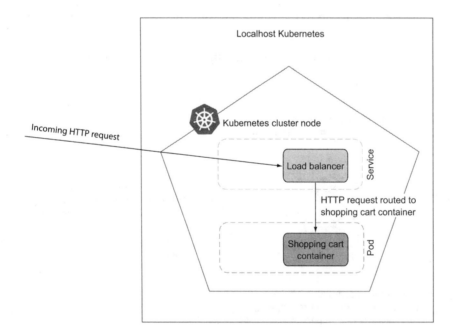

**Figure 3.3
Running the shopping cart on Kubernetes on localhost is almost the same as on Azure.**

3.3.1 *Setting up Kubernetes localhost*

How to set up Kubernetes on your development machine depends on the operating system you are using. If you are on Windows or Mac, I recommend using Docker Desktop, which comes with the option to enable Kubernetes. If you are on Linux, there are numerous options; one easy option is MicroK8S.

Enabling Kubernetes in Docker Desktop

To enable Kubernetes in Docker Desktop, make sure you are using Linux, not Windows, containers. Open the Docker Desktop settings, choose Kubernetes and click "Enable Kubernetes," as shown in the following figure. This will take a while the first time, since Docker Desktop will download, install, and start Kubernetes.

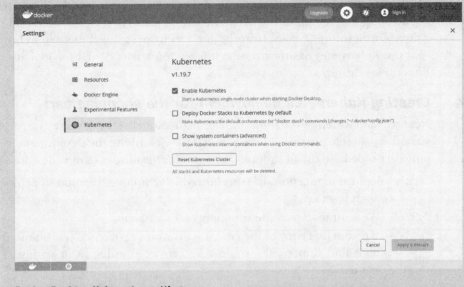

Docker Desktop Kubernetes settings

Once the UI indicates that Kubernetes is running, you are ready to start working with Kubernetes on your localhost.

Installing and starting MicroK8S

To install MicroK8S on a Linux machine, simply run this command:

```
> sudo snap install microk8s --classic
```

This will install and start the Kubernetes cluster. Furthermore, this installs the `microk8s` command-line interface, which includes the `kubectl` command we are going to use. To make it a bit easier to follow along with the work in the following sections, you can create an alias for kubectl:

```
> snap alias microk8s.kubectl kubectl
```

When Kubernetes is running, you can go to the command line and check that Kubernetes is indeed running, using this command

```
> kubectl cluster-info
```

which should give you a response similar to this:

```
Kubernetes master is running at https://kubernetes.docker.internal:6443
KubeDNS is running at https://kubernetes.docker.internal:6443/api/v1/
   namespaces/kube-system/services/kube-dns:dns/proxy

To further debug and diagnose cluster problems, use 'kubectl cluster-info
   dump'.
```

The kubectl command is the command line interface to control Kubernetes, and we will be using that to deploy the shopping cart to Kubernetes, both on localhost and on Azure. Furthermore, kubectl can be used to inspect the Kubernetes cluster and to start the Kubernetes dashboard, which gives you a friendly UI for looking inside the Kubernetes cluster.

3.4   *Creating Kubernetes deployment for the shopping cart*

Next, we want to deploy the shopping cart to the Kubernetes cluster we just installed and started. To do that, we need add a manifest file describing the deployment to the shopping cart code base called shopping-cart.yaml. This file contains two major sections:

1   A deployment section that specifies which container we want to deploy and how we want it set up:
    – We want to deploy the shopping cart container.
    – We want one copy of the container running. We could set this number differently and Kubernetes would take care of running as many instances as we wanted.
    – The port the container communicates on, port 80 in the case of the shopping cart, just like we saw earlier.
2   A service section that configures load balancing in front of the shopping cart. The load balancer makes the shopping cart accessible outside the Kubernetes cluster by giving it an external IP. If we were deploying more than one instance of the shopping cart container, the load balancer would balance the incoming traffic between the shopping cart instances.

These are contents of the shopping-cart.yaml file:

```
kind: Deployment                          ◁──┐  Start of the section specifying
apiVersion: apps/v1                          │  the container deployment
metadata:
  name: shopping-cart
spec:
  replicas: 1
  selector:
    matchLabels:
      app: shopping-cart
  template:
    metadata:
      labels:
        app: shopping-cart
    spec:
```

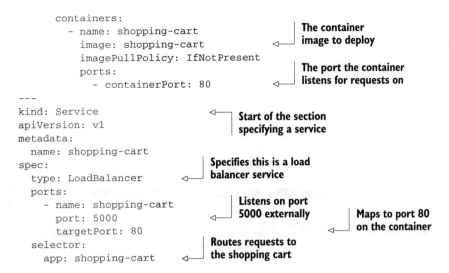

Using this manifest to deploy and run the shopping cart in Kubernetes is as simple as running this from the command line:

```
> kubectl apply -f shopping-cart.yaml
```

This command tells Kubernetes to run everything described in the manifest, so Kubernetes will start the load balancer and the shopping cart. To check if both of these are running, we can use the command kubectl get all, which will list every-thing running in the Kubernetes cluster. If the deployment went well, the output from kubectl get all should be similar to this:

```
NAME                                    READY      STATUS       RESTARTS    AGE
pod/shopping-cart-f4c8f4b94-4j48v       1/1        Running      0           15h


NAME                        TYPE           CLUSTER-IP     EXTERNAL-IP    PORT(S)          AGE
service/kubernetes          ClusterIP      10.96.0.1      <none>         443/TCP          36d
service/shopping-cart       LoadBalancer   10.103.8.64    localhost      5000:31593/TCP   6d20h


NAME                              READY    UP-TO-DATE    AVAILABLE    AGE
deployment.apps/shopping-cart     1/1      1             1            6d20h


NAME                                        DESIRED    CURRENT    READY    AGE
replicaset.apps/shopping-cart-f4c8f4b94     1          1          1        15h
```

If you prefer to have a UI, you can install and start the Kubernetes dashboard. First install the Kubernetes dashboard using this command:

```
> kubectl apply -f https://raw.githubusercontent.com/kubernetes/dashboard/
  v2.2.0/aio/deploy/recommended.yaml
```

At the time of writing, the Kubernetes dashboard in version 2.2.0, which is part of this command. Please consult the Kubernetes dashboard project documentation on GitHub at https://github.com/kubernetes/dashboard for the current version.

Running the command `kubectl proxy` will start the dashboard and make it available on the somewhat complex URL, http://localhost:8001/api/v1/namespaces/kubernetes-dashboard/services/https:kubernetes-dashboard:/proxy/#/overview?namespace=default. This dashboard should also show that the shopping cart is running as shown in figure 3.4.

NOTE If the Kubernetes dashboard asks for a login token, you can get one by running command `kubectl -n kube-system describe secret default` and copying the token from the response.

Figure 3.4   Docker Desktop Kubernetes settings

We are pretty sure Kubernetes is running the shopping cart just fine based on what we see in the dashboard and from `kubectl`, but to make sure it runs as expected, let's test the shopping cart's endpoints. First, let's add a couple of items to a cart:

```
POST http://localhost:5000///shoppingcart/15/items
Accept: application/json
Content-Type: application/json

[1, 2]
```

Next, let's read the same cart back:

```
GET http://localhost:5000///shoppingcart/15
```

The body of the response from the GET request should be the list of items in the cart:

```
{
  "userId": 15,
  "items": [
    {
      "productCatalogueId": 1,
      "productName": "Basic t-shirt",
      "description": "a quiet t-shirt",
      "price": {
        "currency": "eur",
        "amount": 40
      }
    },
    {
      "productCatalogueId": 2,
      "productName": "Fancy shirt",
      "description": "a loud t-shirt",
      "price": {
        "currency": "eur",
        "amount": 50
      }
    }
  ]
}
```

This tells us that the shopping cart indeed works on Kubernetes, just as we expected, since it is the same container image we already ran and tested earlier.

Once done with the shopping cart we can clean up by removing the shopping cart from Kubernetes using this command:

```
kubectl delete -f shopping-cart.yaml
```

Looking at the Kubernetes manifest we used to run the shopping cart on Kubernetes, we can notice that, apart from the name ShoppingCart, the manifest would also work for other microservices. This means that we now have a template for creating Docker-files for our microservices and for creating Kubernetes manifests for them. This puts us in a good position to quickly get all our microservices deployed to Kubernetes.

We are still on localhost, though, so let's move ahead to get the shopping cart up and running on Azure.

3.5 *Running the shopping cart container on Azure Kubernetes Service*

The next goal is to run the shopping cart on Azure Kubernetes Service (AKS). When we have done that, by the end of this section, we will have reached the goal of running our first microservice in a production-like environment, and will have created the setup illustrated in figure 3.1. We need to do the following to get there:

- Set up AKS. We need to create all the Azure resources for a Kubernetes cluster in AKS. This includes the cluster itself, networking, and a private container registry where we will store the container images for our microservices.

- Push the shopping cart container image to our private container registry.
- Deploy the shopping cart to the AKS cluster using the shopping cart's Kubernetes manifest.

Alternatives to Azure Kubernetes Service

Azure is by no means the only place we can run Kubernetes. The other major public clouds—Google Cloud, Amazon Web Services, Digital Ocean, and others—offer similar managed Kubernetes services. All of these are easy to set up, and they all offer tools to scale and monitor the clusters. The reason I use Azure is familiarity; the others are equally viable options.

If you prefer to manage your own servers, you can also choose to set up Kubernetes on your own cloud or on-premise servers. The differences compared to the managed Kubernetes services are in the setup and management of the Kubernetes cluster. The management of the containers we deploy to Kubernetes is the same in all cases.

3.5.1   *Setting up AKS*

The setup we need in order to be ready to work with a Kubernetes cluster in AKS consists of four parts:

1 Creating a *resource group* in Azure. A resource group is just a grouping of things in Azure. We are putting all the resources for the Kubernetes cluster and the container registry in one resource group. This will group everything together in the Azure portal and will make it easy for us to clean everything up once we are done.
2 Creating a private container registry.
3 Creating a Kubernetes cluster in AKS. We will create a small cluster with just one node, and we attach it to the private container registry to allow Kubernetes to pull containers from our registry.
4 Logging our local Kubernetes command line—kubectl—into the newly created AKS cluster.

Each of these four parts is performed by an Azure command with the Azure command line tool az. The end result in Azure is shown in figure 3.5, an Azure resource group

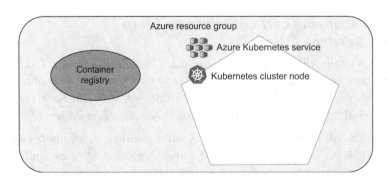

Figure 3.5   Running the shopping cart on Kubernetes on localhost is almost the same as on Azure.

with a private Azure Container Registry and single node Kubernetes cluster in AKS. This is our production environment.

> **NOTE** To follow along with the set up of AKS, you need to have the Azure CLI installed and logged into your Azure account. In appendix A you will find instructions on installing the Azure CLI.

To make the AKS setup easy to repeat, I have gathered the commands needed to set up AKS in a PowerShell script called create-aks.ps1 that looks like this:

```
az group create --name MicroservicesInDotnet --location northeurope

az acr create --resource-group MicroservicesInDotnet --name
   YOUR_UNIQUE_REGISTRY_NAME --sku Basic

az aks create --resource-group MicroservicesInDotnet --name
   MicroservicesInDotnetAKSCluster --node-count 1 --enable-addons monitoring
   --generate-ssh-keys --attach-acr YOUR_UNIQUE_REGISTRY_NAME

az aks get-credentials --resource-group MicroservicesInDotnet --name
   MicroservicesInDotnetAKSCluster
kubectl get nodes
```

The first four lines correspond exactly to the four parts listed: creating a resource group, creating a container registry, creating the AKS cluster, and logging kubectl into the cluster. The last line shows the nodes in the cluster, so we know the cluster is up and running.

> **NOTE** The az acr create . . . command needs a unique registry name. If the name is not unique, you'll get an error about the name already being in use. You can check if the name is already claimed using the API documented here: http://mng.bz/PXZg.

Running the script takes a while—about 5–10 minutes. It also produces a lot of output, although in a burst, so don't be surprised if there is no feedback for a few minutes followed by a burst of output. The last lines of the output are the output from the line kubectl get nodes and should look similar to this:

```
NAME                                STATUS   ROLES   AGE    VERSION
aks-nodepool1-32786309-vmss000000   Ready    agent   107s   v1.14.8
```

This a list of the nodes in the Kubernetes cluster your kubectl command line is attached to. The name of your node will differ from mine but should start with aks-.

> **NOTE** If you want some more background and detail on the steps involved in setting up AKS, refer to Microsoft's documentation, such as the article "Quickstart: Deploy an Azure Kubernetes Service Cluster Using the Azure CLI" at http://mng.bz/J6ZP.

When you are done with the Kubernetes cluster in AKS, you can delete the cluster as well as the container registry with this command:

```
> az group delete --name MicroservicesInDotnet --yes --no-wait
```

At this point, the Kubernetes cluster in AKS is up and running. Before we move on, we will get the Kubernetes dashboard up and running, too. There are two steps toward running the Kubernetes dashboard: first we must allow the dashboard to access the cluster, and then we start the dashboard.

This command will give the dashboard access by telling Kubernetes to assign the role `cluster-admin` to the account `kube-system:kubernetes-dashboard`:

```
> kubectl create clusterrolebinding kubernetes-dashboard
  --clusterrole=cluster-admin
  --serviceaccount=kube-system:kubernetes-dashboard
```

The Kubernetes dashboard uses the `kube-system:kubernetes-dashboard` account, so now it will have cluster admin rights.

With the access in place we can start the Kubernetes dashboard with the Azure command line like this:

```
> az aks browse --resource-group MicroservicesInDotnet  --name
  MicroservicesInDotnetAKSCluster
```

This will start the Kubernetes dashboard and open a browser tab with the dashboard, as shown in figure 3.6

> **NOTE** If you have any trouble with getting the Kubernetes dashboard up and running, refer to Microsoft's documentation, which has the article "Access the Kubernetes Web Dashboard in Azure Kubernetes Service (AKS)" at http://mng.bz/wQxW, which has troubleshooting information.

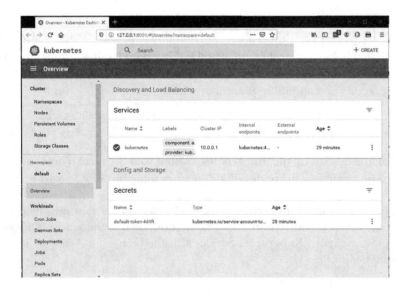

**Figure 3.6
The Kubernetes
dashboard**

Now we have a Kubernetes cluster running in Azure, and we have the dashboard running, so we have a friendly interface to what's running the cluster. We also have the shopping cart container image and a Kubernetes manifest file for the shopping cart. With all this in place, we are ready to deploy the shopping cart to our AKS cluster. Not only that, since the way we built the shopping cart container easily extends to building containers for other microservices and since the Kubernetes manifest also easily extends to other microservices, we are ready to deploy the microservice we will build in the upcoming chapter to AKS.

> **NOTE** To switch back and forth between working with Kubernetes on localhost and on Azure, you can change the *context* of kubectl with the command kubctl config use-context <name-of-context>, and you can see which context you have available by running kubectl config get-contexts.

3.5.2 *Running the shopping cart in AKS*

With the infrastructure to run microservices in AKS in place, we return to the shopping cart microservice. We have already put the shopping cart into a container, and we have run that container in Kubernetes on localhost by applying the Kubernetes manifest for the shopping cart to the localhost Kubernetes. Deploying the shopping cart to AKS is mostly reusing the things we have already made, but there are a few tweaks. The remaining steps to deploying and running the shopping cart in AKS are as follows:

- Tag the shopping cart container image, so we have a precise identification of the container image.
- Push the tagged container image to our container registry in Azure.
- Modify the shopping cart's Kubernetes manifest to refer to the tagged container.
- Apply the modified manifest to AKS.
- Test that the shopping cart runs correctly.

As listed we need to tag the shopping cart container image that we built in section 3.2.2. The tag we will give the container is your_unique_registry_name.azurecr.io/shopping-cart:1.0.0. The first part of the tag is the address of our container registry in Azure, your_unique_registry_name.azurecr.io; the second part is the name and version of the container image. We set the tag as follows:

```
> docker tag shopping-cart your_unique_registry_name.azurecr.io/
  shopping-cart:1.0.0
```

We have to push the container image to a container registry to make it available for AKS to pull down and run. AKS cannot pull a container image from my or your localhost. The registry we use in Azure is private, so any service pulling from it or pushing to it must be authenticated. When we created the AKS cluster, we used the option --attach-acr MicroservicesInDotnetRegistry, which connects the AKS cluster with the container registry called YOUR_UNIQUE_REGISTRY_NAME and allows AKS to pull images. Likewise, the Docker client on our localhost needs to be authenticated with the container registry before it is allowed to push container images to the registry. This authentication is done using the Azure CLI like this:

```
> az acr login --name YOUR_UNIQUE_REGISTRY_NAME
```

Now the tagged container image can be pushed to our private Docker registry in Azure with this Docker command:

```
> docker push your_unique_registry_name.azurecr.io/shopping-cart:1.0.0
```

The shopping cart container image is now available for our AKS cluster to pull, but we have to tell it to do so. To that end, we have to modify the manifest file, shopping-cart.yaml, to refer to the container by the tag `your_unique_registry_name.azurecr.io/shopping-cart:1.0.0`, which means the manifest becomes:

```
kind: Deployment
apiVersion: apps/v1
metadata:
  name: shopping-cart
spec:
  replicas: 1
  selector:
    matchLabels:
      app: shopping-cart
  template:
    metadata:
      labels:
        app: shopping-cart
    spec:
      containers:
        - name: shopping-cart
          image: your_unique_registry_name.azurecr.io/
            shopping-cart:1.0.0              ⟵┐  Points to the container
          imagePullPolicy: IfNotPresent         │  in our private registry
          ports:
            - containerPort: 80
---
apiVersion: v1
kind: Service
metadata:
  name: shopping-cart
spec:
  type: LoadBalancer
  ports:
    - name: shopping-cart
      port: 5000
      targetPort: 80
  selector:
    app: shopping-cart
```

The only change is the image name, which now refers to the image in our private container registry in Azure. All that remains is to apply this manifest to the Kubernetes cluster in AKS:

```
> kubectl apply -f shopping-cart.yaml
```

After a short while, the shopping cart will be running in AKS. To verify this, we need the IP address of the shopping cart in AKS so we can call its endpoints. We can either find the IP address of the shopping cart in the Kubernetes dashboard or with the command line.

Using the command line the command `kubectl get all` will show the information about everything running in the cluster. The output should be similar to this:

```
NAME                                READY    STATUS     RESTARTS    AGE
pod/shopping-cart-f4c8f4b94-vnmn9   1/1      Running    0           107s

NAME                     TYPE           CLUSTER-IP     EXTERNAL-IP     PORT(S)           AGE
service/kubernetes       ClusterIP      10.0.0.1       <none>          443/TCP           15m
service/shopping-cart    LoadBalancer   10.0.100.183   52.142.83.184   5000:31552/TCP    107s

NAME                             READY    UP-TO-DATE    AVAILABLE    AGE
deployment.apps/shopping-cart    1/1      1             1            107s

NAME                                       DESIRED    CURRENT    READY    AGE
replicaset.apps/shopping-cart-f4c8f4b94    1          1          1        107s
```

The IP address of the shopping cart load balancer is in the external IP column in the list of services. In this case, the IP address is `52.142.83.184` and the port is `5000`, just like it was on localhost. We can call the shopping cart through the load balancer, in this case at `52.142.83.184:5000`.

Similarly, the IP address can be found in the Kubernetes dashboard under Services, as shown in figure 3.7.

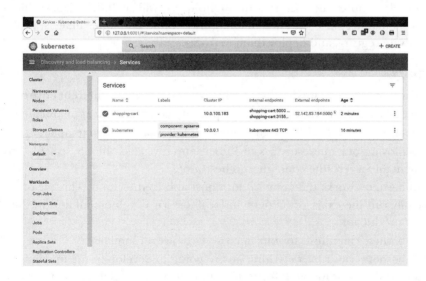

Figure 3.7 Find the address of the shopping cart under services.

To verify that the shopping cart is indeed running, we can test its endpoint by, for instance, adding items to a cart using the shopping cart's POST endpoint

```
POST http:52.142.83.184:5000///shoppingcart/15/items
Accept: application/json
```

```
Content-Type: application/json
```

```
[1, 2]
```

and then reading the same cart using the GET endpoint:

```
GET http:52.142.83.184:5000///shoppingcart/15
```

The response from this endpoint is the list of items in the cart for user number 15, confirming that the shopping cart works just the same on AKS as it did on Kubernetes on localhost, and when we ran the shopping cart directly with `dotnet run`.

Over time, we will create many microservices in a microservice system, which, in turn, means we will have many pods in Kubernetes; following the pattern I have laid out in this chapter, each one also has an associated load balancer in Kubernetes, which allows balancing traffic between multiple copies of the containers. For instance, we might run 3, 10, or 100 copies of the shopping cart container and let the shopping carts load balancer spread the incoming traffic between them. With a load balancer for each service that each exposes endpoints to the outside and each with a different IP address, a problem arises: How do we manage all these different entry points into our Kubernetes cluster? There is a security aspect to this question that we will return to in chapter 10, and there is a question of how end user applications know where to send requests, which we will return to in chapter 12.

This concludes the setup of a production-like environment and the deployment of the first microservice to that environment. This positions us well for continuing working with microservices. The AKS cluster is set up and ready to run more microservices. As we develop more microservices throughout, we will include a Dockerfile and a Kubernetes manifest in each one, enabling us to build container images, push them to the private registry, and deploy them to AKS.

Summary
- The microservices we develop can be deployed to many different environments.
- .NET-based microservices are easily put into containers and run as containers.
- Dockerfiles for .NET-based microservices follow a common template.
- Deploying our microservices to Kubernetes gives us a highly scalable environment and a versatile container orchestrator.
- Kubernetes works the same on localhost and in the cloud. This means we can easily run the exact containers on localhost for development and in the cloud for production.
- Kubernetes manifests for our microservices are all similar.
- Kubernetes can run everything we are going to develop in the upcoming chapters while providing tools for scaling, monitoring, and debugging microservices.
- Azure Kubernetes Services is an easy-to-set-up managed Kubernetes offering that enables us to get up and running with Kubernetes quickly.

Part 2

Building microservices

In this part of the book, you'll learn how to design and code a microservice. The assorted diverse topics all go into designing and coding good, maintainable, reliable microservices:

- Chapter 4 explains how to slice and dice a system into a cohesive set of microservices. You will learn three rules of thumb that help you decide what belongs in each microservice.
- Chapter 5 shows you how microservices can collaborate to provide functionality for end users. You'll also be introduced to three categories of collaboration and when to use each of them.
- Chapter 6 explores where the data goes in a microservice system and which microservices should take responsibility for which data.
- Chapter 7 teaches you some simple techniques to make a microservice system more robust than it would be otherwise. Using these techniques, you can create a system that keeps running in the face of network failures and individual microservice crashes.
- Chapter 8 turns to testing. You'll learn how to create an effective automated test suite for a microservice system, all the way from broad system-level tests to narrowly focused unit tests.

By the end of part 2, you'll know how to design microservices, how to use .NET to code them, and Kubernetes to run them.

Identifying and scoping microservices

4

This chapter covers

- Scoping microservices for business capability
- Scoping microservices to support technical capabilities
- Scoping microservices to support efficient development work
- Managing when scoping microservices is difficult
- Carving out new microservices from existing ones

To succeed with microservices, it's important to be good at scoping each microservice appropriately. If your microservices are too big, the turnaround on creating new features and implementing bug fixes becomes longer than it needs to. If they're too small, the coupling between microservices tends to grow. If they're the right size but have the wrong boundaries, coupling also tends to grow, and higher coupling also leads to longer turnaround. In other words, if you aren't able to scope your microservices correctly, you'll lose much of the benefit microservices offer. In this chapter, I'll teach you how to find a good scope for each microservice so it stays loosely coupled and efficient to work with.

The primary driver in identifying and scoping microservices is business capabilities, the secondary driver is supporting technical capabilities, and the tertiary driver is efficiency of work. Following these drivers leads to microservices that align nicely with the list of microservice characteristics from chapter 1:

- A microservice is responsible for a single capability.
- A microservice is individually deployable.
- A microservice consists of one or more processes.
- A microservice owns its own data store.
- A small team can maintain a handful of microservices.
- A microservice is replaceable.

Of these characteristics, the first two and last two can only be realized if the microservice's scope is good. There are also implementation-level concerns that come into play, but getting the scope wrong will prevent the service from adhering to those four characteristics.

4.1   *The primary driver for scoping microservices: Business capabilities*

Each microservice should implement exactly one capability. For example, a shopping cart microservice should keep track of the items in the user's shopping cart. The primary way to identify capabilities for microservices is to analyze the business problem and determine the business capabilities. Each business capability should be implemented by a separate microservice.

4.1.1   *What is a business capability?*

A *business capability* is something an organization does that contributes to business goals. For instance, handling a shopping cart on an e-commerce website is a business capability that contributes to the broader business goal of allowing users to purchase items. A given business will have a number of business capabilities that together make the overall business function.

When mapping a business capability to a microservice, the microservice models the business capability. In some cases, the microservice implements the entire business capability and automates it completely. In other cases, the microservice implements only part of the business capability, because some part of the capability is carried out by people in the real world and thus the microservice only partly automates the business capability. In both cases, the scope of the microservice is the business capability.

Business capabilities and bounded contexts

Domain-driven design is an approach to designing software systems that's based on modeling the business domain. An important step is identifying the language used by domain experts to talk about the domain. It turns out that the language used by domain experts isn't consistent in all cases.

In different parts of a domain, different things are in focus, so a given word like *customer* may have different foci in different parts of the domain. For instance, for a company selling photocopiers, a customer in the sales department may be a company that buys a number of photocopiers and may be primarily represented by a procurement officer. In the customer service department, a customer may be an end user having trouble with a photocopier. When modeling the domain of the photocopier company, the word *customer* means different things in different parts of the model.

A *bounded context* in domain-driven design is part of a larger domain within which words mean the same things. Bounded contexts are related to but different from business capabilities. A bounded context defines an area of a domain within which the language is consistent. Business capabilities, on the other hand, are about what the business needs to get done. Within one bounded context, the business may need to get several things done. Each of these things is likely a business capability.

Since the business capabilities within a bounded context are related, we can accept a higher degree of coupling between capabilities within the same bounded context than we can between capabilities in different bounded context.

4.1.2 Identifying business capabilities

A good understanding of the domain will enable you to understand how the business functions. Understanding how the business functions means you can identify the business capabilities that make up the business and the processes involved in delivering the capabilities. In other words, the way to identify business capabilities is to learn about the business's domain. You can gain this type of knowledge by talking with the people who know the business domain best: business analysts, the end users of your software, and so on—all the people directly involved in the day-to-day work that drives the business.

A business's organization usually reflects its domain. Different parts of the domain are handled by different groups of people, and each group is responsible for delivering certain business capabilities; so, this organization can give you hints about how the microservices should be scoped. For one thing, a microservice's responsibility should probably lie within the purview of only one group. If it crosses the boundary between two groups, it's probably too widely scoped and will be difficult to keep cohesive, leading to low maintainability. These observations are in line with what is known as *Conway's law*:[1]

> *Any organization that designs a system (defined broadly) will produce a design whose structure is a copy of the organization's communication structure.*

Sometimes you may uncover parts of the domain where the organization and the domain are at odds. In such situations, there are two approaches you can take, both of which respect Conway's law. You can accept that the system can't fully reflect the domain and implement a few microservices that aren't well aligned with the domain but are well aligned with the organization; or you can change the organization to

---

[1] Melvin Conway, "How Do Committees Invent?" *Datamation Magazine*, April 1968.

reflect the domain. Both approaches can be problematic. The first risks building microservices that are poorly scoped and that might become highly coupled. The second involves moving people and responsibilities between groups. Those kinds of changes can be difficult. Your choice should be a pragmatic one, based on an assessment of which approach will be least troublesome.

To get a better understanding of what business capabilities are, it's time to look at an example.

4.1.3   Example: Point-of-sale system

The example we'll explore in this chapter is a point-of-sale system (POS), illustrated in figure 4.1. I'll briefly introduce the domain, and then we'll look at how to identify business capabilities within it. Finally, we'll consider the scope of one of the microservices in the system in more detail.

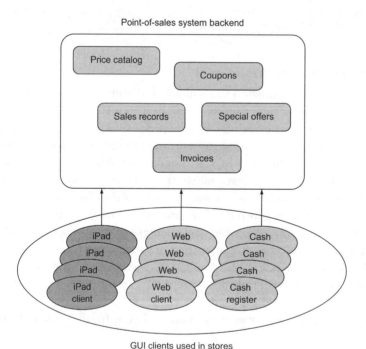

Figure 4.1   A POS system for a large chain of stores, consisting of a backend that implements all the business capabilities in the system and thin GUI clients cashiers use in the stores. Microservices in the backend implement the business capabilities.

This POS system is used in all the stores of a large chain. Cashiers at the stores interact with the system through a thin GUI client—it could be a tablet application, a web application, or a physical purpose-built cash register. The GUI client is just a thin layer in front of the backend. The backend is where all the business logic (the business capabilities) is implemented, and it will be our focus.

The system offers cashiers a variety of functions:

- Scan products and add them to the invoice.
- Prepare an invoice.

- Charge a credit card via a card reader attached to the client.
- Register a cash payment.
- Accept coupons.
- Print a receipt.
- Send an electronic receipt to the customer.
- Search in the product catalog.
- Scan one or more products to show prices and special offers related to the products.

These functions are things the system does for the cashier, but they don't directly match the business capabilities that drive the POS system.

IDENTIFYING BUSINESS CAPABILITIES IN THE POINT-OF-SALE DOMAIN

To identify the business capabilities that drive the POS system, you need to look beyond the list of functions. You must determine what needs to go on behind the scenes to support the functionality.

Starting with the "Search in the product catalog" function, an obvious business capability is maintaining a product catalog. This is the first candidate for a business capability that could be the scope of a microservice. Such a product catalog microservice would be responsible for providing access to the current product catalog. The product catalog needs to be updated every so often, but the chain of stores uses another system to handle that functionality. The product catalog microservice would need to reflect the changes made in that other system, so the scope of the product catalog microservice would include receiving updates to the product catalog.

The next business capability you might identify is applying special offers to invoices. Special offers give the customer a discounted price when they buy a bundle of products. A bundle may consist of a certain number of the same product at a discounted price (for example, three for the price of two), or it may be a combination of different products (say, buy A and get 10% off B). In either case, the invoice the cashier gets from the POS GUI client must take any applicable special offers into account automatically. This business capability is the second candidate to be the scope for a microservice. A special offers microservice would be responsible for deciding when a special offer applies and what the discount for the customer should be.

Looking over the list of functionality again, notice that the system should allow cashiers to "scan one or more products to show prices and special offers related to the products." This indicates that there's more to the special offers business capability than just applying special offers to invoices; it also includes the ability to look up special offers based on products.

If you continued the hunt for business capabilities in the POS system, you might end up with this list:

- Product catalog
- Price catalog
- Price calculation

- Special offers
- Coupons
- Sales records
- Invoice
- Payment

Figure 4.2 shows a map from functionalities to business capabilities. The map is a logical one, in the sense that it shows which business capabilities are needed to implement each function, but it doesn't indicate any direct technical dependencies. For instance, the arrow from prepare invoice to coupons doesn't indicate a direct call from some prepare invoice code in a client to a coupons microservice. Rather, the arrow indicates that in order to prepare an invoice, coupons need to be taken into account, so the prepare invoice function depends on the coupons business capability.

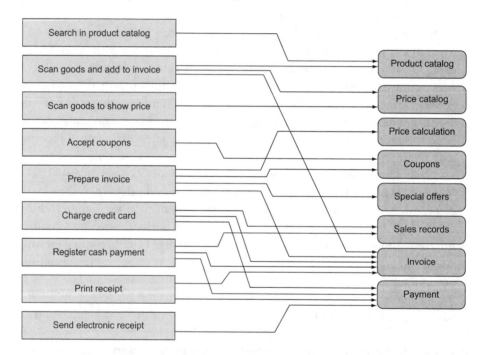

Figure 4.2   The functions on the left depend on the business capabilities on the right. Each arrow indicates a dependency between a function and a capability.

Finding the business capabilities in real domains can be hard work and often requires a good deal of iterating. The list of business capabilities isn't a static list made at the start of development; rather, it's an emergent list that grows and changes over time as your understanding of the domain and the business grows and deepens.

Now that we've gone through the first iteration of identifying business capabilities, let's take a closer look at one of these capabilities and how it defines the scope of a microservice.

THE SPECIAL OFFERS MICROSERVICE

The special offers microservice is based on the special offers business capability. To narrow the scope of this microservice, we'll dive deeper into this business capability and identify the processes involved, illustrated in figure 4.3. Each process delivers part of the business capability.

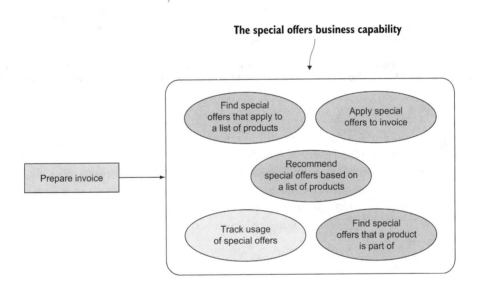

Figure 4.3   The special offers business capability includes a number of different processes.

The special offers business capability is broken down into five processes. Four of these are oriented toward the POS GUI clients. The fifth—tracking the use of special offers—is oriented toward the business itself, which is interested in tracking which special offers customers are taking advantage of.

Implementing the business capability as a microservice means you need to do the following:

- Expose the four client-oriented processes as API endpoints that other microservices can call.
- Implement the usage-tracking process through an event feed. The business intelligence parts of the POS system can subscribe to these events and use them to track which special offers customers use.

The components of the special offers microservice are shown in figure 4.4.

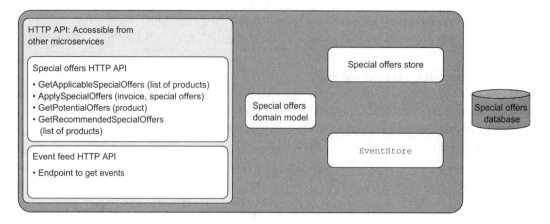

Figure 4.4   The processes in the special offers business capability are reflected in the implementation of the special offers microservice. The processes are exposed to other microservices through the microservice's HTTP API.

The components of the special offers microservice are similar to the components of the shopping cart microservice in chapter 2, which is shown again in figure 4.5. This is no coincidence. These are the components our microservices typically consist of: an HTTP API that exposes the business capability implemented by the microservice, an event feed (explained and implemented in chapter 5), a domain model implementing the business logic involved in the business capability, a data store component, and a database.

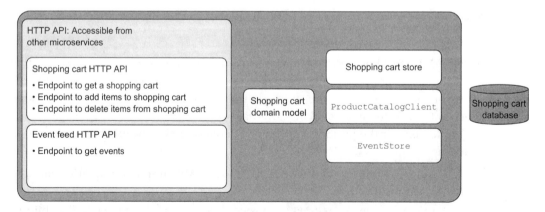

Figure 4.5   The components of the shopping cart microservice from chapter 2 are similar to the components of the special offers microservice.

4.2　The secondary driver for scoping microservices: Supporting technical capabilities

The secondary way to identify scopes for microservices is to look at supporting technical capabilities. A *supporting technical capability* is something that doesn't directly contribute to a business goal but supports other microservices, such as integrating with another system or scheduling an event to happen some time in the future.

4.2.1　What is a technical capability?

Supporting technical capabilities are secondary drivers in scoping microservices because they don't directly contribute to the system's business goals. They exist to simplify and support the other microservices that implement business capabilities.

Remember, one characteristic of a good microservice is that it's replaceable; but if a microservice that implements a business capability also implements a complex technical capability, it may grow too large and too complex to be replaceable. In such cases, you should consider implementing the technical capability in a separate microservice that supports the original one. Before discussing how and when to identify supporting technical capabilities, a couple of examples would probably be helpful.

4.2.2　Examples of supporting technical capabilities

To give you a feel for what I mean by supporting technical capabilities, let's consider two examples: an integration with another system, and the ability to send notifications to customers.

INTEGRATING WITH AN EXTERNAL PRODUCT CATALOG SYSTEM

In the example POS system, you identified the product catalog as a business capability. I also mentioned that product information is maintained in another system, external to the microservice-based POS system. That other system is an enterprise resource planning (ERP) system. This implies that the product catalog microservice must integrate with the ERP system, as illustrated in figure 4.6.

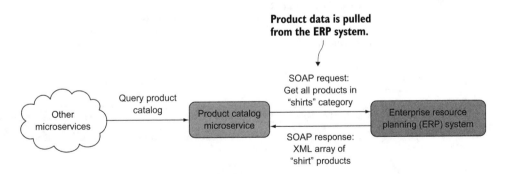

Figure 4.6　Product data flows from the ERP system to the product catalog microservice. The protocol used to get product information from the ERP system is defined by the ERP system. It could expose a SOAP web service for fetching the information, or it might export product information to a proprietary file format.

Let's assume that you aren't in a position to make changes to the ERP system, so the integration must be implemented using whatever interface the ERP system has. It might use a SOAP web service to fetch product information, or it might export all the product information to a proprietary file format. In either case, the integration must happen on the ERP system's terms. Depending on the interface the ERP system exposes, this may be a smaller or larger task. In any case, it's a task primarily concerned with the technicalities of integrating with some other system, and it has the potential to be at least somewhat complex. The purpose of this integration is to support the product catalog microservice.

We'll take the integration out of the product catalog microservice and implement it in a separate ERP integration microservice that's responsible solely for that one integration, as illustrated in figure 4.7. We'll do this for two reasons:

- By moving the technical complexities of the integration to a separate microservice, we keep the scope of the product catalog microservice narrow and focused.
- By using a separate microservice to deal with how the ERP data is formatted and organized, we keep the ERP system's view of what a product is separate from the POS system. Remember that in different parts of a large domain, there are different views of what terms mean. It's unlikely that the product catalog microservice and the ERP system agree on how the product entity is modeled. A translation between the two views is needed and is best done by the new microservice. In domain-driven design terms, the new microservice acts as an *anticorruption layer*.

NOTE The anticorruption layer is a concept borrowed from domain-driven design. It can be used when two systems interact: it protects the domain model in one system from being polluted with language or concepts from the model in the other system.

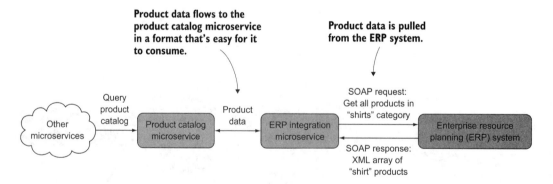

Figure 4.7 The ERP integration microservice supports the product catalog microservice by handling the integration with the ERP system. It translates between the way the ERP system exposes product data and the way the product catalog microservice consumes it.

An added benefit of placing the integration in a separate microservice is that it's a good place to address any reliability issues related to the integration. If the ERP system is unreliable, the place to handle that is in the ERP integration microservice. If the ERP system is slow, the ERP integration microservice can deal with that. Over time, you can tweak the policies used in the ERP integration microservice to address any reliability issues with the ERP system without touching the product catalog microservice at all. This integration with the ERP system is an example of a supporting technical capability, and the ERP integration microservice is an example of a microservice implementing that capability.

SENDING NOTIFICATIONS TO CUSTOMERS

Now let's consider extending the POS system with the ability to send notifications about new special offers to registered customers via email, SMS, or push notification to a mobile app. We can put this capability into one or more separate microservices.

At the moment, the POS system doesn't know who the customers are. To drive better customer engagement and customer loyalty, the company decides to start a small loyalty program where customers can sign up to be notified about special offers. The customer loyalty program is a new business capability and will be the responsibility of a new loyalty program microservice. Figure 4.8 shows this microservice, which is responsible for notifying registered customers every time a new special offer is available to them.

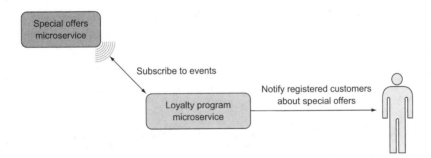

Figure 4.8   The loyalty program microservice subscribes to events from the special offers microservice and notifies registered customers when new offers are available.

As part of the registration process, customers can choose to be notified by email, SMS, or, if they have the company's mobile app, push notification. This introduces some complexity in the loyalty program microservice in that it must not only choose which type of notification to use, but also deal with how each one works. As a first step, we'll introduce a supporting technical microservice for each notification type. This is shown in figure 4.9.

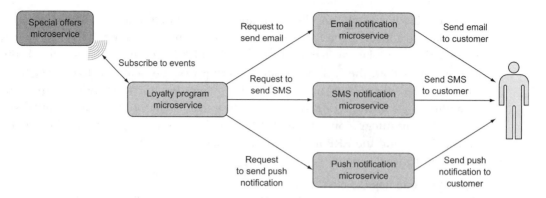

Figure 4.9   To avoid bogging down the loyalty program microservice in technical details for handling each type of notification, we'll introduce three supporting technical microservices, one for each type of notification.

This is better. The loyalty program microservice doesn't have to implement all the details of dealing with each type of notification, which keeps the microservice's scope narrow and focused. The situation isn't perfect, though: the microservice still has to decide which of the supporting technical microservices to call for each registered customer.

This leads us to introducing one more microservice, which acts as a front for the three microservices handling the three types of notifications. This new notifications microservice is depicted in figure 4.10 and is responsible for choosing which type of notification to use each time a customer needs to be notified.

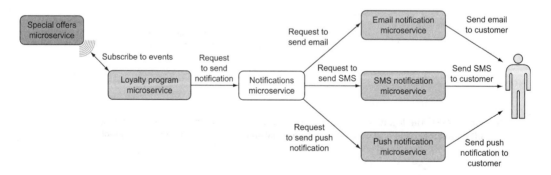

Figure 4.10   To remove more complexity from the loyalty program microservice, we'll introduce a notifications microservice that's responsible for choosing a type of notification based on customer preferences.

This example of a supporting technical capability differs from the previous example of the ERP integration in that other microservices may also need to send notifications to specific customers. For instance, one of the functionalities of the POS system is to send the customer an electronic receipt. The microservice in charge of that business capability can also take advantage of the notifications microservice. Part of the motivation for moving this to a separate microservice is that you can reuse the implementation.

While sending emails, text messages, or push notifications are technical capabilities, sending notifications is likely a business capability with business rules on how and when to notify customers. Thus, we have discovered a separate business capability by driving out the technical capabilities into their own microservices. This is not unusual: in practice the three drivers for scoping microservices interact, and driving along one axis—in this case the axis of technical capabilities—exposes things along the other axes—in this case the axis of business capabilities. This realization leads us to revise our understanding of the domain and introduce a *notifications*-bounded context that contains the business capability of notifying users as well as the technical capabilities of sending emails, SMS messages, and push notifications. This new bounded context and the microservices in it is shown in figure 4.11.

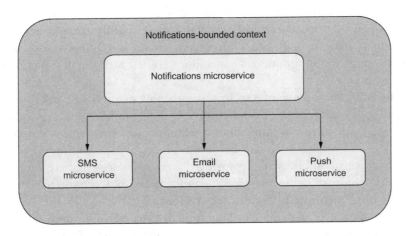

Figure 4.11 The new notifications-bounded context contains the business capability of handling notifications and the technical capabilities of sending emails, SMS messagess, and push notifications.

The notifications microservice is different from the other three microservices in the notifications-bounded context because it handles the business rules around notifications, such as respecting customers preferences about how they want to be notified, when they should be notified, how often they should be notified, and so on. For instance, the notification microservice might implement rules that adjust the time of day customers are notified about special offers based on their purchasing patterns, so we send them notifications just when they are about to go shopping anyway. Another rule could be that we do not notify any customer about more than three special offers a day to avoid annoying them.

Introducing a notifications-bounded context has the added benefit of clarifying that the three technical capabilities—sending emails, text messages, and push notifications—are contained in that bounded context and exist as microservices to serve that bounded context. As a consequence, microservices in other bounded contexts should not collaborate with the three supporting technical microservices; they should instead collaborate with the business-oriented notifications microservices. This helps keep the coupling between the bounded contexts low, since microservices in other bounded contexts do not know or care about the fact that there are three ways to send notifications. Thus, for instance, the email microservice is only used by the notification microservice and is not coupled to any other microservice.

4.2.3 *Identifying technical capabilities*

When you introduce supporting technical microservices, your goal is to simplify the microservices that implement business capabilities. Sometimes—such as with sending notifications—you identify a set of technical capabilities that several microservices need, and you turn that into a bounded context with microservices of its own, so other microservices can share the implementation. Other times—as with the ERP integration—you identify a technical capability that unduly complicates a microservice and turn that capability into a microservice of its own. In both cases, the other microservices implementing business capabilities are left with one less technical concern to take care of.

When deciding to implement a technical capability in a separate microservice, be careful that you don't violate the microservice characteristic of being individually deployable. It makes sense to implement a technical capability in a separate microservice only if that microservice can be deployed and redeployed independently of any other microservices. Likewise, deploying the microservices that are supported by the microservice providing the technical capability must not force you to redeploy the microservice implementing the technical capability.

Identifying business capabilities and microservices based on business capabilities is a strategic exercise, but identifying technical supporting capabilities that could be implemented by separate microservices is an opportunistic exercise. The question of whether a supporting technical capability should be implemented in its own microservice is about what will be easiest in the long run. You should ask these questions:

- If the supporting technical capability stays in a microservice scoped to a business capability, is there a risk that the microservice will no longer be replaceable with reasonable effort?
- Is the supporting technical capability implemented in several microservices scoped to business capabilities?
- Will a microservice implementing the supporting capability be individually deployable?
- Will all microservices scoped to business capabilities still be individually deployable if the supporting technical capability is implemented in a separate microservice?

If your answer is yes to the last two questions and to at least one of the others, you have a good candidate for a microservice scope.

4.3 *The tertiary driver for scoping microservices: Supporting efficiency of work*

The third driver when we find the scope and boundaries of microservices is supporting efficiency of work. The microservices we design and create should be efficient to work with and should let teams that develop and maintain the microservices work efficiently. This, largely, is a matter of respecting and using Conway's law, which you may recall from earlier:

> *Any organization that designs a system (defined broadly) will produce a design whose structure is a copy of the organization's communication structure.*

If we have an already defined organization that we cannot change, the system of microservices we create must align with the organization. On the other hand, if the organization can be changed we should do so in accordance with the overall system of microservices.

First and foremost, respecting Conway's law means we should make sure that there is a clear ownership of each microservice: we should assign one team to the development and maintenance of each microservice. This is in line with the microservices characteristic that a small team can maintain a few handfuls of microservices. Each can be be assigned a few handfuls of services to be responsible for. It is important that the responsibility is clear. If the responsibility for a microservice is split between two or more teams, we introduce a need for those teams to coordinate closely whenever changes to that microservices need to happen. That coordination takes time and means that none of the teams involved can work autonomously. This is a form of inefficiency, and it is something we can avoid if we make sure each microservices is assigned to one team.

Allowing teams to work autonomously plays into defining the scope and boundary of the microservices. First, the team must have the skills and knowledge necessary. For instance, a team that gets assigned the notifications microservice from earlier in this chapter must have the understanding of the business rules related to notifying users.

Second, the teams must be able to work without too much and too detailed coordination with other teams. For example, when a team is assigned the notifications microservice, they will probably also be assigned the supporting technical microservices for sending SMS messages, emails, and push notifications because there is a certain level of coupling between those and the notifications microservices. Because of that coupling, assigning the supporting technical microservices to another team introduces a need for coordination and makes both teams less autonomous, so we will probably assign them all to the same team, which therefore takes responsibility for the whole notifications-bounded context. Once they take on the supporting technical microservices, the team on top of the knowledge about the business rules around notifications needs to have the skills necessary to create integrations to the SMS's gateway, the email system, and push notifications. We need to be aware of this, and if we cannot find or form a team with the necessary combination of knowledge and skills, we may have to change scopes of our microservices.

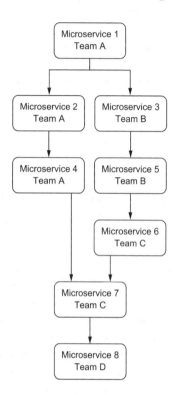

Figure 4.12   **Dependencies between microservices are mirrored as dependencies between the teams maintaining the microservices. The arrows are dependencies and the boxes are microservices annotated with the teams maintaining them.**

To make sure we do not create inefficiencies for the teams developing the microservices, it pays to keep an eye on the dependency chains that exist. In figure 4.12 a dependency chain is depicted: the boxes are microservices and the arrows are dependencies.

If each of the microservices in figure 4.12 are assigned to teams A, B, C, and D, as indicated inside the boxes, the team assigned to the microservice at top of the chain—team A—is in a very different situation than the team assigned to the microservice at the bottom of the chain—team D. This is because the dependencies between the microservices are mirrored by dependencies between the teams. Team A maintaining the microservices at the top can change anything it wants without ever thinking about breaking anything for other teams maintaining microservices further down the chain. Team D maintaining the microservice at the bottom, on the other hand, risks breaking all the other microservices in the dependency chain if they introduce a breaking change. At the same time, team A that is maintaining the microservice at the top may not be able to get much done without coordinating with the other teams in the dependency chain because it may depend on the other teams to implement stuff. In other words, we may be setting both team A and team B up for inefficiency if we create dependency chains that are too long. This is in part combatted by getting the scopes and boundaries for microservices right, and in part by designing the collaboration between microservices in a way that favors low coupling. We will go in depth with designing the collaboration between microservices in chapter 5.

> **NOTE** In chapter 5, we will see how event-based collaboration can help break dependency chains.

4.4   *What to do when the correct scope isn't clear*

At this point, you may be thinking that scoping microservices correctly is difficult: you need to get the business capabilities just right, which requires a deep understanding of the business domain; you also have to judge the complexity of supporting technical capabilities correctly; and you need to make sure the teams can work efficiently. And you're right: it is difficult, and you *will* find yourself in situations where the right scoping for your microservices isn't clear. This lack of clarity can have several causes, including the following:

- *Insufficient understanding of the business domain*—Analyzing a business domain and building up a deep knowledge of that domain is difficult and time-consuming. You'll sometimes need to make decisions about the scope of microservices before you've been able to develop sufficient understanding of the business to be certain you're making the correct decisions.
- *Confusion in the business domain*—It's not only the development side that can be unclear about the business domain. Sometimes the business side is also unclear about how the business domain should be approached. Maybe the business is moving into new markets and must learn a new domain along the way. Other times, the existing business market is changing because of what competitors are doing or what the business itself is doing. Either way, on both the business side and the development side, the business domain is ever changing, and your understanding of it is emergent.
- *Incomplete knowledge of the details of a technical capability*—You may not have access to all the information about what it takes to implement a technical capability. For instance, you may need to integrate with a badly documented system, in which case you'll only know how to implement the integration once you're finished.
- *Inability to estimate the complexity of a technical capability*—If you haven't previously implemented a similar technical capability, it can be difficult to estimate how complex the implementation of that capability will be.

None of these problems mean you've failed. They're all situations that occur time and again. The trick is to know how to move forward despite the lack of clarity. In this section, I'll discuss what to do when you're in doubt.

4.4.1 Starting a bit bigger

When in doubt about the scope of a microservice, it's best to err on the side of making the microservice's scope bigger than it would be ideally. This may sound weird—I've talked a lot about creating small, narrowly focused microservices and about the benefits that come from keeping microservices small. And it's true that significant benefits can be gained from keeping microservices small and narrowly focused. But you must also look at what happens if you err on the side of too narrow a scope.

Consider the special offers microservice discussed earlier in this chapter. It implements the special offers business capability in a POS system and includes five different business processes, as illustrated in figure 4.3 and reproduced in the top part of figure 4.13. If you were uncertain about the boundaries of the special offers business capability and chose to err on the side of too small a scope, you might split the business capability, as shown in the bottom part of figure 4.13.

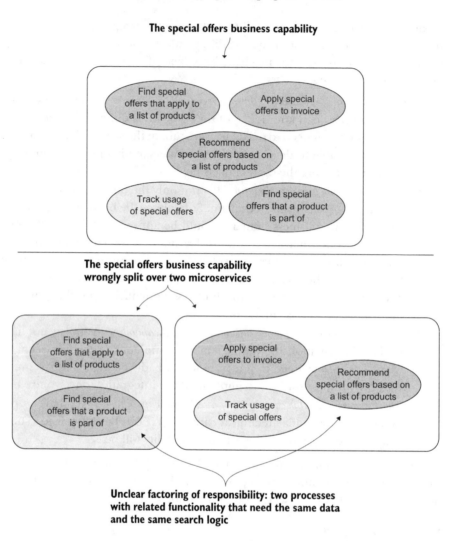

Figure 4.13   If you make the scope of a microservice too small, you'll find that a single business capability becomes split over several highly coupled parts.

If you base the scope of your microservices on only part of the special offers business capability, you'll incur some significant costs:

- *Data and data model duplication between the two microservices*—Both parts of the implementation need to store all the special offers in their data stores.
- *Unclear factoring of responsibility*—One part of the divided business capability can answer whether a given product is part of any special offers, whereas the other part can recommend special offers to customers based on past purchases. These two functions are closely related, and you'll quickly get into a situation where it's unclear in which microservice a piece of code belongs.

- *Obstacles to refactoring the code for the business capability*—This can occur because the code is spread across the code bases for the two microservices. Such cross-code base refactorings are difficult because it's hard to get a complete picture of the consequences of the refactoring and because tooling support is poor.
- *Difficulty deploying the two microservices independently*—After refactoring or implementing a feature that involves both microservices, the two microservices may need to be deployed at the same time or in a particular order. Either way, coupling between versions of the two microservices violates the characteristic of microservices being individually deployable. This makes testing, deployment, and production monitoring more complicated.

These costs are incurred from the time the microservices are first created until you've gained enough experience and knowledge to more correctly identify the business capability and a better scope for a microservice (the entire special offers business capability, in this case). Added to those costs is the fact that the difficulty in refactoring and implementing changes to the business capability will result in you doing less of both, so it will take you longer to learn about the business capability. In the meantime, you pay the cost of the duplicated data and data model and the cost of the lack of individual deployability.

We've established that preferring to err on the side of too narrow a scope easily leads to scoping microservices in a way that creates costly coupling between the microservices. To see if this is better or worse than erring on the side of too big a scope, we need to look at the costs of that approach.

If you err on the side of bigger scopes, you might decide on a scope for the special offers microservice that also includes handling coupons. The scope of this bigger special offers microservice is shown in figure 4.14.

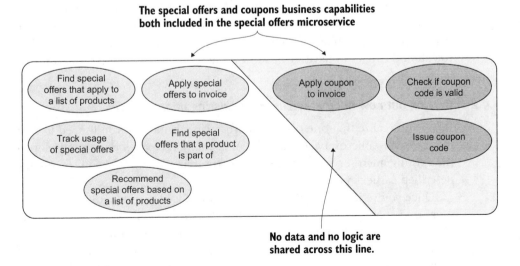

Figure 4.14 If you choose to err on the side of bigger scopes, you might decide to include the handling of coupons in the special offers business capability.

There are costs associated with including too much in the scope of a microservice:

- The code base becomes bigger and more complex, which can lead to changes being more expensive.
- The microservice is harder to replace.

These costs are real, but they aren't overwhelming when the scope of the microservice is still fairly small. Beware, though, because these costs grow quickly with the size of each microservice's scope and become overwhelming when the scope is so big that it approaches a monolithic architecture.

Nevertheless, refactoring within one code base is much easier than refactoring across two code bases. This gives you a better chance to experiment and to learn about the business capability through experiments. If you take advantage of this opportunity, you can arrive at a good understanding of both the special offers business capability and the coupons business capability more quickly than if you scoped your microservices too narrowly.

This argument holds true when your microservices are a bit too big, but it falls apart if they're much too big, in which case we will lose the speed and flexibility we want from microservices.

> **WARNING** Don't get lazy and lump several business capabilities together in one microservice. You'll quickly have a large, hard-to-manage code base with many of the drawbacks of a full-on monolith.

All in all, microservices that are slightly bigger than they should ideally be are both less costly and allow for more agility than if they're slightly smaller than they should ideally be. Thus, the rule of thumb is to err on the side of slightly bigger scopes.

Once you accept that you'll sometimes—if not often—be in doubt about the best scope for a microservice and that in such cases you should lean toward a slightly bigger scope, you can also accept that you'll sometimes—if not often—have microservices in your system that are somewhat larger than they should ideally be. This means you should expect to have to carve new microservices out of existing ones from time to time.

4.4.2 *Carving out new microservices from existing microservices*

When you realize that one of your microservices is too big, you'll need to look at how to carve a new microservice out of it. First, you need to identify a good scope for both the existing microservice and the new microservice. To do this, you can use the drivers described earlier in this chapter.

Once you've identified the scopes, you must look at the code to see if the way it's organized aligns with the new scopes. If not, you should begin refactoring toward that alignment. Figure 4.15 illustrates on a high level the refactorings needed to prepare to carve out a new microservice from an existing one. First, everything that will eventually go into the new microservice is moved to its own class library. Then, all communication between code that will stay in the existing microservice and code that will be moved to the new microservice is refactored to go through an interface. This interface will become part of the public HTTP interface of the two microservices once they're split apart.

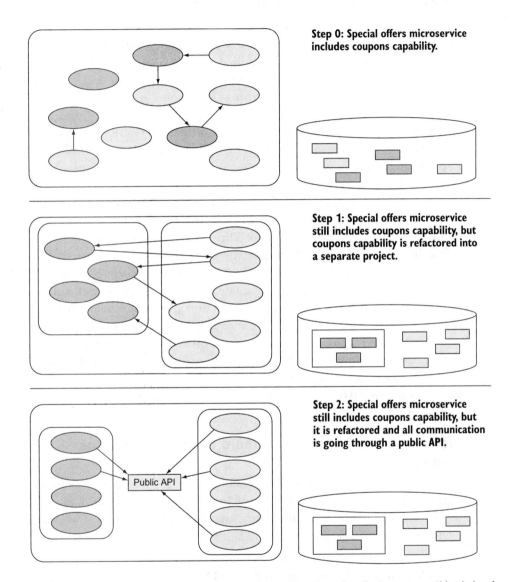

Step 0: Special offers microservice includes coupons capability.

Step 1: Special offers microservice still includes coupons capability, but coupons capability is refactored into a separate project.

Step 2: Special offers microservice still includes coupons capability, but it is refactored and all communication is going through a public API.

Public API

Figure 4.15 Preparing to carve out a new microservice by refactoring: first move everything belonging to the new microservice into its own project, and then make all communication go through a public API, similar to the one the new microservice will end up having.

When you've reached step 2 in figure 4.15, the new microservice can be split out from the old one with a manageable effort. Create a new microservice, move the code that needs to be carved out of the existing microservice over to the new microservice, and change the communication between the two parts to go over HTTP.

4.4.3   *Planning to carve out new microservices later*

Because you consciously err on the side of making your microservices a bit too big when you're in doubt about the scope of a microservice, you have a chance to foresee which microservices will have to be divided at some point. If you know a microservice is likely to be split later, it would be nice if you could plan for that split in a way that will save you one or two of the refactoring steps shown in figure 4.15. It turns out you can frequently make that kind of plan.

Often you'll be unsure whether a particular function is a separate business capability, so you'll follow the rule of thumb and include it in a larger business capability, implemented within a microservice scoped to that larger business capability. But you can remain conscious of the fact that this area *might* be a separate business capability.

Think about the definition of the special offers business capability that includes processes for dealing with coupons. You may well have been in doubt about whether handling coupons was a business capability on its own, so the special offers business capability was modeled as including all the processes shown in figure 4.14.

When you first implement a special offers microservice scoped to the understanding of the special offers business capability illustrated in figure 4.14, you don't know whether the coupons functionality will eventually be moved to a coupons microservice. You do know, however, that the coupon's functionality isn't as closely related to the rest of the microservice as some of the other areas. It's therefore a good idea to put a clear boundary around the coupon's code in the form a well-defined public API and to put the code in a separate class library. This is sound software design, and it will also pay off if one day you end up carving out the coupon code to create a new coupons microservice.

4.5   *Well-scoped microservices adhere to the microservice characteristics*

I've talked about scoping microservices by identifying business capabilities first and supporting technical capabilities second. In this section, I'll discuss how this approach to scoping aligns with these four characteristics of microservices mentioned at the beginning of this chapter:

- A microservice is responsible for a single capability.
- A microservice is individually deployable.
- A small team can maintain a handful of microservices.
- A microservice is replaceable.

NOTE It's important to note that the relationship between the drivers for scoping microservices and the characteristics of microservices goes both ways. The primary and secondary drivers lead toward adhering to the characteristics, but the characteristics also tell you whether you've scoped your microservices well or need to push the drivers further to find better scopes for your microservices.

4.5.1 Primary scoping to business capabilities leads to good microservices

The primary driver for scoping microservices is identifying business capabilities. Let's see how that makes for microservices that adhere to the microservice characteristics.

RESPONSIBLE FOR A SINGLE CAPABILITY

A microservice scoped to a single business capability by definition adheres to the first microservice characteristic: it's responsible for a single capability. As you saw in the examples of identifying supporting technical capabilities, you have to be careful: it's easy to let too much responsibility slip into a microservice scoped to a business capability. You have to be diligent in making sure that what a microservice implements is just one business capability and not a mix of two or more. You also have to be careful about putting supporting technical capabilities in their own microservices. As long as you're diligent, microservices scoped to a single business capability adhere to the first characteristic of microservices.

INDIVIDUALLY DEPLOYABLE

Business capabilities are those that can be performed by largely independent groups within an organization, so the business capabilities themselves must be largely independent. As a result, microservices scoped to business capabilities are largely independent. This doesn't mean there's no interaction between such microservices—there can be a lot of interaction, both through direct calls between services and through events. The point is that the interaction happens through well-defined public interfaces that can be kept backward compatible. If implemented well, the interaction is such that other microservices continue to work even if one has a short outage. This means well-implemented microservices scoped to business capabilities are individually deployable.

REPLACEABLE AND MAINTAINABLE BY A SMALL TEAM

A business capability is something a small group in an organization can handle. This limits its scope and thus also limits the scope of microservices scoped to business capabilities. Again, if you're diligent about making sure a microservice handles only one business capability and that supporting technical capabilities are implemented in their own microservices, the microservices' scope will be small enough that a small team can maintain at least a handful of microservices and a microservice can be replaced fairly quickly if need be.

4.5.2 Secondary scoping to support technical capabilities leads to good microservices

The secondary driver for scoping microservices is identifying supporting technical capabilities. Let's see how that makes for microservices that adhere to the microservice characteristics.

RESPONSIBLE FOR A SINGLE CAPABILITY

Just as with microservices scoped to business capabilities, scoping a microservice to a single supporting technical capability by definition means it adheres to the first characteristic of microservices: it's responsible for a single capability.

INDIVIDUALLY DEPLOYABLE

Before you decide to implement a technical capability as a separate supporting technical capability in a separate microservice, you need to ask whether that new microservice will be individually deployable. If the answer is no, you shouldn't implement it in a separate microservice. Again, by definition, a microservice scoped to a supporting technical capability adheres to the second microservice characteristic.

REPLACEABLE AND MAINTAINABLE BY A SMALL TEAM

Microservices scoped to a supporting technical capability tend to be narrowly and clearly scoped. On the other hand, part of the point of implementing such capabilities in separate microservices is that they can be complex. In other words, microservices scoped to a supporting technical capability tend to be small, which points toward adhering to the microservice characteristics of replaceability and maintainability; but the code inside them may be complex, which makes them harder to maintain and replace.

This is an area where there's a certain back and forth between using supporting technical capabilities to scope microservices on one hand, and the characteristics of microservices on the other. If a supporting technical microservice is becoming so complex that it will be hard to replace, this is a sign that you should probably look closely at the capability and try to find a way to break it down further, as in the example about notification (see section 4.2.2).

4.5.3 *Tertiary scoping to support efficiency of work*

The third driver for scoping microservices is supporting the efficiency of work. Let's see how making sure teams can work efficiently aligns with the microservice characteristics.

INDIVIDUALLY DEPLOYABLE

Part of making sure that teams can work efficiently and autonomously is to make sure that they can deliver their work all the way to production. This aligns nicely to the second microservice characteristic. When a microservices is individually deployable, the team can deploy it to production without coordinating with other teams. This is part of making sure that the team can work efficiently.

A SMALL TEAM CAN MAINTAIN A FEW HANDFULS OF MICROSERVICES

Teams should have knowledge necessary to maintain the microservices they are responsible for. Otherwise, they cannot work efficiently and autonomously. When they have the knowledge needed, they can maintain their microservices by themselves end-to-end, which supports the fifth microservices characteristic.

Summary

- The primary driver in scoping microservices is identifying business capabilities. Business capabilities are the things an organization does that contribute to fulfilling business goals.

- You can use techniques from domain-driven design to identify business capabilities. Domain-driven design is a powerful tool for gaining better and deeper understanding of a domain. That kind of understanding enables you to identify business capabilities.

- The secondary driver in scoping microservices is identifying supporting technical capabilities. A supporting technical capability is a technical function needed by one or more microservices scoped to business capabilities.

- Supporting technical capabilities should be moved to their own microservices only if they're sufficiently complex to be a problem in the microservices they would otherwise be part of, and if they can be individually deployed.

- Identifying supporting technical capabilities is an opportunistic form of design. You should only pull a supporting technical capability into a separate microservice if it will be an overall simplification.

- The tertiary driver in scoping microservices is efficiency of work. A team assigned to develop and maintain microservices should be able to work efficiently and autonomously.

- When you're in doubt about the scope of a microservice, lean toward making the scope slightly bigger rather than slightly smaller.

- Because scoping microservices well is difficult, you'll probably be in doubt sometimes. You're also likely to get some of the scopes wrong in your first iteration.

- You must expect to have to carve new microservices out of existing ones from time to time.

- You can use your doubt about scope to organize the code in your microservices so that they lend themselves to carving out new microservices at a later stage.

Microservice collaboration 5

This chapter covers

- Understanding how microservices collaborate through commands, queries, and events
- Comparing event-based collaboration with collaboration based on commands and queries
- Implementing an event feed
- Implementing command-, query-, and event-based collaboration
- Deploying collaborating microservices to Kubernetes

Each microservice implements a single capability, but to deliver end-user functionality, microservices need to collaborate. Microservices can use three main communication styles for collaboration: *commands, queries,* and *events.* Each style has its strengths and weaknesses, and understanding the tradeoffs between them allows you to pick the appropriate one for each microservice collaboration. When you get the collaboration style right, you can implement loosely coupled microservices with clear boundaries.

In this chapter, I'll show you how to implement all three collaboration styles in code using HTTP GET, POST, PUT, and DELETE endpoints. I will also show how to deploy several collaborating microservices to Kubernetes and have them collaborate as intended using all three collaboration styles.

5.1 Types of collaboration: Commands, queries, and events

Microservices are fine grained and narrowly scoped. To deliver functionality to an end user, microservices need to collaborate.

As an example, consider the loyalty program microservice from the POS system in chapter 4. The loyalty program microservice is responsible for the loyalty program business capability. The program is simple: customers can register as users with the loyalty program; once registered, they receive notifications about new special offers and earn loyalty points when they purchase something. Still, the loyalty program business capability depends on other business capabilities, and other business capabilities depend on it. As illustrated in figure 5.1, the loyalty program microservice needs to collaborate with a number of other microservices.

Figure 5.1 The loyalty program microservice collaborates with several other microservices. In some cases, the loyalty program microservice receives requests from other microservices; at other times, it sends requests to other microservices.

As stated in the list of microservice characteristics in chapter 1, a microservice is responsible for a single capability; and as discussed in chapter 4, that single capability is typically a business capability. End-user functionalities—or use cases—often involve several business capabilities, so the microservices implementing these capabilities must collaborate to deliver functionality to the end user.

When two microservices collaborate, there are three main styles:

- *Commands*—Commands are used when one microservice needs another microservice to perform an action. For example, the loyalty program microservice sends a command to the notifications microservice when it needs a notification to be sent to a registered user.
- *Queries*—Queries are used when one microservice needs information from another microservice. Because customers with many loyalty points receive a discount, the invoice microservice queries the loyalty program microservice for the number of loyalty points a user has.
- *Events*—Events are used when a microservice needs to react to something that happened in another microservice. The loyalty program microservice subscribes to events from the special offers microservice so that when a new special offer is made available, it can have notifications sent to registered users.

The collaboration between two microservices can use one, two, or all three of these collaboration styles. Each time two microservices need to collaborate, you must decide which style to use. Figure 5.2 shows the collaborations of loyalty program again, but this time identifying the collaboration style I chose for each one.

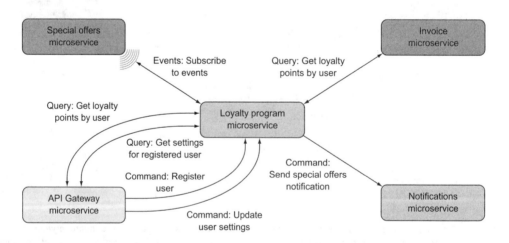

Figure 5.2 The loyalty program microservice uses all three collaboration styles: commands, queries, and events.

Collaboration based on commands and queries should use relatively coarse-grained commands and queries. The calls made between microservices are remote calls, meaning they cross at least a process boundary and usually also a network. This means calls between microservices are relatively slow. Even though the microservices are fine-grained, you must not fall into the trap of thinking of calls from one microservice to another as being like function calls in a microservice.

Furthermore, you should prefer collaboration based on events over collaboration based on commands or queries. Event-based collaboration is more loosely coupled than the other two forms of collaboration because events are handled asynchronously. That means two microservices collaborating through events aren't temporally coupled; the handling of an event doesn't have to happen immediately after the event is raised. Rather, handling can happen when the subscriber is ready to do so. In contrast, commands and queries are synchronous and therefore need to be handled immediately after they're sent.

5.1.1 Commands and queries: Synchronous collaboration

Commands and queries are both synchronous forms of collaboration. Both are implemented as HTTP requests from one microservice to another. Queries are implemented with HTTP GET requests, whereas commands are implemented with HTTP POST, PUT, or DELETE requests.

> ### Commands and Queries over gRPC
>
> As mentioned briefly in chapter 1, gRPC is a strong candidate for an alternative to using HTTP. gRPC is a protocol for performing remote procedure calls (RPC), which means that it offers a model for allowing one microservice to call a method in another microservice. This maps directly to commands and queries—commands are calls to methods that perform an action in the receiving microservices, and queries are methods that return some information to the calling microservices.
>
> Working with gRPC starts with defining a contract in the form of a *proto* file where procedure calls are described. The proto file is used to generate code for both the client and server side using the Grpc.Tools NuGet package.
>
> The main benefits of using gRPC for microservice collaboration are as follows:
>
> - *Efficiency*—gRPC uses HTTP/2 and protobuf. Protobuf is a much more compact format than JSON. Likewise HTTP/2 offers more efficiency than HTTP/1. In high-load systems this can make a significant difference and make gRPC very appealing.
> - *Explicit contracts*—The proto files define the contract between the calling microservice and the receiving microservice, and the gRPC libraries will check the contract at runtime. This is a double-edged sword: we can gain some safety by making the contracts explicit, but we also lose some flexibility to evolve microservices in isolation by checking the contracts in detail.
> - *Good .NET support*—With the Grpc.tools NuGet package for generating code from the proto files and the Grpc.AspNetCore NuGet package for hosting gRPC endpoints in ASP.NET, using gRPC fits nicely into .NET-based microservices.

The loyalty program microservice can answer queries about registered users and can handle commands to create or update registered users. Figure 5.3 shows the command- and query-based collaborations that loyalty program takes part in.

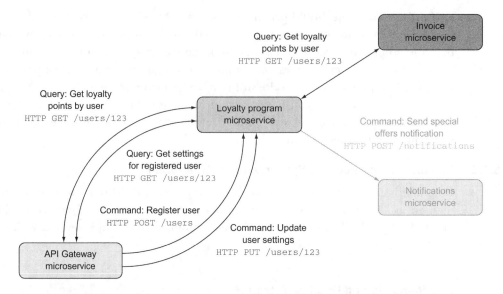

Figure 5.3   The loyalty program microservice collaborates with three other microservices using commands and queries. The queries are implemented as HTTP GET requests, and the commands are implemented as HTTP POST or PUT requests. The command collaboration with the notifications microservice is grayed out because I'm not going to show its implementation—it's done exactly the same way as the other collaborations.

Figure 5.3 includes two different queries: "Get loyalty points for registered user" and "Get settings for registered user." You'll handle both of these with the same endpoint that returns a representation of the registered user. The representation includes both the number of loyalty points and the settings. You do this for two reasons: it's simpler than having two endpoints, and it's also cleaner because the loyalty program microservice gets to expose just one representation of the registered user instead of having to come up with specialized formats for specialized queries.

Two commands are sent to loyalty program in figure 5.3: one to register a new user, and one to update an existing registered user. You'll implement the first with an HTTP POST and the second with an HTTP PUT. This is standard usage of POST and PUT HTTP methods. POST is often used to create a new resource, and PUT is defined in the HTTP specification to update a resource.

All in all, the loyalty program microservice needs to expose three endpoints:

- An HTTP GET endpoint at URLs of the form /users/{userId} that responds with a representation of the user. This endpoint implements both queries in figure 5.3.
- An HTTP POST endpoint at "/users/" that expects a representation of a user in the body of the request and then registers that user in the loyalty program.
- An HTTP PUT endpoint at URLs of the form "/users/{userId}" that expects a representation of a user in the body of the request and then updates an already registered user.

The loyalty program microservice is made up of the same set of standard components you've seen before, as shown in figure 5.4. The endpoints are implemented in the HTTP API component.

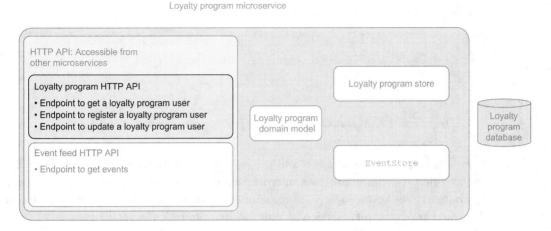

Figure 5.4 The endpoints exposed by the loyalty program microservice are implemented in the HTTP API component.

The other sides of these collaborations are microservices that most likely follow the same standard structure, with the addition of a `LoyaltyProgramClient` component. For instance, the invoice microservice might be structured as shown in figure 5.5.

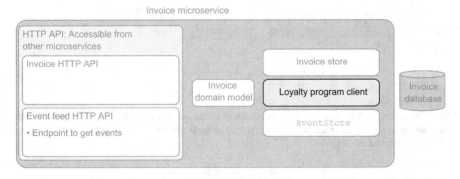

Figure 5.5 The invoice microservice has a `LoyaltyProgramClient` component responsible for calling the loyalty program microservice.

The representation of a registered user that the loyalty program will expect to receive in the commands and with which it will respond to queries is a serialization of the following `LoyaltyProgramUser`.

Listing 5.1   The loyalty program microservice's user representation

```
public record LoyaltyProgramUser(
  int Id,
  string Name,
  int LoyaltyPoints,
  LoyaltyProgramSettings Settings);

public record LoyaltyProgramSettings()
{
  public LoyaltyProgramSettings(string[] interests) : this()
  {
    this.Interests = interests;
  }

  public string[] Interests { get; init; } = Array.Empty<string>();
}
```

The definitions of the endpoints and the two classes in this code effectively form the contract that the loyalty program microservice publishes: the LoyaltyProgramClient component. The invoice microservice adheres to this contract when it makes calls to the loyalty program microservice, as illustrated in figure 5.6.

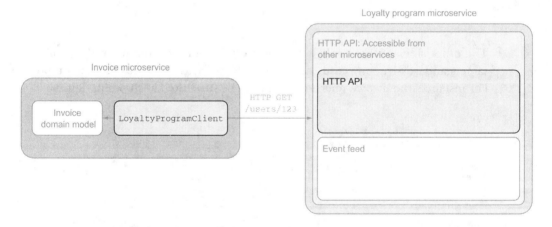

Figure 5.6   The LoyaltyProgramClient component in the invoice microservice is responsible for making calls to the loyalty program microservice. It translates between the contract published by the loyalty program and the domain model of invoice.

NOTE   The invoice microservice is not part of the code download, but you will find an implementation of the LoyaltyProgramClient in the ApiGateway-Mock in the code download.

Commands and queries are powerful forms of collaboration, but they both suffer from being synchronous by nature. As mentioned earlier, that creates coupling between the microservices that expose the endpoints and the microservices that call the endpoints. Next, we'll turn our attention to asynchronous collaboration through events.

5.1.2 Events: Asynchronous collaboration

Collaboration based on events is asynchronous. That is, the microservice that publishes the events doesn't call the microservices that subscribe to the events. Rather, the subscribers process new events when they're ready to process them. When we use HTTP to implement this style of collaboration, the subscribers poll for new events. That polling is what I'll call *subscribing* to an event feed. Although the polling is made out of synchronous requests, the collaboration is asynchronous because publishing events is independent of any subscriber polling for events.

In figure 5.7, you can see the loyalty program microservice subscribing to events from the special offers microservice. Special offers can publish events whenever some-

thing happens in its domain, such as every time a new special offer becomes active. Publishing an event, in this context, means storing the event in the special offers data store. The loyalty program won't see the event until it makes a call to the event feed on special offers. When that happens is entirely up to the loyalty program. It can happen right after the event is published or at any later point in time.

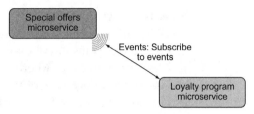

Figure 5.7   The loyalty program microservice processes events from the special offers microservice when it's convenient for the loyalty program.

As with the other types of collaboration, there are two sides to event-based collaboration. One side is the microservice that publishes events through an event feed, and the other is the microservices that subscribe to those events.

EXPOSING AN EVENT FEED

A microservice can publish events to other microservices via an *event feed*, which is just an HTTP endpoint—at "/events," for instance—to which that other microservice can make requests and from which it can get event data. Figure 5.8 shows the components

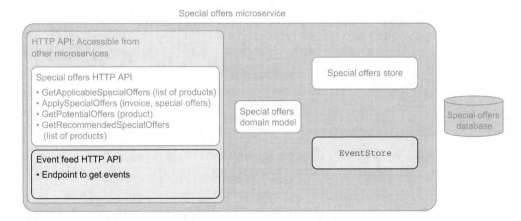

Figure 5.8   The event feed in the special offers microservice is exposed to other microservices over HTTP and is based on the event store.

in the special offers microservice. Once again, the microservice has the same standard set of components that you've seen several times already. In figure 5.8, the components involved in implementing the event feed are highlighted.

The events published by the special offers microservice are stored in its database. The `EventStore` component has the code that reads events from that database and that writes them to the database. The domain model code can use `EventStore` to store the events it needs to publish. The `Event Feed` component is the implementation of the HTTP endpoint that exposes the events to other microservices: that is, the /events endpoint.

The `Event Feed` component uses `EventStore` to read events from the database and then returns the events in the body of an HTTP response. Subscribers can use query parameters to control which and how many events are returned.

SUBSCRIBING TO EVENTS

Subscribing to an event feed essentially means you poll the events endpoint of the microservice that you subscribe to. At intervals, you send an HTTP GET request to the /events endpoint to check whether there are any events you haven't processed yet.

Figure 5.9 is an overview of the loyalty program microservice, which shows that it consists of two processes. We've already talked about the web process, but the event-subscriber process is new.

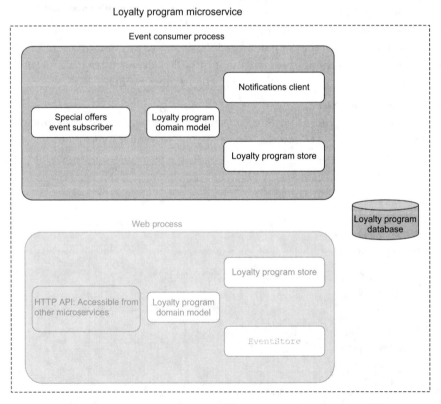

Figure 5.9 The event subscription in the loyalty program microservice is handled in an event-subscriber process.

The event-subscriber process is a background process that periodically makes requests to the event feed on the special offers microservice to get new events. When it gets back a batch of new events, it processes them by sending commands to the notifications microservice to notify registered users about new special offers. The `SpecialOffers-Subscriber` component is where the polling of the event feed is implemented, and the `Notifications-Client` component is responsible for sending the command to notifications. The rate at which the event subscribes gets events can differ quite a bit based on the specific use case. Often, events are fetched every 30 seconds or every few minutes, but there are also cases where fetching events occur frequently, like every second, or where fetching events seldom occur, like every hour, and is the right thing to do.

This is the way you implement event subscriptions: microservices that need to subscribe to events have a subscriber process with a component that polls the event feed. When new events are returned from the event feed, the subscriber process handles the events based on business rules.

> ### Events over queues
>
> An alternative to publishing events over an event feed is to use a queue technology, like RabbitMQ, AWS SQS, or Azure Queue Storage. In this approach, microservices that publish events push them to a queue, and subscribers read them from the queue. Events must be routed from the publisher to multiple subscribers, and how that's done depends on the choice of queue technology and may require additional technologies on top of the queue. As with the event-feed approach, the microservice subscribing to events has an event-subscriber process that reads events from the queue and processes them. Event replay can also be built with queues but may require a bit of extra work depending on the queue technology.
>
> This is a viable approach to implementing event-based collaboration between microservices. But this book uses HTTP-based event feeds for event-based collaboration because it allows events to be replayed at any time and it's a simple yet robust and scalable solution.
>
> ### Event over gRPC
>
> As mentioned, command and queries map directly to gRPC's remote procedure calls. But what about events? gRPC has a concept of *streaming* that allows for keeping an HTTP/2 connection open and sending data through the connection. Streaming in gRPC works in both directions—from client to server or from server to client. To model events using gRPC streaming, you can create a remote procedure that works somewhat like an event feed: it allows event subscribers to call the procedure and get events back in a response stream.

5.1.3 *Data formats*

So far, we've focused on exchanging data in JSON format. JSON works well in many situations, but there are reasons you might want to use something else:

- If you need to exchange a lot of data, a more compact format may be needed. Text-based formats such as JSON and XML are a lot more verbose than binary formats like protocol buffers.

- If you need a more structured format than JSON that's still human readable, you may want to use YAML.
- If your company uses proprietary data formatting, you may need to support that format.

In all these cases, you need endpoints capable of receiving data in another format than JSON, and they also need to be able to respond in that other format. As an example, a request to register a user with the loyalty program microservice using YAML in the request body looks like this:

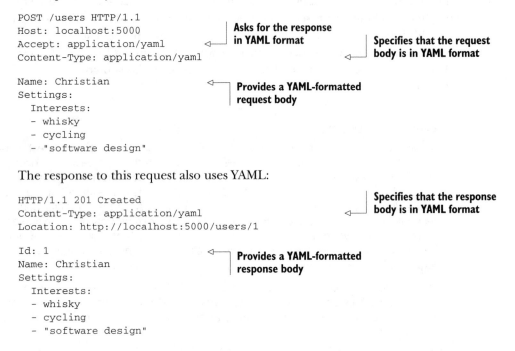

```
POST /users HTTP/1.1
Host: localhost:5000                    Asks for the response
Accept: application/yaml                 in YAML format             Specifies that the request
Content-Type: application/yaml                                      body is in YAML format

Name: Christian                         Provides a YAML-formatted
Settings:                                request body
  Interests:
  - whisky
  - cycling
  - "software design"
```

The response to this request also uses YAML:

```
HTTP/1.1 201 Created                               Specifies that the response
Content-Type: application/yaml                      body is in YAML format
Location: http://localhost:5000/users/1

Id: 1                                   Provides a YAML-formatted
Name: Christian                          response body
Settings:
  Interests:
  - whisky
  - cycling
  - "software design"
```

Both the preceding request and response have YAML-formatted bodies, and both specify that the body is YAML in the `Content-Type` header. The request uses the `Accept` header to ask for the response in YAML. This example shows how microservices can communicate using different data formats and how they can use HTTP headers to tell which formats are used.

5.2 *Implementing collaboration*

This section will show you how to code the collaborations you saw earlier in figure 5.2. I'll use the loyalty program microservice as a starting point, but I'll also go into some of its collaborators—the API Gateway microservice, the invoice microservice, and the special offers microservice—in order to show both ends of the collaborations.

Three steps are involved in implementing the collaboration:

1 Set up a project for the loyalty program. Just as you've done before, you'll create an empty ASP.NET application and add ASP.NET MVC.

2 Implement the command- and query-based collaborations shown in figure 5.2. You'll implement all the commands and queries that the loyalty program can handle, as well as the code in collaborating microservices that use them.

3 Implement the event-based collaboration shown in figure 5.2. You'll start with the event feed in special offers and then move on to implement the subscription in the loyalty program. The subscription will be in a new project in the loyalty program and will be controlled by a Kubernetes CronJob. After these steps, you'll have implemented all the collaborations of the loyalty program.

The loyalty program microservice consists of a web process that has the same structure you've seen before. This is illustrated at the bottom of figure 5.10. Later, when you implement the event-based collaboration, you'll add another component that I call the *event subscriber*. This is shown at the top of figure 5.10.

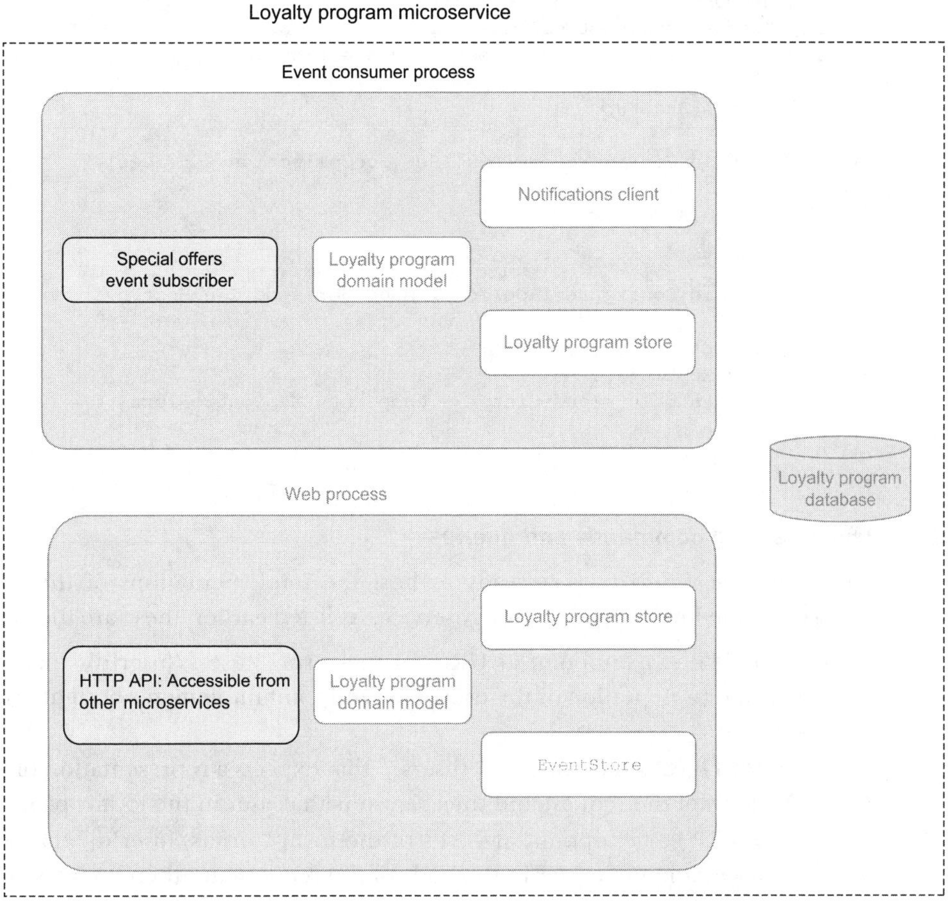

Loyalty program microservice

Figure 5.10 The loyalty program microservice has a web process that follows the structure you've seen before and an event subscriber that handles the subscription to events from the special offers microservice. I'll only show the code for the highlighted components in this chapter.

In the interest of focusing on the collaboration, I won't show all the code in the loyalty program microservice. Rather, I'll include the code for the HTTP API in the web process and the special offers event subscriber in the event-subscriber process.

5.2.1   Setting up a project for the loyalty program

The first thing to do in implementing the loyalty program microservice is to create an empty ASP.NET application and add MVC to it. You've already done this a couple of times—in chapters 1 and 2—so I won't go over the details again here, but only remind you that your Startup.cs should look like this.

Listing 5.2   Startup class with MVC

```
namespace LoyaltyProgram
{
  using Microsoft.AspNetCore.Builder;
  using Microsoft.AspNetCore.Hosting;
  using Microsoft.Extensions.DependencyInjection;

  public class Startup
  {
    public void ConfigureServices(IServiceCollection services)
    {
      services.AddControllers();
    }

    public void Configure(IApplicationBuilder app, IWebHostEnvironment env)
    {
      app.UseHttpsRedirection();
      app.UseRouting();
      app.UseEndpoints(endpoints => endpoints.MapControllers());
    }
  }
}
```

5.2.2   Implementing commands and queries

You now have a web project ready to host the implementations of the endpoints exposed by the loyalty program microservice. As listed earlier, these are the endpoints:

- An HTTP GET endpoint at URLs of the form "/users/{userId}" that responds with a representation of the user. This endpoint implements both queries in figure 5.3.
- An HTTP POST endpoint at "/users/" that expects a representation of a user in the body of the request and then registers that user in the loyalty program.
- An HTTP PUT endpoint at URLs of the form "/users/{userId}" that expects a representation of a user in the body of the request and then updates an already registered user.

You'll implement the command endpoints first and then the query endpoint.

5.2.3 *Implementing commands with HTTP POST or PUT*

The code needed in the loyalty program microservice to implement the handling of the two commands—the HTTP POST to register a new user and the HTTP PUT to update one—is similar to the code you saw in chapter 2. You'll start by implementing an action method for the command to register a user. A request to loyalty program to register a new user is shown in the following listing.

Listing 5.3 Request to register a user named Christian

```
POST /users HTTP/1.1
Host: localhost:5001
Content-Type: application/json
Accept: application/json

{
  "name":"Christian",
  "loyaltyPoints":0,
  "settings":{ "interests" : ["whisky", "cycling"] }
}
```

JSON representation of the user being registered

To handle the command for registering a new user, you need to add an MVC controller to the loyalty program by adding a file called UsersController.cs and putting the following code in it.

Listing 5.4 POST endpoint for registering users

```
using System;
  using System.Collections.Generic;
  using Microsoft.AspNetCore.Mvc;

  [Route("/users")]
  public class UsersController : ControllerBase
  {
    [HttpPost("")]
    public ActionResult<LoyaltyProgramUser> CreateUser(
      [FromBody] LoyaltyProgramUser user)
    {
      if (user == null)
        return BadRequest();
      var newUser = RegisterUser(user);
      return Created(
        new Uri($"/users/{newUser.Id}", UriKind.Relative),
        newUser);
    }

    private LoyaltyProgramUser RegisterUser(LoyaltyProgramUser user)
    {
      // store the new user to a data store
    }
  }
```

The request must include a LoyaltyProgramUser in the body.

Uses the 201 Created status code for the response

Returns the user in the response for convenience

Adds a location header to the response because this is expected by HTTP for 201 Created responses

The response to the preceding request looks like this:

```
HTTP/1.1 201 Created
Content-Type: application/json; charset=utf-8
Location: /users/4
{
  "id": 4,
  "name": "Christian",
  "loyaltyPoints": 0,
  "settings": { "interests": ["whisky", "cycling"]
  }
}
```

The status code
is **201 Created**.

ASP.NET sets the
Content-Type.

**The Location header points to
the newly created resource.**

There isn't much new to notice here, except that we are using the method `Created` to control the HTTP response. There are many such convenience methods on the `ControllerBase` base class, and throughout the book we will use them to easily create the HTTP responses we want.

With the action method for the register-user command in place, let's turn our attention to implementing an action method for the update user command by adding this to the `UsersController`. (There's nothing in this code you haven't seen before.)

Listing 5.5   PUT endpoint for updating users

```
private static readonly IDictionary<int, LoyaltyProgramUser>
    RegisteredUsers = new Dictionary<int, LoyaltyProgramUser>();

    [HttpPut("{userId:int}")]
    public LoyaltyProgramUser UpdateUser(
      int userId,
      [FromBody] LoyaltyProgramUser user)
      => RegisteredUsers[userId] = user;
```

**Returns the new user and lets ASP.NET
turn it into an HTTP response**

The actions for the commands are only one side of the collaboration. The other side is the code that sends the commands. Figure 5.2 shows that the API Gateway microservice sends commands to the loyalty program microservice. You won't build a complete API Gateway microservice here, but in the code download for this chapter, you'll find a console application that acts as API Gateway with regard to collaborating with the loyalty program. Here, we'll focus only on the code that sends the commands.

In the API Gateway microservice, you'll create a class called `LoyaltyProgramClient` that's responsible for dealing with communication with the loyalty program microservice. That class encapsulates building and sending HTTP requests to the loyalty program microservice.

The code for sending the register user command takes a user name as input, creates an HTTP `POST` with a user object in the body, and sends that to the loyalty program microservice. After the response comes back from the loyalty program, we will just return the whole thing as an `HttpResponseMessage`. That's an easy solution for the current needs, but often a client class like this would also check the status code of the response, deserialize the body if the status code is as expected, and possibly even perform error handling if the status code indicates an error. The following listing shows the implementation.

Listing 5.6 The API Gateway microservice registering new users

```
using System.Net.Http;
  using System.Text;
  using System.Threading.Tasks;
  using System.Text.Json;

  public class LoyaltyProgramClient
  {
    private readonly HttpClient httpClient;

    public LoyaltyProgramClient(HttpClient httpClient)
    {
      this.httpClient = httpClient;
    }

    public async Task<HttpResponseMessage> RegisterUser(string name)
    {
      var user = new {name, Settings = new { }};
      return await this.httpClient.PostAsync("/users/",       ⟵ Sends the command
        CreateBody(user));                                        to loyalty program
    }

    private static StringContent CreateBody(object user)
    {
      return new StringContent(              ⟵ Serializes user
        JsonSerializer.Serialize(user),,          as JSON
        Encoding.UTF8,
        "application/json");                ⟵ Sets the Content-
    }                                            Type header
  }
```

Similarly, `LoyaltyProgramClient` has a method for sending the update user command. This method also encapsulates the HTTP communication involved in sending the command.

Listing 5.7 The API Gateway microservice updating users

```
public async Task<HttpResponseMessage> UpdateUser(dynamic user) =>
    await this.httpClient.PutAsync(        ⟵ Sends the UpdateUser
      $"/users/{user.id}",                     command as a PUT request
      CreateBody(user));
```

This code is similar to the code for the register user command, except this HTTP request uses the PUT method. With the command handlers implemented in the loyalty program microservice and a `LoyaltyProgramClient` implemented in the API Gateway microservice, the command-based collaboration is implemented. The API Gateway can register and update users, but it can't yet query users.

5.2.4   *Implementing queries with HTTP GET*

The loyalty program microservice can handle the commands it needs to handle, but it can't answer queries about registered users. Remember that the loyalty program only needs one endpoint to handle queries. As mentioned previously, the endpoint handling queries is an HTTP GET endpoint at URLs of the form "/users/{userId}," and it responds with a representation of the user. This endpoint implements both queries in figure 5.3.

> #### Listing 5.8   GET endpoint to query a user and their loyalty point by user ID

```
namespace LoyaltyProgram.Users
{
  using System;
  using System.Collections.Generic;
  using Microsoft.AspNetCore.Mvc;

  [Route("/users")]
  public class UsersController : ControllerBase
  {
    private static readonly Dictionary<int, LoyaltyProgramUser>
      RegisteredUsers = new();

    [HttpGet("{userId:int}")]
    public ActionResult<LoyaltyProgramUser> GetUser(int userId) =>
      RegisteredUsers.ContainsKey(userId)
        ? (ActionResult<LoyaltyProgramUser>) Ok(RegisteredUsers[userId])
        : NotFound();

    ...
  }
}
```

There's nothing about this code that you haven't already seen several times. Likewise, the code needed in the API Gateway microservice to query this endpoint shouldn't come as a surprise:

```
public class LoyaltyProgramClient
{
  ...

    public async Task<HttpResponseMessage> QueryUser(string arg) =>
      await this.httpClient.GetAsync($"/users/{int.Parse(arg)}");
}
```

This is all that's needed for the query-based collaboration. You've now implemented the command- and query-based collaborations of the loyalty program microservice.

5.2.5 *Implementing an event-based collaboration*

Now that you know how to implement command- and query-based collaborations between microservices, it's time to turn our attention to the event-based collaboration. Figure 5.11 repeats the collaborations that the loyalty program microservice is involved in. The loyalty program subscribes to events from special offers, and it uses the events to decide when to notify registered users about new special offers.

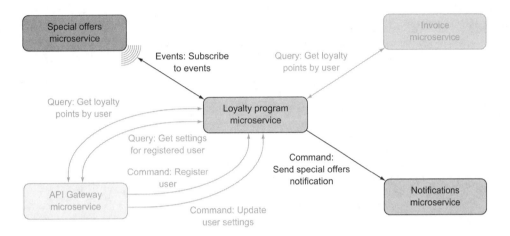

Figure 5.11 The event-based collaboration in the loyalty program microservice is the subscription to the event feed in the special offers microservice.

We'll first look at how special offers exposes its events in a feed. Then, we'll return to the loyalty program and add a second process to that service, which will be responsible for subscribing to and handling events.

IMPLEMENTING AN EVENT FEED

You saw a simple event feed in chapter 2. The special offers microservice implements its event feed the same way: it exposes an endpoint—"/events"—that returns a list of sequentially numbered events. The endpoint can take two query parameters—start and end—that specify a range of events. For example, a request to the event feed can look like this:

```
GET /events?start=10&end=110 HTTP/1.1

Host: localhost:5002
Accept: application/json
```

The response to this request might be the following, except that I've cut off the response after five events:

```
HTTP/1.1 200 OK
Content-Type: application/json; charset=utf-8
```

```
[
  {
    "sequenceNumber": 1,
    "occuredAt": "2020-06-16T20:13:53.6678934+00:00",
    "name": "SpecialOfferCreated",
    "content": {
      "description": "Best deal ever!!!",
      "id": 0
    }
  },
  {
    "sequenceNumber": 2,
    "occuredAt": "2020-06-16T20:14:22.6229836+00:00",
    "name": "SpecialOfferCreated",
    "content": {
      "description": "Special offer - just for you",
      "id": 1
    }
  },
  {
    "sequenceNumber": 3,
    "occuredAt": "2020-06-16T20:14:39.841415+00:00",
    "name": "SpecialOfferCreated",
    "content": {
      "description": "Nice deal",
      "id": 2
    }
  },
  {
    "sequenceNumber": 4,
    "occuredAt": "2020-06-16T20:14:47.3420926+00:00",
    "name": "SpecialOfferUpdated",
    "content": {
      "oldOffer": {
        "description": "Nice deal",
        "id": 2
      },
      "newOffer": {
        "description": "Best deal ever - JUST GOT BETTER",
        "id": 0
      }
    }
  },
  {
    "sequenceNumber": 5,
    "occuredAt": "2020-06-16T20:14:51.8986625+00:00",
    "name": "SpecialOfferRemoved",
    "content": {
      "offer": {
        "description": "Special offer - just for you",
        "id": 1
      }
    }
  }
]
```

Notice that the events have different names (`SpecialOfferCreated`, `Special-OfferUpdated`, and `SpecialOfferRemoved`), and the different types of events don't have the same data fields. This is normal: different events carry different information. It's also something you need to be aware of when you implement the subscriber in the loyalty program microservice. You can't expect all events to have the exact same shape.

> **NOTE** I only include the most important parts of the special offers code here. The rest is available in the code download.

The implementation of the "/events" endpoint in the special offers microservice is a simple controller, just like the one in chapter 2.

Listing 5.9 Endpoint that reads and returns events

```
namespace SpecialOffers.Events
{
  using System.Linq;
  using Microsoft.AspNetCore.Mvc;

  [Route(("/events"))]
  public class EventFeedController : ControllerBase
  {
    private readonly IEventStore eventStore;

    public EventFeedController(IEventStore eventStore)
    {
      this.eventStore = eventStore;
    }

    [HttpGet("")]
    public ActionResult<EventFeedEvent[]> GetEvents([FromQuery] int start,
        [FromQuery] int end)
    {
      if (start < 0 || end < start)
        return BadRequest();

      return this.eventStore.GetEvents(start, end).ToArray();
    }
  }
}
```

This controller only uses ASP.NET features that we've already discussed. You may notice, however, that it returns the result of eventStore.GetEvents. ASP.NET serializes it as an array. The EventFeedEvent is a class that carries a little metadata and a Content field that's meant to hold the event data.

Listing 5.10 `EventFeedEvent` record that represents events

```
public record EventFeedEvent(
    long SequenceNumber,
    DateTimeOffset OccuredAt,
    string Name,
    object Content);
```

The `Content` property is used for event-specific data and is where the difference between a `SpecialOfferCreated` event, a `SpecialOfferUpdated`, and a `Special-OfferRemoved` event appears. Each has its own type of object in `Content`.

This is all it takes to expose an event feed. This simplicity is the great advantage of using an HTTP-based event feed to publish events. Event-based collaboration can be implemented over a queue system, but that introduces another complex piece of technology that you have to learn to use and administer in production. That complexity is warranted in some situations, but certainly not always.

CREATING AN EVENT-SUBSCRIBER PROCESS

Subscribing to an event feed essentially means you'll poll the events endpoint of the microservice you subscribe to. At intervals, you'll send an HTTP GET request to the "/events" endpoint to check whether there are any events you haven't processed yet.

We will implement this periodic polling as two main parts:

- A simple console application that reads one batch of events
- A Kubernetes CronJob to run the console application at intervals

Putting these two together implements the event subscription: the CronJob makes sure the console application runs at an interval, and each time the console application runs, it sends the HTTP GET request to check whether there are any events to process.

The first step in implementing an event-subscriber process is to create a console application with the following `dotnet` command:

```
PS> dotnet new console -n EventConsumer
```

and run it with `dotnet` too:

```
PS> dotnet run
```

The application is empty, so nothing interesting happens yet, but in the next section we will make it read events.

SUBSCRIBING TO AN EVENT FEED

You now have an `EventConsumer` console application. All it has to do is read one batch of events and track where the starting point of the next batch of events is. This is done as follows.

Listing 5.11   Reading a batch of events from an event feed

```
using System;
using System.IO;
using System.Net.Http;
using System.Net.Http.Headers;
using System.Text.Json;
using System.Threading.Tasks;
                                               Read the starting point of
var start = await GetStartIdFromDatastore();  ◁──┘ this batch from a database.
var end = 100;
var client = new HttpClient();
```

```
client.DefaultRequestHeaders
  .Accept
  .Add(new MediaTypeWithQualityHeaderValue("application/json"));
using var resp = await client.GetAsync(
  new Uri($"http://special-offers:5002/events?start={start}&end={end}"));
await ProcessEvents(await resp.Content.ReadAsStreamAsync());
await SaveStartIdToDataStore(start);

Task<long> GetStartIdFromDatastore(){...}
async Task ProcessEvents(Stream content){...}
Task SaveStartIdToDataStore(long startId){...}
```

Send GET request to the event feed.

Save the starting point of the next batch of events.

Call the method to process the events in this batch. ProcessEvents also updates the start variable.

With this code above, the EventConsumer can read a batch of events, and every time it is called, it reads the next batch of events. The remaining part is to process the events, as shown next.

Listing 5.12 Deserializing and then handling events

```
async Task ProcessEvents(Stream content)
{
  var events =
    await JsonSerializer.DeserializeAsync<SpecialOfferEvent[]>(content)
    ?? new SpecialOfferEvent[0];
  foreach (var @event in events)
  {
    Console.WriteLine(@event);
    start = Math.Max(start, @event.SequenceNumber + 1);
  }
}
```

This is where the event would be processed.

Keeps track of the highest event number handled

There are a few things to notice here:

- This method keeps track of which events have been handled. This makes sure you don't request events from the feed that you've already processed.
- As you saw earlier, not all events carry the same data in the Content property, so depending on the Name property, the event handling can expect different data in the Content object. You want to be liberal in accepting incoming data in the 'Content' property—it shouldn't cause problems if the special offers microservice decides to add an extra field to the event JSON. As long as the data you *need* is there, the rest can be ignored.
- The events are deserialized into the type SpecialOfferEvent. This is a different type than the EventFeedEvent type used to serialize the events in special offers. This is intentional and is done because the two microservices don't need to have the exact view of the events. As long as the loyalty program doesn't depend on data that isn't there, all is well.

The SpecialOfferEvent type used here is simple and contains only the fields used in the loyalty program:

```
public record SpecialOfferEvent(
  long SequenceNumber,
  DateTimeOffset OccuredAt,
  string Name,
  object Content);
```

This concludes your implementation of the C# part of event subscriptions. The other part—the Kubernetes CronJob—is implemented in the next section.

5.2.6   *Deploying to Kubernetes*

In this section, we will deploy the loyalty program and special offers microservices to Kubernetes. To that end there are three steps we need to perform:

- We will build Docker containers for both microservices. The container for special offers is similar to what we saw in chapter 3. The container for the loyalty program has a twist: based on an environment variable it can act either as an HTTP API exposing the POST, PUT, and GET endpoints we implemented earlier, or it can act as the event consumer we implemented in the previous section. This is explained in detail next.
- We will deploy the special offers microservice similarly to how we deployed to Kubernetes in chapter 3.
- We will deploy the loyalty program, which will consist of deploying the loyalty program container in two copies of different configurations: one running as the API and one running as the event consumer.

> **NOTE** You can find the code for the special offers microservice in the code download. Here I only show the deployment bits for the special offers microservice.

With those three steps done we will have three parts running in Kubernetes:

- A pod for the special offers microservice
- A pod for the API part of the loyalty program microservice
- A CronJob for the event consumer part of the loyalty program

We will also have two deployments in Kubernetes, one for the special offers microservice and one for the loyalty program microservice. Since we consider the loyalty program API and the loyalty program event consumer as parts of the same loyalty program microservice, we will always deploy these two together, and by the same token, we will put them into the same Kubernetes manifest file. At runtime they run independently, though, which allows us to, for instance, scale up the API part to deal with the higher load while still only running one event consumer.

5.2.7   *Building a Docker container special offers microservice*

Before we can deploy the special offers microservice to Kubernetes, we need to build a Docker container for it. To do that, we use the following Dockerfile, which is similar to the Dockerfile for the shopping cart we saw in chapter 2.

Listing 5.13 Dockerfile for special offers microservice

```
FROM mcr.microsoft.com/dotnet/sdk:5.0 AS build
WORKDIR /src
COPY . .
RUN dotnet restore "SpecialOffers.csproj"
WORKDIR "/src"
RUN dotnet build "SpecialOffers.csproj" -c Release -o /api/build

FROM build AS publish
WORKDIR "/src"
RUN dotnet publish "SpecialOffers.csproj" -c Release -o /api/publish

FROM mcr.microsoft.com/dotnet/aspnet:5.0 AS final
WORKDIR /app
EXPOSE 80
COPY --from=publish /api/publish ./api
ENTRYPOINT dotnet api/SpecialOffers.dll
```

This builds the special offers microservice and when started will run the special offers microservice. There is nothing new here—we are just applying what we learned in chapter 2.

NOTE Recall from chapter 2 that the docker build command builds a container from a Dockerfile.

5.2.8 *Building a Docker container for both parts of the loyalty program*

Next up, we build a container image for the loyalty program microservice. The loyalty program has two parts: the API and the event consumer. We will build one container that is capable of running as either the API or the event consumer based on an environment variable. To do that, we create a Dockerfile in the loyalty program code base where the ENTRYPOINT is controlled by an environment variable.

Listing 5.14 One Docker image for the loyalty program API and event consumer

```
FROM mcr.microsoft.com/dotnet/sdk:5.0 AS build
WORKDIR /src
COPY . .
RUN dotnet restore "LoyaltyProgram/LoyaltyProgram.csproj"
RUN dotnet restore "EventConsumer/EventConsumer.csproj"
WORKDIR "/src/LoyaltyProgram"                                      Builds
RUN dotnet build "LoyaltyProgram.csproj" -c Release -o /api/build    ◁┘ the API
WORKDIR "/src/EventConsumer"
RUN dotnet build "EventConsumer.csproj" -c Release -o /consumer/build/
  consumer                                     ◁─┐ Builds the
                                                 │ event consumer
FROM build AS publish
WORKDIR "/src/LoyaltyProgram"                                      Publishes
RUN dotnet publish "LoyaltyProgram.csproj" -c Release -o /api/publish ◁┘ the API
WORKDIR "/src/EventConsumer"
RUN dotnet publish "EventConsumer.csproj" -c Release -o /consumer/   Publishes the
  publish                                       ◁─┘ event consumer
```

```
FROM mcr.microsoft.com/dotnet/aspnet:5.0 AS final
WORKDIR /app
EXPOSE 80
COPY --from=publish /api/publish ./api
COPY --from=publish /consumer/publish ./consumer
ENTRYPOINT dotnet $STARTUPDLL
```

Uses the value of the STARTUPDLL environment variable as the entry point

This Dockerfile is a little different from what we have seen before. The Dockerfiles we have seen before have built and published one ASP.NET application. This one builds and publishes an ASP.NET application—the loyalty program—and a .NET console application—the event consumer. The image built with this Dockerfile will therefore have both the `LoyaltyProgram.dll` and the `EventConsumer.dll` in it. The last line of the Dockerfile, `ENTRYPOINT dotnet $STARTUPDLL`, says that when the images built with this Dockerfile start up, they should run `dotnet` on whatever the environment variable `$STARTUPDLL` points to. So if `$STARTUPDLL` is equal to the path to the Loyalty-Program.dll, the image will run the loyalty program API, and if `'$STARTUPDLL'` is equal to the path to the `EventConsumer.dll`, the image will run the loyalty program event consumer.

Let's see this Dockerfile in action. First we build a loyalty program Docker image:

```
> docker build . -t loyalty-program
```

Now we run the loyalty program image as either the API part or the event consumer part. Let's first try to run it as the API by passing in the path to the `LoyaltyProgram.dll` in the `$STARTUPDLL`:

```
> docker run --rm -p 5001:80 -e STARTUPDLL="api/LoyaltyProgram.dll"
  loyalty-program
```

That command also maps port 5001 on your localhost to port 80 in the container. The loyalty program API is now running, and you can call it on localhost port 5001. Let's run the same Docker image again, but start it up as the Event Consumer:

```
> docker run --rm -e STARTUPDLL="consumer/EventConsumer.dll" loyalty-program
```

This will run the event consumer, but it will fail to fetch events from the special offers event feed, because we do not have one running. We fix that by running the special offers microservice in a container and putting that on the same Docker network as the event consumer. To do that, we create a new Docker network called "microservices":

```
> docker network create --driver=bridge microservices
```

The containers we add to the microservices network can communicate using the container and host names. We will take advantage of that when we run the special offers microservice by adding it to the microservices network and giving it the name special-offers. To do just that, run this command:

```
> docker run --rm -p 5002:80 --network=microservices --name=special-offers
  special-offers
```

Now we can rerun the event consumer, this time on the microservices network, and it will succeed:

```
docker run --rm -e STARTUPDLL="consumer/EventConsumer.dll"
  --network=microservices loyalty-program
```

This runs the event consumer once, and it will consume one batch of events. Later we will set up a Cron schedule in Kubernetes that triggers the event consumer periodically.

We are now able to run all the parts in Docker on localhost, the special offers microservice and both parts of the loyalty program microservice at the same time, and have them collaborate as intended. This confirms that we have successfully created Docker container images for the loyalty program and the special offers microservices. Next we will deploy those container images to our Kubernetes cluster in Azure.

5.2.9 *Deploying the loyalty program API and the special offers*

In chapter 3, we set up a Kubernetes cluster on Azure. We will continue to use that cluster throughout the book, and now we will deploy the loyalty program microservice and the special offers microservice to it.

NOTE Remember that in chapter 3 we created a script called `create-aks.ps1` for setting up the Kubernetes cluster and container registry in Azure. The script can be found in the code download. In case you did not create a Kubernetes cluster in chapter 3, I recommend you create one now.

First, we add a file called "loyalty-program.yaml" to the loyalty program's code base and put the Kubernetes manifest for the loyalty program API into it. This is just like the Kubernetes manifest file we saw in chapter 3, except this one uses the loyalty program container image.

> **Listing 5.15 Kubernetes manifest for the `LoyaltyProgram` API**

```
kind: Deployment
apiVersion: apps/v1
metadata:
  name: loyalty-program            The number of copies
spec:                              of the LoyaltyProgram
  replicas: 1              ◁────┘   API we want deployed
  selector:
    matchLabels:
      app: loyalty-program
  template:
    metadata:
      labels:
        app: loyalty-program
    spec:
      containers:
        - name: loyalty-program
          image: your_unique_registry_name.azurecr.io/
            loyalty-program:1.0.2
```

```
        imagePullPolicy: IfNotPresent
        ports:
          - containerPort: 80
        env:
          - name: STARTUPDLL
            value: "api/LoyaltyProgram.dll"
---
apiVersion: v1
kind: Service
metadata:
  name: loyalty-program
spec:
  type: LoadBalancer
  ports:
    - name: loyalty-program
      port: 5001
      targetPort: 80
  selector:
    app: loyalty-program
```

> **Override the STARTUPDLL environment variable to control how the container starts up.**

> **Point to the LoyaltyProgram.dll, which will run the LoyaltyProgram API.**

With this file in place, we are ready deploy the loyalty program API to Kubernetes with this command:

```
> kubectl apply -f loyalty-program.yaml
```

The Kubernetes manifest for the special offers microservice is similar and is also deployed using the kubectl apply command.

Once the loyalty program API and the special offers microservice are deployed, we should see both running in the Kubernetes dashboard (which we configured in chapter 3) and in the kubectl command line:

```
> kubectl get pods
NAME                                READY   STATUS    RESTARTS   AGE
loyalty-program-5d87df4656-9x89c    1/1     Running   0          55s
special-offers-67d6b78998-mttp6     1/1     Running   0          43s
```

We can also find the IP addresses and ports where the two APIs are available:

```
> kubectl get services
NAME             TYPE          CLUSTER-IP     EXTERNAL-IP    PORT(S)         AGE
kubernetes       ClusterIP     10.0.0.1       <none>         443/TCP         20d
loyalty-program  LoadBalancer  10.0.137.255   40.127.231.56  5001:32553/TCP  2m28s
special-offers   LoadBalancer  10.0.76.165    52.142.115.22  80:32391/TCP    2m16s
```

In my case, the loyalty programs API is available at http://40.127.231.56:5001 and the special offers API is at http://52.142.115.22/. The IP addresses will be different in your case since they are assigned dynamically by AKS.

That's all we need to deploy the two API.

5.2.10 Deploy EventConsumer

The remaining work is to deploy the loyalty programs event consumer. This is done by extending the Kubernetes manifest for the loyalty program and reapplying it using kubectl. As mentioned, we will deploy the event consumer as a CronJob that will be called on a schedule. To do that, we add the following to the end of the "loyalty-progam.yaml" file created in the previous section:

Listing 5.16 Kubernetes manifest for the loyalty program event consumer

```
---
apiVersion: batch/v1beta1
kind: CronJob
metadata:
  name: loyalty-program-consumer
spec:
  schedule: "*/1 * * * *"
  jobTemplate:
    spec:
      template:
        spec:
          containers:
            - name: loyalty-program
              image: your_unique_registry_name.azurecr.io/
                loyalty-program:1.0.2
              imagePullPolicy: IfNotPresent
              env:
                - name: STARTUPDLL
                  value: "consumer/EventConsumer.dll"
          restartPolicy: Never
      concurrencyPolicy: Forbid
```

- The Kubernetes API version needed to specify a CronJob
- Indicate that this is a CronJob.
- Define the schedule for this job.
- Point to the event consumer dll.
- Make sure consumer runs only one copy at the time of the event.

The schedule defined here means the event consumer will run once every minute. This can be adjusted based on the specifics of the event consumer. Some events are rare and do not require immediate reaction. In those cases, the schedule can be much slower. Some events happen often, in which case we might want to keep a one-minute schedule but read larger batches every time the event consumer runs.

To deploy the event consumer, we use loyalty-program.yaml again:

```
> kubectl apply -f loyalty-program.yaml
```

Rerunning this command is quite fine. Kubernetes will figure out if there are any changes to make and apply only the changes.

Now that the event consumer has also been deployed, we should see a CronJob in Kubernetes too:

```
> kubectl get cronjob
NAME                       SCHEDULE    SUSPEND  ACTIVE  LAST SCHEDULE  AGE
loyalty-program-consumer   */1 * * * * False    0       20s            1m20s
```

We can also see the loyalty program event consumer by looking at the last schedule column. In my case, the CronJob was triggered 20 seconds ago.

We can also see a list of recent invocations of the loyalty program event consumer by looking at the Kubernetes jobs list:

```
> kubectl get jobs
NAME                                       COMPLETIONS   DURATION   AGE
loyalty-program-consumer-1590755940        1/1           2s         11s
loyalty-program-consumer-1590757080        1/1           2s         1m11s
loyalty-program-consumer-1590757140        1/1           3s         2m11s
```

This concludes the deployment of the loyalty program microservice. The API part as well as the event consumers part is running in our Kubernetes cluster in AKS. The Kubernetes manifest we have created for the loyalty program is the template for the manifests for all the microservices we will create; only the container images will have different names, and the event consumer schedules will vary.

If we want to convince ourselves that the event consumer is indeed running, we can inspect the logs of one of the instantiations of the CronJob:

```
> kubectl logs job.batch/loyalty-program-consumer-1590755940
[{"sequenceNumber":1,"occuredAt":"2020-06-18T18:07:13.7973414+00:00","name":
"SpecialOfferCreated","content":{"description":"Nice deal","id":0}},
{"sequenceNumber":2,"occuredAt":"2020-06-18T18:07:17.7957514+00:00",
"name":"SpecialOfferCreated","content":{"description":"Nice deal","id":1}},
{"sequenceNumber":3,"occuredAt":"2020-06-18T18:07:47.4246091+00:00","name":
"SpecialOfferUpdated","content":{"oldOffer":{"description":"Nice deal",
"id":1},"newOffer":{"description":"Best deal ever - JUST GOT BETTER","id":
0}}},{"sequenceNumber":4,"occuredAt":"2020-06-18T18:08:04.5908816+00:00",
"name":"SpecialOfferRemoved","content":{"offer":{"description":"Nice deal",
"id":0}}}]
```

Looking at these logs, we will be able to see the special offers event being consumed shortly after we make calls to the special offers API.

With both the special offers microservice and the loyalty program microservice running in AKS, we have finished implementing examples of all three styles of collaboration: commands, queries, and events.

Summary

- There are three types of microservice collaboration:
  - Command-based collaboration, where one microservice uses an HTTP POST, PUT, or DELETE to make another microservice perform an action
  - Query-based collaboration, where one microservice uses an HTTP GET to query the state of another microservice
  - Event-based collaboration, where one microservice exposes an event feed that other microservices can subscribe to by polling the feed for new events
- Event-based collaboration is more loosely coupled than command- and query-based collaboration.
- You can use HttpClient to send commands to other microservices and to query other microservices.

- You can use MVC controllers to expose the endpoints for receiving and handling commands and queries.
- An MVC controller can expose a simple event feed.
- You can create a process that subscribes to events by
  - Creating a .NET console application
  - Using `HttpClient` to read events from an event feed
  - Running this application as a CronJob in Kubernetes

Data ownership
and data storage

6

This chapter covers

- Which data microservices store
- Understanding how data ownership follows business capabilities
- Using data replication for speed and robustness
- Building read models from event feeds with event subscribers
- Implementing data storage in microservices

Software systems create, use, and transform data. Without the data, most software systems wouldn't be worth much, and that's true for microservice systems, too. In this chapter, you'll learn where a piece of data should be stored and which microservice should be responsible for keeping it up to date. Furthermore, you'll learn how you can use data replication to make your microservice system both more robust and faster.

6.1   Each microservice has a data store

One of the characteristics of microservices identified in chapter 1 is that each microservice should own its data store. The data in that data store is solely under the control of the microservice, and it's exactly the data the microservice needs. First, it's data that belongs to the capability the microservice implements, but it's also supporting data, like cached data and read models created from event feeds.

The fact that each microservice owns a data store means you don't need to use the same database technology for all microservices. You can choose a database technology that's suited to the data that each microservice needs to store.

A microservice typically needs to store three types of data:

- Data belonging to the capability the microservice implements. This is data that the microservice is responsible for and must keep safe and up-to-date.
- Events raised by the microservice. During command processing, the microservice may need to raise events to inform the rest of the system about updates to the data the microservice is responsible for.
- Read models based on data in events from other microservices or occasionally on data from queries to other microservices.

These three types of data may be stored in different databases and even in different types of databases.

6.2 Partitioning data between microservices

When you're deciding where to store data in a microservice system, competing forces are at play. The two main forces are data ownership and locality:

- *Ownership of data* means being responsible for keeping the data correct, safe, and up-to-date.
- *Locality of data* refers to where the data a microservice needs is stored. Often, the data should be stored nearby—preferably in the microservice itself.

These two forces may be at odds, and in order to satisfy both, you'll often have to store data in several places. That's okay, but it's important that only one of those places be considered the authoritative source. Figure 6.1 illustrates that; whereas one microservice stores the authoritative copy of a piece of data, other microservices can mirror that data in their own data stores.

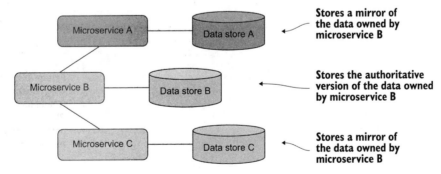

Figure 6.1   Microservices A and C collaborate with microservice B. Microservices A and C can store mirrors of the data owned by microservice B, but the authoritative copy is stored in microservice B's own data store.

6.2.1   *Rule 1: Ownership of data follows business capabilities*

The first rule when deciding where a piece of data belongs in a microservices system is that ownership of data follows business capabilities. As discussed in chapter 4, the primary driver in deciding on the responsibility of a microservice is that it should handle a business capability. The business capability defines the boundaries of the microservice—everything belonging to the capability should be implemented in the microservice. This includes storing the data that falls under the business capability.

Domain-driven design teaches that some concepts can appear in several business capabilities and that the meaning of the concepts may differ slightly. Several microservices may have the concept of a customer, and they will work on and store customer entities. There may be some overlap between the data stored in different microservices, but it's important to be clear about which microservice is in charge of what.

For instance, only one microservice should own the home address of a customer. Another microservice could own the customer's purchase history, and a third the customer's notification preferences. The way to decide which microservice is responsible for a given piece of data—the customer's home address, for instance—is to figure out which business process keeps that data up-to-date. The microservice responsible for the business capability is responsible for storing the data and keeping it up-to-date.

Let's consider again the e-commerce site from chapters 1 and 2. Figure 6.2 shows an overview of how that system handles user requests for adding an item to a shopping

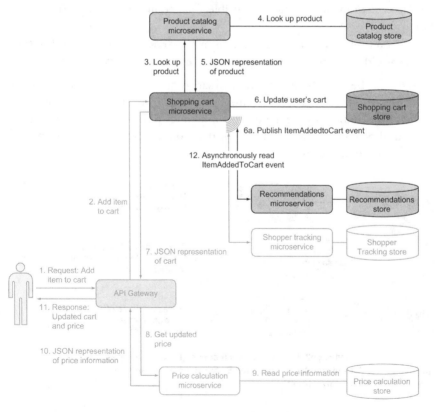

Figure 6.2   In this e-commerce example (from chapters 1 and 2), we'll focus on partitioning data between the shopping cart microservice, the product catalog microservice, and the recommendations microservice.

cart. Most of the microservices in figure 6.2 are dimmed to put the focus on three microservices: shopping cart, product catalog, and recommendations.

Each of the highlighted microservices in figure 6.2 handles a business capability: the shopping art microservice is responsible for keeping track of users' shopping carts; the product catalog microservice is responsible for giving the rest of the system access to information from the product catalog; and the recommendations microservice is responsible for calculating and giving product recommendations to users of the e-commerce site. Data is associated with each of these business capabilities, and each microservice *owns* and is responsible for the data associated with its capability. Figure 6.3 shows the data that each of the microservices owns. Saying that a microservice owns a piece of data means it must store that data and be the authoritative source for that piece of data.

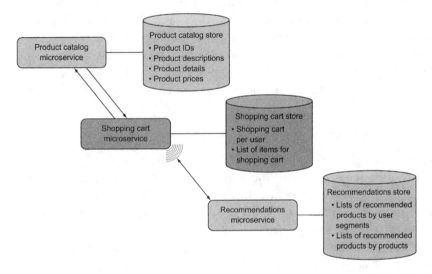

Figure 6.3   Each microservice owns the data belonging to the business capability it implements.

6.2.2   *Rule 2: Replicate for speed and robustness*

The second force at play when deciding where a piece of data should be stored in a microservices system is locality. There's a big difference between a microservice querying its own database for data and a microservice querying another microservice for that same data. Querying its own database is generally both faster and more reliable than querying another microservice.

Once you've decided on the ownership of data, you'll likely discover that your microservices need to ask each other for data. This type of collaboration creates a certain coupling: one microservice querying another means the first is *coupled* to the other. If the second microservice is down or slow, the first microservice will suffer.

To loosen this coupling, you can cache query responses. Sometimes you'll cache the responses as they are, but other times you can store a read model based on query responses. In both cases, you must decide when and how a cached piece of data becomes invalid. The microservice that owns the data is in the best position to decide when a piece of data is still valid and when it has become invalid. Therefore, endpoints responding to queries about data owned by the microservice should include cache headers in the response telling the caller how long it should cache the response data.

USING HTTP CACHE HEADERS TO CONTROL CACHING

HTTP defines a number of headers that can be used to control how HTTP responses can be cached. The purpose of the HTTP caching mechanisms is twofold:

- To eliminate the need, in many cases, to request information the caller already has
- To eliminate the need, in some other situations, to send full HTTP responses

To eliminate the need to make requests for information the caller already has, the server can add a `cache-control` header to responses. The HTTP specification defines a range of controls that can be set in the `cache-control` header. The most common are the `private|public` and the `max-age` directives. The first indicates whether only the caller—private—may cache the response or if intermediaries—proxy servers, for instance—may cache the response, too. The `max-age` directive indicates the number of seconds the response may be cached. For example, the following `cache-control` header indicates that the caller, and only the caller, can cache the response for 3,600 seconds:

```
cache-control: private, max-age:3600
```

In other words, the caller may reuse the response any time it wants to make an HTTP request to the same URL with the same method—GET, POST, PUT, DELETE—and the same body within 3,600 seconds. In this book, I will only use caching for queries, which means only for GET requests. It's worth noting that the query string is part of the URL, so caching takes query strings into account.

To eliminate the need to send a full response in cases where the caller has a cached but stale response, the `ETag` and `If-None-Match` headers can be used: the server can add an `ETag` header to responses. This is an identifier for the response. When the caller makes a later request to the same URL using the same method and the same body, it can include the `ETag` in a request header called `If-None-Match`. The server can read the `ETag` and know which response the caller has cached. If the server decides the cached response is still valid, it can return a response with the "304 Not Modified" status code to tell the client to use the already cached response. Furthermore, the server can add a `cache-control` header to the 304 response to prolong the period the response may be cached. Note that the `ETag` is set by the server and later read again by the same server.

Let's consider the microservices in figure 6.3 again. The shopping cart microservice uses product information that it gets by querying the product catalog microservice. How long the product catalog information for any given product is likely to be correct is best decided by product catalog, which owns the data. Therefore, the product catalog should add cache headers to its responses, and the shopping cart should use them to decide how long it can cache a response. Figure 6.4 shows a sequence of requests to the product catalog that the shopping cart wants to make.

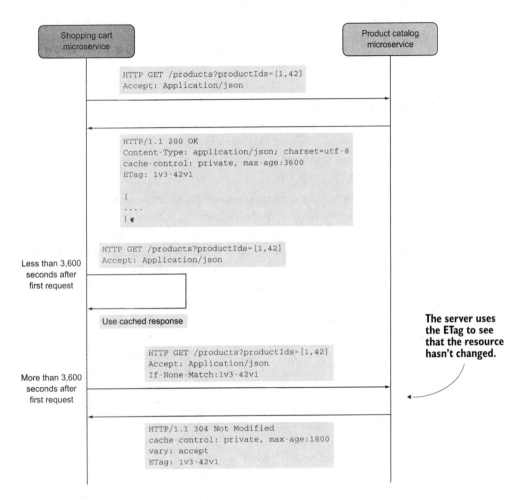

Figure 6.4 **The product catalog microservice can allow its collaborators to cache responses by including cache headers in its HTTP responses. In this example, it sets `max-age` to indicate how long responses may be cached, and it also includes an `etag` built from the product IDs and versions.**

In figure 6.4, the cache headers on the response to the first request tell the shopping cart microservice that it can cache the response for 3,600 seconds. The second time shopping cart wants to make the same request, the cached response is reused because fewer than 3,600 seconds have passed. The third time, the request to the product catalog microservice is made because more than 3,600 seconds have passed. That request includes the ETag from the first response in the If-None-Match header. Product catalog uses the ETag to decide that the response would still be the same, so it sends back the shorter "304 Not Modified" response instead of a full response, and includes a new set of cache headers that allows the shopping cart to cache the already-cached response for an additional 1,800 seconds.

In the context of microservices running relatively close to each other (e.g., within the same data center), eliminating requests for information the caller already has by using `cache-control` headers is often sufficient to get the speed and robustness benefits we are after. The need to also use `ETags` to eliminate unnecessary response bodies arises in situations where the responses to queries are big and therefore require significant bandwidth or when the distance between the microservices is larger (e.g., they are in different data centers or in different zones in a cloud).

In sections 6.3.4 and 6.3.5, we'll discuss how to include `cache-control` headers in responses from action methods in our controllers. We'll also look at reading them on the client side from the response.

USING READ MODELS TO MIRROR DATA OWNED BY OTHER MICROSERVICES

It's normal for a microservice to query its own database for data it owns, but querying its database for data it doesn't own may not seem as natural. The natural way to get data owned by another microservice may seem to be to query that microservice. But it's often possible to replace a query to another microservice with a query to the microservice's own database by creating a *read model*: a data model that can be queried easily and efficiently. This is in contrast to the model used to store the data owned by the microservice, where the purpose is to store an authoritative copy of the data and be able to easily update it when necessary.

Data is, of course, also written to read models—otherwise they'd be empty—but the data is written as a consequence of changes somewhere else. You trade some additional complexity at write time for less complexity at read time.

Read models are often based on events from other microservices. One microservice subscribes to events from another microservice and updates its own model of the event data as events arrive.

Read models can also be built from responses to queries to other microservices. In this case, the lifetime of the data in the read model is decided by the cache headers on those responses, just as in a straight cache of the responses. The difference between a straight cache and a read model is that to build a read model, the data in the responses is transformed and possibly enriched to make later reads easy and efficient. This means the shape of the data is determined by the scenarios in which it will be read instead of the scenario in which it was written.

Let's consider an example. The shopping cart microservice publishes events every time an item is added to or removed from a shopping cart. Figure 6.5 shows a shopper tracking microservice that subscribes to those events and updates a read model based on the events. Shopper tracking allows business users to query how many times specific items are added to or removed from shopping carts.

The events published from the shopping cart microservice aren't in themselves an efficient model to query when you want to find out how often a product has been

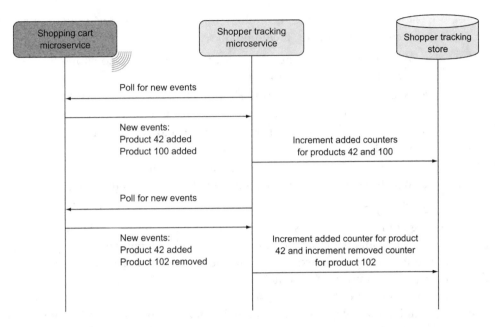

Figure 6.5   The shopper tracking microservice subscribes to events from the shopping cart microservice and keeps track of how many times products are added to or removed from shopping carts.

added to or removed from shopping carts. But the events are a good source from which to build such a model. The shopper tracking microservice keeps two counters for every product: one for how many times the product has been added to a shopping cart, and one for how many times it's been removed. Every time an event is received from the shopping cart, one of the counters is updated; and every time a query is made about a product, the two counters for that product are read.

6.2.3   Where does a microservice store its data?

A microservice can use one, two, or more databases. Some of the data stored by the microservice may fit well into one type of database, and other data may fit better into another type. Many viable database technologies are available, and I won't get into a comparison here. There are, however, some broad database categories that you can consider when you're making a choice, including relational databases, key/value stores, document databases, column stores, and graph databases.

If your production environment is in one of the major public clouds, there are some very compelling database services you can take advantage of. These offerings differ in terms of database category—relation databases, document databases, and so on—but also in terms of operational characteristics. Some are "server-less" and require very little in terms of maintenance; others are more traditional. These also should be taken into consideration.

The choice of database technology (or technologies) for a microservice can be influenced by many factors, including these:

- What shape is your data? Does it fit well into a relational model, a document model, or a key/value store, or is it a graph?
- What are the write scenarios? How much data is written? Do the writes come in bursts, or are they evenly distributed over time?
- What are the read scenarios? How much data is read at a time? How much is read altogether? Do the reads come in bursts?
- How much data is written compared to how much is read?
- Which databases do the team already know how to develop against *and* run in production?

Asking yourself these questions—and finding the answers—will not only help you decide on a suitable database, but will also likely deepen your understanding of the nonfunctional qualities expected from the microservice. You'll learn how reliable the microservice must be, how much load it must handle, what the load looks like, how much latency is acceptable, and so on.

Gaining that deeper understanding is valuable, but note that I'm not recommending you undertake a major analysis of the pros and cons of different databases each time you create a new microservice. You should be able to get a new microservice going and deployed to production quickly. The goal isn't to find a database technology that's perfect for the job—you just want to find one that's suitable given your answers to the previous questions. You may be faced with a situation in which a document base seems like a good choice and in which you're confident that Couchbase, CosmosDB, and MongoDB would be well suited. In that case, choose one of them. It's better to get the microservice to production with one of them quickly, and at a later stage, possibly replace the microservice with an implementation that uses the other, instead of delaying release of the first version of the microservice to production because you're analyzing Couchbase, CosmosDB, and MongoDB in detail.

How many database technologies in the system?

The decision about which database you should use in a microservice isn't solely a matter of what fits well in that microservice. You need to take the broader landscape into consideration. In a microservice system, you'll have many microservices and many data stores. It's worth considering how many different database technologies you want to have in the system. There's a tradeoff between standardizing a few database technologies and having a free-for-all.

On the side of standardizing are goals like these:

- Running the databases reliably in production and continuing to do so in the long run
- Developers being able to get into and work effectively in the codebase of a microservice they haven't touched before

Favoring a free-for-all have these types of goals:

- Being able to choose the optimal database technology for each microservice in terms of maintainability, performance, security, reliability, and so on.
- Keeping microservices replaceable. If new developers take over a microservice and don't agree with the choice of database, they should be able to replace the database or even the microservice as a whole.

How these goals are weighed against each other changes from organization to organization. It's important to be aware that there are tradeoffs, but I will go as far as recommending some standardization within an organization.

6.3 *Implementing data storage in a microservice*

We've discussed where data should go in a microservice system, including which data a microservice should own and which it should mirror. It's time to switch gears and look at the code required to store the data.

I'll focus on how a microservice can store the data it owns, including how to store the events it raises. I'll first show you how to do this using SQL Server and the lightweight Dapper data access library. Then I'll show you how to store events in a database specifically designed for storing events—the aptly named EventStoreDB.

New technologies used in this chapter

In this chapter, you'll begin using a couple of new technologies:

- *SQL Server*—Microsoft's SQL database. For purposes of this chapter many different databases would work fine. I am choosing SQL Server because I suspect it will be familiar to many readers.
- *Dapper* (https://github.com/StackExchange/dapper-dot-net)—A lightweight object-relational mapper (ORM).
- *EventStoreDB* (https://www.eventstore.com/eventstoredb)—A database product specifically designed to store events.

Dapper: A lightweight O/RM

Dapper is a simple library for working with data in a SQL database from C#. It's part of a family of libraries sometimes referred to as *micro ORMs*, which also includes Simple.Data and Massive. These libraries focus on being simple to use and fast, and they embrace SQL.

Whereas a more traditional ORM writes all the SQL required to read data from and write it to the database, Dapper expects you to write your own SQL. I find this liberating when dealing with a database with a simple schema.

In the spirit of choosing lightweight technologies for microservices, I choose Dapper over a full-fledged ORM like Entity Framework or NHibernate. Often the database for a microservice is simple, and in such cases, I find it easiest to add a thin layer—like Dapper—on top of it for a simpler solution overall. I could have chosen to use any of

(continued)

the other micro ORMs, but I like Dapper. In this chapter, you'll use Dapper to talk to SQL Server, but Dapper also works with other SQL databases like PostgreSQL, MySQL, or Azure SQL.

EventStoreDB: A dedicated event database

EventStoreDB is an open source database server designed specifically for storing events. EventStoreDB stores events as JSON documents, but it differs from a document database by assuming that the JSON documents are part of a stream of events. Although EventStoreDB is a niche product because it's so narrowly focused on storing events, it's in widespread use and has proven itself in heavy-load production scenarios.

In addition to storing events, EventStoreDB has facilities for reading and subscribing to events. For instance, EventStoreDB exposes its own event feeds—as ATOM feeds—that clients can subscribe to. If you don't mind depending on EventStoreDB, using its ATOM event feed to expose events to other microservices can be a viable alternative to the way you'll implement event feeds in this book.

EventStoreDB works by exposing an HTTP API for storing, reading, and subscribing to events. There are a number of EventStoreDB client libraries in various languages—including C#, F#, Java, Scala, Erlang, Haskell, and JavaScript—that make it easier to work with the database.

6.3.1   *Preparing a development setup*

Before we dive into implementation, we will need to run the SQL Server on localhost, which we will do in a Docker container.

First, pull down the latest SQL Server docker image to your machine

```
docker pull mcr.microsoft.com/mssql/server
```

and then run it:

```
docker run -e 'ACCEPT_EULA=Y' -e 'SA_PASSWORD=yourStrong(!)Password' -p
  1433:1433 -d mcr.microsoft.com/mssql/server
```

Last, confirm that SQL is indeed running by listing the locally running container and checking that SQL Server is in the list:

```
docker ps

CONTAINER ID       IMAGE                              COMMAND
    CREATED              STATUS          PORTS                  NAMES
3388b710892f       mcr.microsoft.com/mssql/server     "/opt/mssql/bin/
    perm…"    52 minutes ago     Up 52 minutes      0.0.0.0:1433->1433/
    tcp      friendly_bell
```

If the SQL Server container did not start up, you may need to use double quotes instead of single quotes in the Docker run command.

With this in place we are ready to start implementing data storage in our microservices.

6.3.2 *Storing data owned by a microservice*

Once you've decided which data a microservice owns, storing that data is relatively straightforward. The details of how it's done depend on your choice of database. The only difference specific to microservices is that the data store is solely owned and accessed by the microservice itself.

As an example, let's go back to the shopping cart microservice. It owns the users' shopping carts and therefore stores them. You'll store the shopping carts in SQL Server using Dapper.

You implemented most of the shopping cart microservice in chapter 2. Here, you'll fill in the data store bits.

> **NOTE** We are using SQL Server as an example, but everything we do with SQL Server could just as well be done with any other relational database, be it PostgreSQL, MySQL, or a cloud-hosted relational database like Azure SQL or AWS Aurora.

If you're familiar with storing data in SQL Server, the implementation should be no surprise, and that's the point. Storing the data owned by a microservice doesn't need to involve anything fancy. These are the steps for storing the shopping cart:

1 Create a database.
2 Use Dapper to implement the code to read, write, and update shopping carts.

First, you'll create a simple database for storing shopping carts. It will have two tables, as shown in figure 6.6.

The ShoppingCart database and the two tables—ShoppingCart and ShoppingCartItem—can be created with SQL scripts, which you can execute with various tools, including SQL Management Studio and Visual Studio Code, after connecting to the SQL Server container on localhost port 1433:

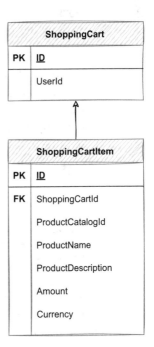

Figure 6.6 ShoppingCart has only two tables: one has a row for each shopping cart, and the other has a row per item in a shopping cart.

```
CREATE DATABASE ShoppingCart
GO

USE [ShoppingCart]
GO

CREATE TABLE [dbo].[ShoppingCart](
  [ID] int IDENTITY(1,1) PRIMARY KEY,
  [UserId] [bigint] NOT NULL,
  CONSTRAINT ShoppingCartUnique UNIQUE([ID], [UserID])
)
GO

CREATE INDEX ShoppingCart_UserId
ON [dbo].[ShoppingCart] (UserId)
GO
```

```
CREATE TABLE [dbo].[ShoppingCartItem](
  [ID] int IDENTITY(1,1) PRIMARY KEY,
    [ShoppingCartId] [int] NOT NULL,
    [ProductCatalogId] [bigint] NOT NULL,
    [ProductName] [nvarchar](100) NOT NULL,
    [ProductDescription] [nvarchar](500) NULL,
    [Amount] [int] NOT NULL,
    [Currency] [nvarchar](5) NOT NULL
)

GO

ALTER TABLE [dbo].[ShoppingCartItem]  WITH CHECK ADD CONSTRAINT [
  FK_ShoppingCart] FOREIGN KEY([ShoppingCartId])
REFERENCES [dbo].[ShoppingCart] ([Id])
GO

ALTER TABLE [dbo].[ShoppingCartItem] CHECK CONSTRAINT [FK_ShoppingCart]
GO

CREATE INDEX ShoppingCartItem_ShoppingCartId
ON [dbo].[ShoppingCartItem] (ShoppingCartId)
GO
```

> **NOTE** If you have issues connecting to the SQL Server in the container, it may be because it uses a development certificate that you will have to trust explicitly.

With the database in place, you can implement the code in the shopping cart micro-service that reads, writes, and updates the database. You'll install the Dapper NuGet package into the microservice. Remember that you do this by adding Dapper to the ShoppingCart project with the dotnet add package dapper command from a command line in the same folder as the ShoppingCart.csproj file. After adding the Dapper package the item group with package references, the ShoppingCart.csproj file should look like this:

```
<ItemGroup>
  <PackageReference Include="Dapper" Version="2.0.35" />        Adds the Dapper
  <PackageReference Include="Microsoft.Extensions.Http.Polly" rsion="3.1.0"/>   library
  <PackageReference Include="Polly" Version="7.2.0" />
  <PackageReference Include="Scrutor" Version="3.1.0" />
</ItemGroup>
```

In chapter 2, the shopping cart microservice was expecting an implementation of an IShoppingCart interface. You'll change that interface slightly to allow the implementation of it to make asynchronous calls to the database. This is the modified interface:

```
public interface IShoppingCartStore
{
  Task<ShoppingCart> Get(int userId);
  Task Save(ShoppingCart shoppingCart);
}
```

Now it's time to look at the implementation of the `IShoppingCartStore` interface. First, let's consider the code for reading a shopping cart from the database.

Listing 6.1   Reading shopping carts with Dapper

```
namespace ShoppingCart.ShoppingCart
{
  using System.Data;
  using System.Data.SqlClient;
  using System.Linq;
  using System.Threading.Tasks;
  using Dapper;

  public interface IShoppingCartStore
  {
    Task<ShoppingCart>Get(int userId);
    Task Save(ShoppingCart shoppingCart);
  }

  public class ShoppingCartStore : IShoppingCartStore
  {
    private string connectionString =
      @"Data Source=localhost;Initial Catalog=ShoppingCart;
User Id=SA; Password=yourStrong(!)Password";

    private const string readItemsSql =
      @"
select ShoppingCart.ID, ProductCatalogId,
ProductName, ProductDescription, Currency, Amount
from ShoppingCart, ShoppingCartItem
where ShoppingCartItem.ShoppingCartId = ShoppingCart.ID
and ShoppingCart.UserId=@UserId";

    public async Task<ShoppingCart> Get(int userId)
    {
      await using var conn = new SqlConnection(this.connectionString);
      var items = (await
        conn.QueryAsync(
          readItemsSql,
          new {UserId = userId}))
        .ToList();
      return new ShoppingCart(
        items.FirstOrDefault()?.ID,
        userId,
        items.Select(x =>
          new ShoppingCartItem(
            (int) x.ProductCatalogId,
            x.ProductName,
            x.ProductDescription,
            new Money(x.Currency, x.Amount)))));
    }
  }
}
```

Annotations:
- **Connection string to the ShoppingCart database in the MS SQL Docker container**
- **Dapper expects and allows you to write your own SQL.**
- **Opens a connection to the ShoppingCart database**
- **Uses a Dapper extension method to execute a SQL query**
- **The result set from the SQL query to ShoppingCartItem**

Dapper is a simple tool that provides some convenient extension methods on
`IDbConnection` to make working with SQL in C# easier. It also provides some basic
mapping capabilities. For instance, when the rows returned by a SQL query have column names equal to the property names in a class, Dapper can automatically map to
instances of the class.

Dapper doesn't try to hide the fact that you're working with SQL, so you see SQL
strings in the code. This may feel like a throwback to the earliest days of .NET. I find
that as long as I'm working with a simple database schema—as I usually am in microservices—the SQL strings in C# code aren't a problem.

Writing a shopping cart to the database is also done through Dapper. The implementation is the following method in `ShoppingCartStore`.

Listing 6.2   Writing shopping carts with Dapper

```
private const string insertShoppingCartSql =
@"insert into ShoppingCart (UserId) OUTPUT inserted.ID VALUES (@UserId)";

    private const string deleteAllForShoppingCartSql =
@"delete item from ShoppingCartItem item
inner join ShoppingCart cart on item.ShoppingCartId = cart.ID
and cart.UserId=@UserId";

    private const string addAllForShoppingCartSql =
@"insert into ShoppingCartItem
(ShoppingCartId, ProductCatalogId, ProductName,
ProductDescription, Amount, Currency)
values
(@ShoppingCartId, @ProductCatalogId, @ProductName,
@ProductDescription, @Amount, @Currency)";

    public async Task Save(ShoppingCart shoppingCart)
    {
      await using var conn = new SqlConnection(this.connectionString);
      await conn.OpenAsync();
      await using (var tx = conn.BeginTransaction())
      {
        var shoppingCartId =
          shoppingCart.Id ??
            await conn.QuerySingleAsync<int>(        ◁─┐ Create a row in the ShoppingCart
              insertShoppingCartSql,                   │ table if the shopping cart does
              new {shoppingCart.UserId}, tx);          │ not already have an Id.

        await conn.ExecuteAsync(                  ◁── Deletes all pre-existing
          deleteAllForShoppingCartSql,                shopping cart items
          new {UserId = shoppingCart.UserId},
          tx);
        await conn.ExecuteAsync(                  ◁── Adds the current
          addAllForShoppingCartSql,                   shopping cart items
          shoppingCart.Items.Select(x =>
            new
            {
              shoppingCartId,
```

```
            x.ProductCatalogId,
            Productdescription = x.Description,
            x.ProductName,
            x.Price.Amount,
            x.Price.Currency
        }),
    tx);
    await tx.CommitAsync();                    ◁──┐ Commits all changes
    }                                             │ to the database
}
```

That concludes the code that stores shopping cart information in the shopping cart microservice. It's similar to storing data in a more traditional setting—like a monolith or traditional SOA service—except that the narrow scope of a microservice means the model is often so simple that little to no mapping between C# code and a database schema is needed.

6.3.3 Storing events raised by a microservice

This section looks at storing the events raised by a microservice. During command processing, a microservice can decide to raise events. Figure 6.7 shows the standard set of components in a microservice; the domain model raises the events. It typically does so when there's a change or a set of changes to the state of the data for which the microservice is responsible.

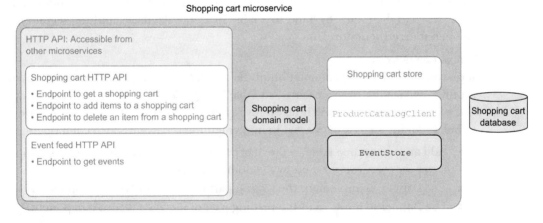

Figure 6.7 The components in the shopping cart microservice involved in raising and saving events are the shopping cart domain model, the `EventStore` component, and the shopping cart database.

The events should reflect a change to the state of the data owned by the microservice. The events should also make sense in terms of the capability implemented by the microservice. For example, in a shopping cart microservice, when a user has added an item to their shopping cart, the event raised is `ItemAddedToShoppingCart`, not `RowAdded-ToShoppingCartTable`. The difference is that the first signifies an event of significance to the system—a user did something that's interesting in terms of the business—whereas the latter would report on a technical detail—a piece of software did something because a programmer decided to implement it that way. The events should be of significance at the level of abstraction of the capability implemented by the microservice, and they will often cover several updates to the underlying database. The events should correspond to business-level transactions, not to database transactions.

Whenever the domain logic in a microservice raises an event, it's stored to the database in the microservice. In figure 6.8, this is done through the `EventStore` component, which is responsible for talking to the database where the events are stored.

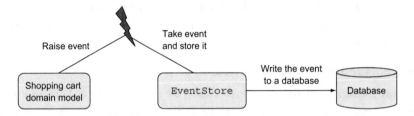

Figure 6.8   When the domain model raises an event, the `EventStore` component code must write it to the database.

The following two sections show two implementations of an `EventStore` component. The first stores the events by hand to a table in a SQL database, and the second uses the open source EventStoreDB.

STORING EVENTS BY HAND

Here, you'll build an implementation of the `EventStore` component in the shopping cart microservice that stores events to a table in SQL Server. The `EventStore` component is responsible for both writing events to and reading them from that database.

The following steps are involved in implementing the `EventStore` component:

1 Add an `EventStore` table to the `ShoppingCart` database. This table will contain a row for every event raised by the domain model.
2 Use Dapper to implement the writing part of the `EventStore` component.
3 Use Dapper to implement the reading part of the `EventStore` component.

Before we dive into implementing the `EventStore` component, here's a reminder of what the `Event` type in the shopping cart looks like.

Listing 6.3   The `Event` type in the ShoppingCart microservice

```
public record Event(
    long SequenceNumber,
    DateTimeOffset OccuredAt,
    string Name,
    object Content);
```

It's events of this type that you'll store in the `ShoppingCart` database. The first step is to go into the `ShoppingCart` database and add a table like the one shown in figure 6.9. The database script in the file Chapter06\ShoppingCart\database-scripts\create-shopping-cart-db.sql in the code download creates this table, along with the other two tables in the `ShoppingCart` database.

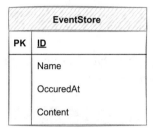

Figure 6.9   The `EventStore` table has four columns for these categories: event ID, event name, the time the event occurred, and the contents of the event.

Next, add a file named EventStore.cs to the shopping cart, and add to it the following code for writing events.

Listing 6.4   Raising an event, which amounts to storing it

```
namespace ShoppingCart.EventFeed
{
  using System;
  using System.Collections.Generic;
  using System.Data.SqlClient;
  using System.Text.Json;
  using System.Threading.Tasks;
  using Dapper;

  public interface IEventStore
  {
    Task<IEnumerable<Event>> GetEvents(long firstEventSequenceNumber,
      long lastEventSequenceNumber);
    Task Raise(string eventName, object content);
  }

  public class EventStore : IEventStore
  {
    private string connectionString =
      @"Data Source=localhost;Initial Catalog=ShoppingCart;
User Id=SA; Password=yourStrong(!)Password";

    private const string writeEventSql =
@"insert into EventStore(Name, OccurredAt, Content)
values (@Name, @OccurredAt, @Content)";

    public async Task Raise(string eventName, object content)
    {
      var jsonContent = JsonSerializer.Serialize(content);
```

```
    await using var conn = new SqlConnection(this.connectionString);
    await conn.ExecuteAsync(                    Uses Dapper to execute a
      writeEventSql,                            simple SQL insert statement
      new
      {
        Name = eventName,
        OccurredAt = DateTimeOffset.Now,
        Content = jsonContent
      });
  }
}
```

This code doesn't compile because the `IEventStore` interface has another method, one for reading events. That side is implemented as shown next.

Listing 6.5 `EventStore` method for reading events

```
private const string readEventsSql =
    @"select * from EventStore where ID >= @Start and ID <= @End";

  public async Task<IEnumerable<Event>> GetEvents(
    long firstEventSequenceNumber,
    long lastEventSequenceNumber)
  {
    await using var conn = new SqlConnection(this.connectionString);
    return await conn.QueryAsync<Event>(         Maps EventStore table
        readEventsSql,                           rows to Event objects
        new
        {
          Start = firstEventSequenceNumber,      Reads EventStore table rows
          End = lastEventSequenceNumber          between start and end
        });
  }
```

NOTE Storing events essentially amounts to storing a JSON serialization of the content of the event in a row in the `EventStore` table, along with the ID of the event, the name of the event, and the time at which the event was raised. The concept of storing events and publishing them through an event feed may be new, but the implementation is pretty simple.

That's all you need to implement a basic event store. The shopping cart microservice can now raise events in the domain model and rely on the `EventStore` component to write them to the `EventStore` table in the `ShoppingCart` database. Furthermore, shopping cart has an event feed that you implemented back in chapter 2, which now uses the `EventStore` component to read events from the database. It will send them to event subscribers when they poll the feed.

This event store implementation is very basic and is not ready for all production use cases. For instance, it may run into lock-contention problems as when the microservice starts raising events from several concurrent threads, especially under high load. This example does, however, show what it means to store events.

> **NOTE** There are several high-quality open source projects that implement an event store on top of a relational database, including SqlStreamStore (https://sqlstreamstore.readthedocs.io) and Marten (https://martendb.io/).

STORING EVENTS USING THE EVENTSTOREDB SYSTEM

You'll now implement another version of the `EventStore` component in the shopping cart microservice, this time using the open source EventStoreDB. The advantage of using EventStoreDB over storing events in SQL Server is that its API is geared specifically toward storing events, reading events, and subscribing to new events. EventStoreDB is an open source, mature, well-tested EventStoreDB implementation that can scale and run stably under load. Furthermore, it comes with some added features out of the box, such as a web interface for inspecting events and Atom event feeds. SQL Server is, of course, also mature, well-tested, scalable, and stable, but it isn't specifically geared toward storing events.

You'll implement this version with the following steps. When you're finished, you'll have a fully working implementation of the `EventStore` component in the shopping cart microservice based on the EventStoreDB:

1 Run EventStoreDB in a Docker container.
2 Write events to EventStoreDB via the `EventStore` component.
3 Read events from EventStoreDB via the `EventStore` component.

> **NOTE** You can learn much more about EventStoreDB than we will cover in this chapter at https://eventstore.com/.

You can pull the EventStoreDB Docker image down with this command:

```
docker pull eventstore/eventstore
```

Once pulled down you can run the EventStoreDB container like this:

```
docker run --name eventstore-node -it -p 2113:2113 -p 1113:1113 --rm
  eventstore/eventstore:latest --run-projections All --enable-external-tcp
  --enable-atom-pub-over-http
```

> **NOTE** If you get the error "TLS is enabled on at least one TCP/HTTP interface—a certificate is required to run EventStoreDB" when running the EventStoreDB container on localhost—you can add the `--insecure` switch to the Docker run command. This removes the security provided by TLS and should not be used in production.

You can check whether the EventStoreDB is running by going to http://127.0.0.1:2113/. You should see a login prompt that lets you log in with the user name "admin" and the password "changeit."

In order to use the EventStoreDB from the shopping cart microservice code, you first need to add the `EventStore.Client` NuGet package to the project. With that installed, you can implement the `EventStore` component against the EventStoreDB. The following listing shows the code for writing events.

Listing 6.6   Storing events to the EventStoreDB

```csharp
namespace ShoppingCart.EventFeed
{
  using System;
  using System.Collections.Generic;
  using System.Linq;
  using System.Text;
  using System.Text.Json;
  using System.Threading.Tasks;
  using EventStore.ClientAPI;

  public class EsEventStore : IEventStore
  {
    private const string ConnectionString =
      "tcp://admin:changeit@localhost:1113";

    public async Task Raise(string eventName, object content)
    {
      using var connection =
        EventStoreConnection.Create(
          ConnectionSettings.Create().DisableTls().Build(),
          new Uri(ConnectionString));
      await connection.ConnectAsync();
      await connection.AppendToStreamAsync(
        "ShoppingCart",
        ExpectedVersion.Any,
        new EventData(
          Guid.NewGuid(),
          "ShoppingCartEvent",
          isJson: true,
          data: Encoding.UTF8.GetBytes(
            JsonSerializer.Serialize(content)),
          metadata: Encoding.UTF8.GetBytes(
            JsonSerializer.Serialize(new EventMetadata
            (
              OccuredAt = DateTimeOffset.UtcNow,
              EventName = eventName
            )))));
    }

    public record EventMetadata(
      DateTimeOffset OccuredAt,
      string EventName);
  }
}
```

Annotations:
- For local development only. In production, TLS should be enabled.
- Creates a connection to EventStore
- Opens the connection to EventStore
- Writes the event to EventStore
- EventData is EventStore's representation of an event.
- Maps OccurredAt and EventName to metadata to be stored along with the event

This code maps the shopping cart microservice's own `Event` type to the Event-StoreDB's `EventData` type and then stores that to the EventStoreDB. The implementation for reading events back from the EventStoreDB is shown next.

Listing 6.7   Reading events from the EventStoreDB

```
public async Task<IEnumerable<Event>>
 GetEvents(long firstEventSequenceNumber, long lastEventSequenceNumber)
{
  using var connection =
    EventStoreConnection.Create(
      ConnectionSettings.Create().DisableTls().Build(),
      new Uri(ConnectionString));
  await connection.ConnectAsync();
  var result = await connection.ReadStreamEventsForwardAsync(      ⟵ Reads events from
    "ShoppingCart",                                                    the EventStoreDB
    start: firstEventSequenceNumber,
    count: (int) (lastEventSequenceNumber - firstEventSequenceNumber),
    resolveLinkTos: false);
  return result.Events          ⟵ Accesses the events on the
    .Select(e =>                   result from the EventStoreDB
      new
      {
        Content = Encoding.UTF8.GetString(e.Event.Data),      ⟵ Gets the content
        Metadata = JsonSerializer.Deserialize<EventMetadata>(      part of each event
          Encoding.UTF8.GetString(e.Event.Metadata),    ⟵ Gets the metadata
          new JsonSerializerOptions                         part of each event
          {
            PropertyNameCaseInsensitive = true
          })!
      })
    .Select((e, i) =>          ⟵ Maps to events from
      new Event(                 EventStoreDB Event objects
        i + firstEventSequenceNumber,
        e.Metadata.OccuredAt,
        e.Metadata.EventName,
        e.Content));
}
```

This code reads the events from EventStoreDB, desterilizes the content and metadata parts of the events, and then maps them back to the shopping cart microservice's own `Event` type.

This completes the implementation of the `EventStore` component based on the EventStoreDB. Let's now look at using caching.

6.3.4   *Setting cache headers in HTTP responses*

Let's consider the microservices in figure 6.2 again. The shopping cart microservice uses product information that it gets by querying the product catalog microservice; you implemented the shopping cart microservice part of that collaboration in chapter 2. Here, you'll first set cache headers in the code implementing the endpoint in the product catalog. Then, you'll rewrite the code in the shopping cart that calls the product catalog to read and use the cache header.

Assume that the /products endpoint in the product catalog microservice is implemented in an MVC controller called `ProductCatalogController`. You'll take a comma-separated list of product IDs as a query parameter. The endpoint returns the product information for each of the products identified by that list of product IDs. The implementation is similar to the MVC controllers you've already seen in this book. The new part is that you'll use the `ResponseCache` attribute to add a cache-control header to the response that allows clients to cache the response for 24 hours.

Listing 6.8   Adding cache headers to the product list

```
namespace ProductCatalog
{
  using System.Collections.Generic;
  using System.Linq;
  using Microsoft.AspNetCore.Mvc;

  [Route("/products")]
  public class ProductCatalogController : ControllerBase
  {
    private readonly IProductStore productStore;

    public ProductCatalogController(IProductStore productStore) =>
      this.productStore = productStore;

    [HttpGet("")]
    [ResponseCache(Duration = 86400)]          ⟵⎯  Adds a cache-control header,
    public IEnumerable<ProductCatalogProduct> Get(     with max-age in seconds
      [FromQuery] string productIds))
    {
      var products = this.productStore.GetProductsByIds(
        ParseProductIdsFromQueryString(productIds));
      return products;
    }

    private static IEnumerable<int>
      ParseProductIdsFromQueryString(string productIdsString) => ...
  }
```

This implementation adds a cache-control header to the response that looks like this:

```
cache-control: public,max-age:86400
```

The header tells callers that the response may be cached for as long as indicated by `max-value`, which is given in seconds. In this case, callers may cache the response for 86,400 seconds (24 hours).

6.3.5   *Reading and using cache headers*

In chapter 2, you saw code make calls to the /products endpoint from the shopping cart microservice. That code is as follows; it's part of the `ProductCatalogClient` class.

> ### Listing 6.9 Calling the product catalog microservice

```
private async Task<HttpResponseMessage>
  RequestProductFromProductCatalog(int[] productCatalogIds)
{
  var productsResource =
    string.Format(getProductPathTemplate,
      string.Join(",", productCatalogIds));
  return await
    this.client.GetAsync(productsResource);
}
```

With this code, an HTTP request is made every time the shopping cart needs product information, regardless of any cache headers. This is inefficient in cases where the shopping cart needs information about the same products several times within 24 hours, because that's the max-age value set in the responses from the product catalog microservice. Such cases will occur every time a user adds an item to their shopping cart that another user has added to theirs within the preceding 24 hours. That's likely to happen often.

Let's extend the code making the call to the /products endpoint in product catalog to take cache headers into account. Add a dependency to ProductCatalogClient on a cache that implements an ICache interface:

```
private readonly HttpClient client;
private readonly ICache cache;
private static string productCatalogueBaseUrl =  @"https://git.io/JeHiE";
private static string getProductPathTemplate = "?productIds=[{0}]";

public ProductCatalogClient(HttpClient client, ICache cache)
{
  client.BaseAddress = new Uri(productCatalogueBaseUrl);
  client.DefaultRequestHeaders.Accept.Add(
    new MediaTypeWithQualityHeaderValue("application/json"));
  this.client = client;
  this.cache = cache;
}
```

As you'll recall, ASP.NET handles dependency injection for you, so as long as there's an implementation of the ICache interface registered in the IServiceCollection, ASP.NET will inject it. Here, I'll only show the interface, but in the code download, you can find a simple static cache implementing the interface. The interface is straightforward and has two methods:

```
public interface ICache
{
  void Add(string key, object value, TimeSpan ttl);    ⟵┐ ttl means
  object Get(string key);                                │ time to live.
}
```

You'll use the cache variable on ProductCatalogClient to check whether there's a valid object in the cache before making an HTTP request.

Listing 6.10   Making requests when there's no valid response in the cache

```
private async Task<HttpResponseMessage>
  RequestProductFromProductCatalog(int[] productCatalogIds)
{
  var productsResource = string.Format(
    getProductPathTemplate,
    string.Join(",", productCatalogIds));
  var response =
    this.cache.Get(productsResource) as HttpResponseMessage;
  if (response is null)
  {
    response = await this.client.GetAsync(productsResource);
    AddToCache(productsResource, response);
  }
  return response;
}

private void AddToCache(string resource, HttpResponseMessage response)
{
  var cacheHeader = response
    .Headers
    .FirstOrDefault(h => h.Key == "cache-control");
  if (!string.IsNullOrEmpty(cacheHeader.Key)
      && CacheControlHeaderValue.TryParse(
        cacheHeader.Value.ToString(), out var cacheControl)
      && cacheControl.MaxAge.HasValue)
    this.cache.Add(resource, response, cacheControl.MaxAge.Value);
}
```

> Tries to retrieve a valid response from the cache

> Only makes the HTTP request if there's no response in the cache

> Reads the cache-control header from the response

> Parses the cache-control value and extracts max-age from it

> Adds the response to the cache if it has a max-age value

With this code in place in the shopping cart microservice, the responses from the product catalog microservice will be used for as long as the max-age value in the cache-control header allows (24 hours, in this example).

Summary

- A microservice stores and owns all the data that belongs to the capability the microservice implements.
- A microservice is the authoritative source for the data it owns.
- A microservice stores its data in its own dedicated database.
- A microservice will often cache data owned by other microservices for several reasons:
  - To reduce coupling to other microservices. This makes the overall system more stable.
  - To speed up processing by avoiding making remote calls.
  - To build up its own custom representations—known as read models—of data owned by another microservice to make its code simpler.
  - To build read models based on events from other microservices to avoid querying the other microservices, thus using an event-based collaboration

style instead of a query-based one. Remember from chapter 5 that event-based collaboration is preferable because of the reduced coupling.

- Which database or databases a microservice uses is a design decision particular to that microservice. Different microservices can use different databases.
- Storing the data owned by a microservice is similar to storing data in other kinds of systems.
- You can use Dapper to read data from and write data to a SQL database.
- Storing events is essentially a matter of storing a serialized event to a database.
- A simple version of an event store involves storing events to a table in a SQL database.
- You can also implement an EventStoreDB by storing events to the open source EventStoreDB, which is specifically designed to store events.

Designing for robustness

7

This chapter introduces strategies for making a system of microservices robust in the face of failures. In general, whenever one microservice communicates with another, the communication may fail. In this chapter, you'll learn about and implement some patterns for dealing with such failures. The strategies are fairly simple, but they'll make the overall system much more robust.

Failures and errors

I'll distinguish between the terms *failure* and *error*. A *failure* happens when something goes wrong in the system and the issue is caused by something outside the system. Some typical sources of failures are as follows:

- Lost network packets cause communication to fail.
- Lost connections cause communication to fail.
- Hardware failures cause microservices to fail.

An *error* happens when the system can't serve its users properly. Some typical examples of errors are these:

- A user sees an error page.
- The system hangs and never responds to a user action.
- The system gives back the wrong response to a user action.

Errors can stem from failures. On the other hand, failures only become errors if the software can't cope properly with failures. It follows that a perfect system would see failures but no errors. Unfortunately, our systems aren't perfect, and we may as well accept that errors will occur but learn to cope with them quickly.

7.1 *Expect failures*

When working with any nontrivial software system, you must expect failures to occur. Hardware can fail. Software may fail due to, for instance, unforeseen usage or corrupt data. A distinguishing factor of a microservice system is that there's a lot of communication between microservices. Figure 7.1 repeats the diagram from chapter 1 that shows the communication resulting from a user adding an item to a shopping cart. You see that just one user action results in quite a bit of communication—and a real system will likely have many concurrent users all performing many actions, and thus lots of communication. You must expect communication to fail from time to time. Communication between two microservices may not fail often, but looking at a microservice system as a whole, communication failures are likely to occur often due to the amount of communication.

Because you have to expect that some of the communication in your microservice system will fail, you should design your microservices to be able to cope with those failures. As discussed in chapter 5, you can divide the collaborations between microservices into three categories: query-, command-, and event-based collaborations. When a communication fails, the impact depends on the type of collaboration and the way the microservices cope with it:

- *Query-based collaboration*—When a query fails, the caller doesn't get the information it needs. If the caller copes well with that, the system keeps working, but with degraded functionality. If the caller doesn't cope well, the result could be an error.

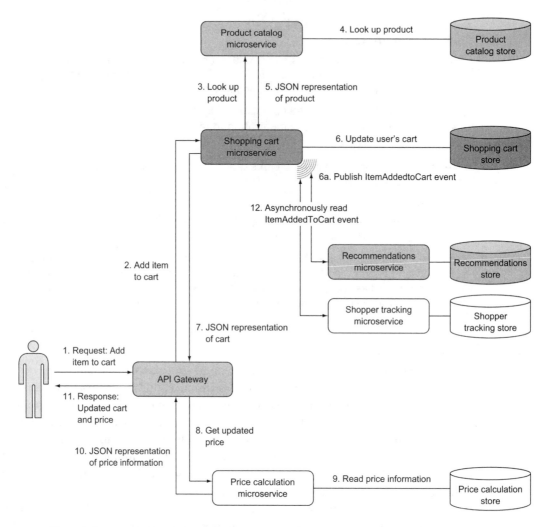

Figure 7.1   In a system of microservices, there will be many communication paths.

- *Command-based collaboration*—When sending a command fails, the sender can't know whether the receiver got the command. Again, depending on how the sender copes, this could result in an error, or it could result in degraded functionality.
- *Event-based collaboration*—When a subscriber polls an event feed but the call fails, the impact is limited. The subscriber will poll the event feed again later and, assuming the event feed is up again, receive the events at that time. In other words, the subscriber will still get all events, but some of them will be delayed. This shouldn't be a problem for an event-based collaboration because it's asynchronous anyway.

The following subsection discusses some important ways to prepare for handling failure well.

7.1.1 Keeping good logs

Once you accept that failures are bound to happen and that some of them may result not just in a degraded end user experience but also in errors, you must make sure you're able to understand what went wrong when an error occurs. That means you need good logs that allow you to trace what happened in the system and led to an error situation. "What happened" will often span several microservices, which is why you should introduce a central log microservice, as shown in figure 7.2; all other

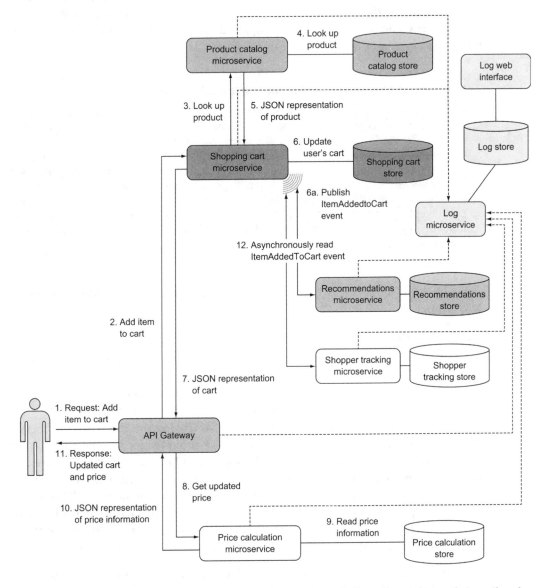

Figure 7.2 **A central log microservice receives log messages from all other microservices and stores them in a database or a search engine. The log data is accessible through a web interface. The dotted arrows show microservices sending log messages to the central log microservice.**

microservices send log messages to it, and you can inspect and search the logs when you need to.

The log microservice is a central component that all other microservices use. You need to make certain that a failure in a log doesn't bring down the whole system by causing all other microservice to fail if they can't log messages. Therefore, sending log messages to a log must be decoupled, so the microservice sending the message shouldn't wait for a response. That decoupling can be achieved in several different ways depending on the choices you make for your productions environment. When using containers, the standard way to decouple from the log microservices is for the other microservices to simply log to standard out and let a *log shipping* tool collect those logs and send them to the log microservice.

Using an off-the-shelf solution for the log microservice

A central log microservice doesn't implement a business capability of a particular system. It's an implementation of generic technical capability. In other words, the requirements for a log microservice in system A aren't that different from the requirements for a log microservice in system B. Therefore, I recommend using an off-the-shelf solution to implement your log microservice. Products in this category include ELK, Datadog, Splunk, Honeycomb, and many more. These are well-established, well-documented products, and I won't dive into how to set them up here, but they all support ingesting logs from microservices with low coupling. In chapter 10, I'll assume that you have a log microservice based on one of these products, and I'll show you how to send useful log messages to it.

Later in this chapter, we'll look at logging unhandled errors by adding handlers to MVCs pipeline.

7.1.2   *Using trace IDs*

To find all log messages related to a particular action in the system, you can use *trace IDs*. A trace ID is an identifier attached, for example, to a request from an end user when it comes into the system. The trace ID is passed along from microservice to microservice in any communication that stems from that end user request. Any time one of the microservices sends a log message to the log microservice, the message should include the trace ID. The log microservice should allow searching for log messages by trace ID. In figure 7.2, the API Gateway would create and assign a trace ID to each incoming request, and the trace ID would then be passed with every microservice-to-microservice communication, including events and log messages. This is a well-established pattern and can be implemented based on an open standard like Open Telemetry (https://opentelemetry.io/), which has the benefit that several of the off-the-shelf logging products mentioned support and understand Open Telemetry.

> **NOTE**   Chapter 9 discusses how to implement request logging and how to include trace IDs in communications and log messages.

7.1.3 *Rolling forward vs. rolling backward*

When errors happen in production, you're faced with the question of how to fix them. In many traditional systems, if errors begin to occur shortly after deployment, the default response is to roll back to the previous version of the system. In a microservice system, the default can be different. As discussed in chapter 1, microservices lend themselves to continuous delivery. With continuous delivery, microservices are deployed frequently, and each deployment should be both fast and easy to perform. Furthermore, microservices are sufficiently small and simple that many bug fixes are also easy. This opens the possibility of *rolling forward* rather than *rolling backward.*

Why would you want to default to rolling forward? In some situations, rolling backward is complicated—in particular when database changes are involved. When a new version that changes the database is deployed, the microservice begins to produce data that fits in the updated database. Once that data is in the database, it has to stay there, which may not be compatible with rolling backward to an earlier version. In such a case, rolling forward may be easier.

7.1.4 *Don't propagate failures*

Sometimes, things happen around a microservice that may disturb its normal operation. We say that the microservice is *under stress* in such situations. There are many sources of stress, including the following:

- One of the machines in the cluster on which the microservice's data store runs has crashed.
- The microservice has lost network connectivity to one of its collaborators.
- The microservice is receiving unusually high amounts of traffic.
- One of its collaborators is down.

In all these situations, the microservice under stress can't continue to operate the way it normally does. That doesn't mean it's down, but it must cope with the situation.

When one microservice fails, its collaborators are put under stress. That means the collaborators are also at risk of failing. While the microservice is failing, its collaborators can't query, send commands, or poll events from the failing microservice. As illustrated in figure 7.3, if the collaborators fail, even more microservices become at risk of failing: the failure begins to propagate through the system of microservices. Such a situation can quickly escalate from one microservice failing to many microservices failing.

Here are some examples of how you can stop failures from propagating:

- When one microservice tries to send a command to another microservice that happens to be failing at that time, the request will fail. If the sender fails too, you get the situation illustrated in figure 7.3, with failures propagating throughout the system. To stop the propagation, the sender can act as if the command succeeded but actually store the command in a list of failed commands. The sending microservice can periodically go through the list of failed commands

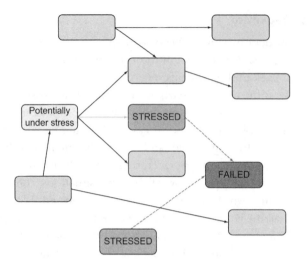

Figure 7.3   If the microservice marked FAILED is failing, so is communication with it. That means the microservices at the other end of those communications are under stress. If the stressed microservices fail due to the stress, the microservices communicating with them are put under stress. In that situation, the failure in one failed microservice can propagate to several other microservices.

and try to send them again. This isn't possible in all situations because the command may need to be handled immediately, but when this approach is feasible, it stops the failure in one microservice from propagating. This approach can be combined with a *circuit breaker*, which we'll talk about later in the chapter.

- When one microservice queries another that's failing, the caller can use a cached response. In chapter 6, you saw how to cache query responses and respect the cache header set by the microservice being queried. If the caller has a stale response in the cache but a query for a fresh response fails, it may decide to use the stale response anyway. Again, this isn't possible in all situations, but when it is, the failure won't propagate.

- An API Gateway that's stressed because of high amounts of traffic from a certain client can throttle that client by not responding to more than a certain number of requests per second from the client. Note that the client may be sending an unusually high number of requests because it's failing internally. When throttled, the client will get a degraded experience but will still receive some responses. Without the throttling, the API Gateway may become slow for all clients or fail completely. Moreover, because the API Gateway collaborates with other microservices, handling all the incoming requests would push the stress of those requests onto other microservices, too. Again, throttling stops the failure in the client from propagating to other microservices.

As you can see from these examples, stopping failure propagation comes in many shapes and sizes. The important takeaway is the idea of building safeguards into your systems that are specifically designed to stop propagation of the kinds of failures you anticipate. How that's realized depends on the specifics of the systems you're building. Building in safeguards may take some effort, but it's often well worth the effort because of the robustness they give the system as a whole.

7.2   *The client side's responsibility for robustness*

When two microservices collaborate, there's a client and server, as shown in figure 7.4. The client is the microservice that sends out HTTP requests, and the server microservice handles them. The request shown in figure 7.4 happens to fail; it may fail because the server fails, or it may fail because it doesn't reach the server. Once the request has failed, the server can't do anything about it. The server can't send a response to a failed request; it is already gone at that point. Responsibility for handling requests therefore must fall on the client. In other words, the client is responsible for making the collaboration robust in the face of failing requests.

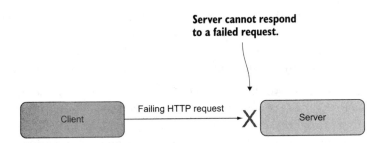

Figure 7.4   All collaborations between microservices have a client and a server. The client sends HTTP requests to the server. The client is responsible for handling failed requests.

When you look at an event-based collaboration, you see a degree of robustness in the face of failing requests built into the collaboration itself. Figure 7.5 shows an event subscriber in one microservice and an event feed in another microservice. As you saw in chapter 4, an event subscriber polls the event feed at intervals for new events. That way of collaborating means that if a request for new events fails, the event subscriber will ask for the same events the next time it polls for events. The subscriber can catch up to events in the event feed even though some requests fail, and thus the subscriber is robust with regard to failing requests for events.

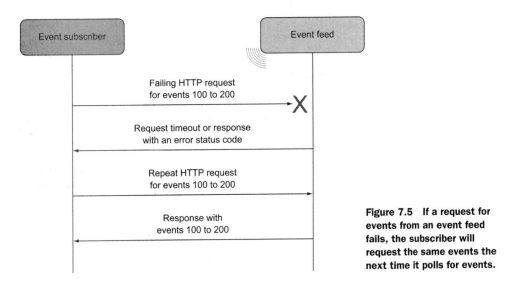

Figure 7.5   If a request for events from an event feed fails, the subscriber will request the same events the next time it polls for events.

You can see that with regard to command- and query-based collaboration, robustness doesn't come easily. The next two sections talk about patterns for building robustness into command- and query-based collaborations.

7.2.1   *Robustness pattern: Retry*

The client in a command- or query-based collaboration may choose to try again when a request fails. If the reason for the failed request is transient, the next attempt may be successful. Transient failures are common, and the reasons for them include the following:

- Network congestion.
- The server microservice being deployed. Depending on how the microservice is deployed, there may be a short window when the microservice is unavailable or slow—for example, while a load balancer is switched over to a new version. Even if the server is slow only during deployment, requests may fail due to timeouts.

Retrying is a double-edged sword. If the reason for the failures isn't transient, retrying requests won't help. On the contrary, retrying indiscriminately puts stress on the server because it's getting not only its usual number of requests, but also the retries (see figure 7.6). This may not seem like a big deal, but imagine a system that's already under high load. During normal operation, the client sends many requests to the server. If requests start failing and the client retries all of them, the client ends up sending more and more requests to the server. If the reason for the failing requests is that the server is already having trouble keeping up with the number of requests it receives, sending even more requests certainly isn't going to help.

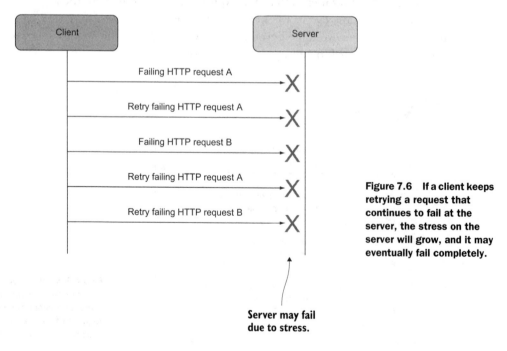

Figure 7.6   If a client keeps retrying a request that continues to fail at the server, the stress on the server will grow, and it may eventually fail completely.

Does this mean retrying is a bad pattern? No; it means you shouldn't continue retrying or retry too aggressively. The first thing to consider is how many times it makes sense to retry. If the request fails three times, is there any reason to believe it will succeed the fourth time? Second, you can use an exponential *backoff* between each retry. That is, instead of retrying after a constant amount of time (say, 100 ms), wait two or three times longer between each retry: maybe 100 ms before the first retry, 200 ms between the first and the second, and 400 ms between the second and third. These two simple additions mean the stress on the server builds more slowly; you should always use them when you retry command or query requests. Later in this chapter, I'll show how the Polly library makes it easy to set up such retry strategies.

You may even want to consider making the interval between retries much longer. Instead of waiting a fraction of a second before retrying, you could wait a few minutes or even hours. Figure 7.7 shows a retry strategy in which the intervals are long and become exponentially longer. This type of retry doesn't place nearly as much stress on the server as the fast retries used in many software systems.

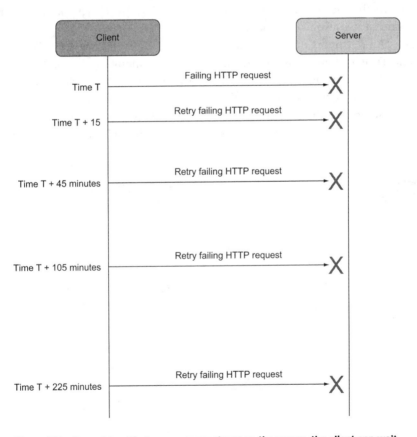

Figure 7.7   To avoid putting unnecessary stress on the server, the client can wait exponentially longer and longer between retries.

This approach clearly doesn't work for all situations. If a user is waiting for a response, it makes no sense to retry an hour later, because the user will have given up long before, so the software should also give up and give a degraded response sooner. On the other hand, if the request is initiated based on something the system does on its own—for example, as part of handling an event—you can often wait a long time.

Next, we'll discuss another useful pattern for making collaborations robust: the circuit breaker pattern. Then we'll move on to code and implement both the fast- and slow-paced styles of retries.

7.2.2 *Robustness pattern: Circuit breaker*

The circuit breaker pattern is a different take on dealing with failing requests. (For further reading about the circuit breaker and related patterns, see Michael T. Nygard's book, *Release It! Design and Deploy Production-Ready Software*, 2nd ed., Pragmatic Programmers, 2018.) As you saw in the previous section, retrying failing requests can add to the problem by putting the server under stress; therefore, you must limit the number of retries. The circuit breaker pattern takes this line of thinking a step further: it assumes that if a number of different requests in a row fail, then the next request is also likely to fail.

Figure 7.8 illustrates this situation. The client has already made HTTP requests A, B, C, and D. Is it then likely that E will succeed? In many cases, no. The fact that a number of requests failed indicates that the problem isn't with the individual requests. Rather, it has to do with the communication: the client can't reach the server, the server is failing, or the client is sending bad requests. The issue with communication may be transient, but even so, request E often also fails.

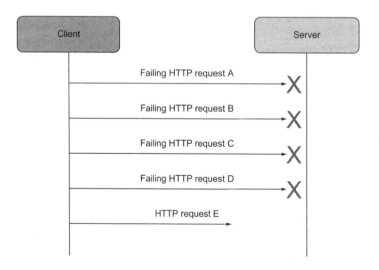

Figure 7.8 If several requests in a row have failed, is the next one likely to fail? In many cases, yes.

The circuit breaker pattern addresses this situation by not making request E at all, but instead assumes it will fail. Not making requests that are likely to fail alleviates stress on both the client and the server:

- The server receives fewer requests.
- The client doesn't have to wait for requests to fail but rather assumes they will, meaning the client doesn't spend resources on waiting and can get its own work done more quickly.

A circuit breaker wraps HTTP requests in a state machine like the one shown in figure 7.9. When the microservice needs to make an HTTP request, it does so through the circuit breaker.

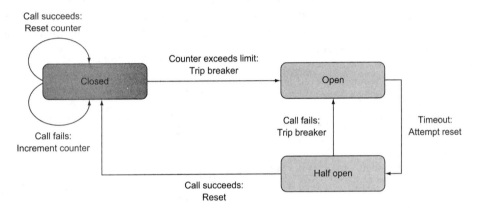

Figure 7.9 A circuit breaker is a state machine with three states. When the circuit breaker is closed, real HTTP requests are made. When the circuit breaker is open, no requests are made. A circuit breaker helps avoid making HTTP requests that are likely to fail.

The circuit breaker state machine starts in the closed state and works as follows:

- While the circuit breaker is in the *closed state*, it makes a real HTTP request when asked. If the HTTP request fails, the circuit breaker increments a counter. If the request succeeds, the circuit breaker resets the counter to zero. When and if that counter exceeds a preset limit—say, five failed requests in a row—the circuit breaker goes to the open state.
- While the circuit breaker is in the *open state*, it doesn't make any HTTP requests. Instead, it errors immediately. The circuit breaker stays in the open state for a preset period—say, 30 seconds—and then goes to the half-open state.
- While the circuit breaker is in the *half-open state*, it makes an HTTP request the first time it's asked. After that one HTTP request, it goes to the closed state if the request succeeded, or to the open state if it failed.

The result of these simple rules is a state machine that stops making HTTP requests when they're likely to fail anyway. Later in this chapter, I'll show you how to use Polly to create circuit breakers around HTTP requests.

TIP   Circuit breakers not only are useful for HTTP requests, but also can be used to add robustness around any other operation that can fail.

For the remainder of the chapter, we'll get down to the code level and see how to implement retry strategies and circuit breakers using Polly and general error handling using MVC's pipelines.

7.3   *Implementing robustness patterns*

To see how to implement the retry and circuit breaker patterns discussed in the previous sections, let's turn our attention back to the point-of-sale system introduced in chapter 4 and zoom in on the collaborations around the loyalty program microservice. You identified these collaborations in chapter 5; figure 7.10 shows them again, annotated with the robustness strategies you'll implement in the following sections. We won't look at code for the robustness strategies of the invoice and log microservices, so they're grayed out.

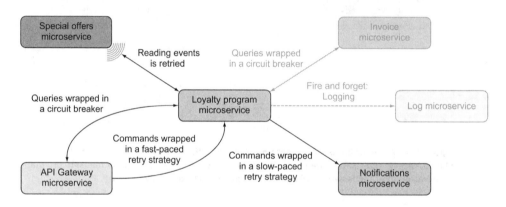

Figure 7.10   The loyalty program microservice collaborates with several other microservices. Each collaboration is annotated with a robustness strategy.

In the following sections, you'll do the following:

- Implement a fast-paced retry strategy in the API Gateway microservice for the commands it sends to the loyalty program microservice. The implementation is based on the Polly library.
- Implement a circuit breaker in the API Gateway microservice for the queries it makes to the loyalty program microservice. This implementation is also based on the Polly library.
- Implement a slow-paced retry strategy in the loyalty program microservice for the commands it sends to the notifications microservice based on the way the event subscription already works.
- Implement general exception handlers in the HTTP API in the loyalty program microservice using facilities in MVC.

Polly

Polly is a convenient library for creating and using error-handling strategies. Creating a strategy with Polly is done in a declarative way via a fluent API. Once created, a strategy can be applied to any `Func` or `Action`, which essentially means you can apply the strategy to any code you want. Furthermore the `HttpClient` class integrates with Polly to make applying error-handling strategies to HTTP requests even easier.

The three basic steps to using Polly are as follows:

- Decide which exceptions to handle, such as `HttpException`.
- Decide which policy to use, such as a retry policy.
- Apply the policy to a function.

The entry point to working with Polly is the `Policy` class:

```
var retryStrategy =
  Policy
    .Handle<HttpException>()        Step 1: Decide which
    .Retry();                       exceptions to handle.   Step 2: Decide which
                                                            policy to use.

retryStrategy.Execute(() => DoHttpRequest());     Step 3: Use the strategy
                                                  to wrap a function call.
```

Polly comes with a number of built-in policies, including variations of retry strategies and various circuit breaker strategies. Furthermore, all strategies come in async as well as sync flavors.

We will leverage Polly and the integration with `HttpClient` to easily implement solid retry and circuit breaker strategies.

The API Gateway microservice consists of the components shown in figure 7.11. In the next two sections, we'll zoom in on `LoyaltyProgramClient`.

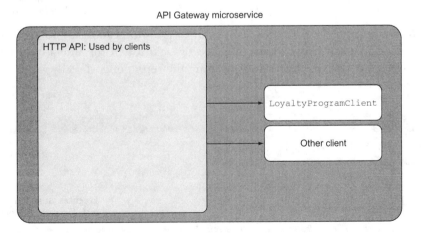

Figure 7.11 The API Gateway microservice consists of the same standard set of components you've seen several times already.

7.3.1 *Implementing a fast-paced retry strategy with Polly*

As shown in figure 7.10, the API Gateway microservice sends commands to the loyalty program microservice. We'll only look at adding a retry strategy to the register-user command here, because the code for adding a retry strategy to the update-user command is essentially the same.

First, you need to add the Polly NuGet package to the API Gateway microservice. The code that sends the commands to the loyalty program microservice is in `Loyalty-ProgramClient` in the API Gateway. You use Polly to set up a retry policy that uses an exponential backoff. Polly splits the setup of a policy from the execution of the policy; that is, Polly allows you to set up different policies—a retry policy, for instance—and then later execute a piece of code under the policy. In the case of a retry strategy, that means retrying the piece of code if it fails. The retry policy for the register-user command is set up as shown.

Listing 7.1 Polly retry policy

```
using System;
using Polly;                                    Code executed under this
                                                policy should return an
public class LoyaltyProgramClient               HttpResponseMessage.
{
    private static readonly IAsyncPolicy<HttpResponseMessage>
      ExponentialRetryPolicy =
        Policy<HttpResponseMessage>                              Handle timeouts
          .Handle<HttpRequestException>()                       and server errors
          .OrTransientHttpStatusCode()                          (5XX status codes)
          .WaitAndRetryAsync(              Chooses an async policy because
            3,                             you'll use it with async code later
            attempt =>
              TimeSpan.FromMilliseconds(100 * Math.Pow(2, attempt))
          );
}                                                           Time span to wait
                                                            before the next retry
```

Handles all HTTP exceptions

Number of retries

With the retry strategy set up, you can use it to wrap the call to the loyalty program microservice. We can chose to do this directly or through the integration between `HttpClient` and Polly. First let's look at using the retry policy directly with `Loyalty-ProgramClient`:

Listing 7.2 Using a Polly policy around an HTTP request

```
public async Task<HttpResponseMessage>
  RegisterUser(string name)
{
  var user = new {name, Settings = new { }};
  return await ExponentialRetryPolicy              Executes an action
    .ExecuteAsync(() =>                            with the retry policy
      this.httpClient.PostAsync("/users/", CreateBody(user)));   Makes the
}                                                                 HTTP request

private static StringContent CreateBody(object user) => ...
```

That is how easy it is to set up a retry policy with Polly and wrap a piece of code in it. We can achieve the same behavior in a slightly different way by configuring the Http-Client used in LoyaltyProgramClient with the retry policy. In this version, Loyalty-ProgramClient is left untouched. Instead, we add the exponentialRetryPolicy to the Startup class where we use it to configure the HttpClient for LoyaltyProgramClient like this:

```
public class Startup
{
  private static readonly IAsyncPolicy<HttpResponseMessage>
    ExponentialRetryPolicy =
      Policy<HttpResponseMessage>                          ◁─┐ The retry
        .Handle<HttpRequestException>()                      │ policy
        .OrTransientHttpStatusCode()
        .WaitAndRetryAsync(
          3,
          attempt =>
            TimeSpan.FromMilliseconds(100 * Math.Pow(2, attempt)));

  public void ConfigureServices(IServiceCollection services)   │ Tell the service collection
  {                                                            │ that LoyaltyProgramClient
    services.AddHttpClient<LoyaltyProgramClient>()        ◁─┘ wraps an HttpClient.
      .AddPolicyHandler(_ => ExponentialRetryPolicy)       ◁─┐ Add retry
      .ConfigureHttpClient(c => c.BaseAddress = new Uri(host)); ◁─┐ policy to the
      ...                                                         │ HttpClient.
  }                              Add other configuration         │
  ...                            to the HttpClient.          ────┘
}
```

This code registers the LoyaltyProgramClient with the service collection, which allows ASP.NET to inject LoyaltyProgramClient into other types as a dependency. Furthermore, the service collection is instructed that the LoyaltyProgramClient needs an HttpClient, which should apply the ExponentialRetryPolicy to all HTTP requests. This also achieves our goal of wrapping the user registration in a retry policy. In fact, this does a little bit more than that: since we set up the HttpClient to wrap all HTTP requests in the retry policy, the retry is also applied to queries made by Loyalty-ProgramClient. We will fix this problem in the next section when we add a circuit breaker to the queries.

Whether you prefer to apply the Polly policy directly in the LoyaltyProgramClient or in configuration when adding the LoyaltyProgramClient to the service collection comes down to taste: which version do you find simpler? Personally I don't have a strong preference either way—as long as we remember to add robustness patterns to all collaboration.

Next, you'll use Polly to create a circuit breaker.

7.3.2 *Implementing a circuit breaker with Polly*

Now you'll add a circuit breaker to the API Gateway microservice's queries to the loyalty program microservice. This time, you'll use Polly's built-in support for circuit breaker policies.

Listing 7.3 Polly circuit breaker policy

```
private static readonly IAsyncPolicy<HttpResponseMessage>
  CircuitBreakerPolicy =
    Policy<HttpResponseMessage>
      .Handle<HttpRequestException>()
      .OrTransientHttpStatusCode()
      .CircuitBreakerAsync(5, TimeSpan.FromMinutes(1));
```

Handles the same errors as the retry policy

Sets the failure limit to 5 minutes and the time-in-open-state limit to 1 minute

Even though the circuit breaker pattern may seem more complicated than retrying, Polly makes it just as easy to set up a circuit breaker policy. Using a policy is the same no matter what the policy is. If you prefer using the policy directly in Loyalty-ProgramClient, you can wrap the queries the same way we wrapped register-user commands. If, on the other hand, you prefer the HttpClient configuration approach, we extend the configuration in Startup to choose the policy based on the type of HTTP request the HttpClient performs.

Listing 7.4 Wrapping a query in a circuit breaker

```
services.AddHttpClient<LoyaltyProgramClient>()
  .AddPolicyHandler(request =>
    request.Method == HttpMethod.Get
      ? CircuitBreakerPolicy
      : ExponentialRetryPolicy)
  .ConfigureHttpClient(c => c.BaseAddress = new Uri(host));
```

Check which HTTP method. A GET is a query; everything else is a command.

Use retry for commands.

Use circuit breaker for queries.

With these two policies in place, API Gateway takes responsibility for adding robustness to the collaboration with loyalty program. Next, we'll move on to the loyalty program microservice.

7.3.3 *Implementing a slow-paced retry strategy*

The loyalty program microservice subscribes to events from the special offers microservice. Based on the events, the loyalty program sends commands to the notifications microservice, asking it to notify users about new special offers. If sending a command to notifications fails, you want to retry. Because sending out notifications isn't particularly time critical, you'll choose not to retry immediately; instead, you'll retry the next time the event subscriber would otherwise poll for new events. To do this, all you have to do is keep track of what the last successful event was.

Remember from chapter 5 that an event subscriber works by periodically waking up and polling the event feed for new events. On each such cycle, the next batch of events is read and handled. The next batch of events will begin one event after the last successfully handled event. This means all failed events are retried. It also means you may as well abort the rest of a batch as soon as one event fails—the rest will be retried later anyway. The code from chapter 5 handles one batch of events and was set up to be called by Kubernetes on a schedule, so we actually already implemented slow-paced retry in chapter 5. To emphasize how the slow-paced retry works, let's reiterate the code from chapter 5. First, there is a small program that handles one batch of events:

Listing 7.5 Single-event subscription cycle

```
using System;
using System.IO;
using System.Net.Http;
using System.Net.Http.Headers;
using System.Text.Json;
using System.Threading.Tasks;

var start = await GetStartIdFromDatastore();        ← Read the starting point of
var end = 100;                                         this batch from a database.
var client = new HttpClient();
client
    .DefaultRequestHeaders
    .Accept
    .Add(new MediaTypeWithQualityHeaderValue("application/json"));    ← Send the GET
using var resp = await client                                          request to the
    .GetAsync(                                                         event feed.
       new Uri($"http://special-offers:5002/events?start={start}&end={end}"));
await ProcessEvents(await resp.Content.ReadAsStreamAsync());          ←
await SaveStartIdToDataStore(start);            ← Save the starting point of
                                                   the next batch of events.

static int GetStartIdFromDataStore() { ... }              Call the method to process
static void SaveStartIdToDataStore(int start) { ... }      the events in this batch.
static void ProcessEvents(string rawEvents) { ... }       ProcessEvents also updates
                                                             the start variable.
public record SpecialOfferEvent(
  long SequenceNumber,
  DateTimeOffset OccuredAt,
  string Name,
  object Content);
```

This programs is called on a schedule and handles reading one batch of events. Once a batch has been read, each event must be processed with code like the following.

Listing 7.6 Handling a batch of events

```
private async Task ProcessEvents(string rawEvents)
{
  var events = await
    JsonSerializer.DeserializeAsync<SpecialOfferEvent[]>(content)
    ?? new SpecialOfferEvent[0];
  foreach (var ev in events)
  {
    dynamic eventData = ev.Content;
    if (ShouldSendNotification(eventData))          All events were assumed to be
      await SendNoitifcation(eventData);             successfully handled, and "start"
    this.start = ev.SequenceNumber + 1;           ← was updated for each one.
  }
}
```

```
private bool ShouldSendNotification(dynamic eventData)
{
  // decide if notification should be sent based on business rules
}

private Task SendNotification(dynamic eventData)
{
  // use HttpClient to send command to notification microservice
}
```

The specifics of the event-handling code will differ with every specific situation—that's where the business logic is implemented.

With this in place, one batch can be handled. The final piece is configuring Kubernetes to call the program on a schedule of once an hour, which is done with this YAML, which defines a CronJob in Kubernetes that calls our event consumer every hour.

Listing 7.7   Kubernetes manifest for the `LoyaltyProgram` event consumer

```
---
apiVersion: batch/v1beta1          ⊲—┐ The Kubernetes API version
kind: CronJob                         └ needed to specify a CronJob
metadata:                          ⊲—┐ Indicate that this
  name: loyalty-program-consumer      └ is a CronJob.
spec:
  schedule: "*/1 * * * *"          ⊲—┐ Define the schedule
  jobTemplate:                        └ for this job.
    spec:
      template:
        spec:
          containers:
            - name: loyalty-program
              image: microservicesindotnetregistry1.azurecr.io/loyalty-
                program:1.0.2
              imagePullPolicy: IfNotPresent
              env:
                - name: STARTUPDLL                    ┐ Point to the event
                  value: "consumer/EventConsumer.dll" ⊲┘ consumer DLL.
          restartPolicy: Never
  concurrencyPolicy: Forbid        ⊲—┐ Make sure only one copy at a time
                                      └ of the event consumers runs.
```

As you can see, we already implemented slow-paced retry, because that is how our event consumers work.

7.3.4   *Logging all unhandled exceptions*

Finally, we'll turn our attention to the HTTP API of the loyalty program microservice. As stated earlier, you want to keep good logs of everything that goes wrong in the system. That means you should log any unhandled exceptions thrown in the controllers in the microservices. In fact, the loyalty program microservice already does this. Part of the default ASP.NET pipeline is to catch all otherwise unhandled exceptions and

log them to standard out. To see this in action, you can add a new endpoint to the
UsersController that simply throws a NotImplementedException:

Listing 7.8 An endpoint that always throws an exception

```
[HttpGet("fail")]
public IActionResult Fail() => throw new NotImplementedException();
```

Then run the loyalty program microservice with dotnet run and call the new endpoint at https://localhost:5001/users/fail. The output in the console will
include an error log caused by the NotImplementedException similar to this.

Listing 7.9 Errors are logged to standard out

```
dotnet run
info: Microsoft.Hosting.Lifetime[0]
      Now listening on: https://localhost:5001
info: Microsoft.Hosting.Lifetime[0]
      Now listening on: http://localhost:5000
info: Microsoft.Hosting.Lifetime[0]
      Application started. Press Ctrl+C to shut down.
info: Microsoft.Hosting.Lifetime[0]
      Hosting environment: Development
info: Microsoft.Hosting.Lifetime[0]
      Content root path: C:\Users\chors\Documents\horsdal3\code\Chapter07\
      LoyaltyProgram\LoyaltyProgram                    ◄─┤ Start of the error log
fail: Microsoft.AspNetCore.Server.Kestrel[13]
      Connection id "0HM2KQ4LI56GR", Request id "0HM2KQ4LI56GR:00000001":
      An unhandled exception was thrown by the application.
System.NotImplementedException: The method or operation is not implemented.
   at LoyaltyProgram.Users.UsersController.Fail() in C:\Users\chors\
   Documents\horsdal3\code\Chapter07\LoyaltyProgram\LoyaltyProgram\Users\
   UsersController.cs:line 13
   at lambda_method(Closure , Object , Object[] )
   at Microsoft.Extensions.Internal.ObjectMethodExecutor.Execute(
     Object target, Object[] parameters)
   at Microsoft.AspNetCore.Mvc.Infrastructure.ActionMethodExecutor.
     SyncActionResultExecutor.Execute(IActionResultTypeMapper mapper,
     ObjectMethodExecutor executor, Object controller, Object[] arguments)
   at Microsoft.AspNetCore.Mvc.Infrastructure.ControllerActionInvoker.
     InvokeActionMethodAsync()
   at Microsoft.AspNetCore.Mvc.Infrastructure.ControllerActionInvoker.
     Next(State& next, Scope& scope, Object& state, Boolean& isCompleted)
   at Microsoft.AspNetCore.Mvc.Infrastructure.ControllerActionInvoker.
     InvokeNextActionFilterAsync()
--- End of stack trace from previous location where exception was thrown ---
   at Microsoft.AspNetCore.Mvc.Infrastructure.ControllerActionInvoker.
     Rethrow(ActionExecutedContextSealed context)
   at Microsoft.AspNetCore.Mvc.Infrastructure.ControllerActionInvoker.
     Next(State& next, Scope& scope, Object& state, Boolean& isCompleted)
   at Microsoft.AspNetCore.Mvc.Infrastructure.ControllerActionInvoker.
     InvokeInnerFilterAsync()
```

```
--- End of stack trace from previous location where exception was thrown ---
    at Microsoft.AspNetCore.Mvc.Infrastructure.ResourceInvoker.<
    InvokeFilterPipelineAsync>g__Awaited|19_0(ResourceInvoker invoker, Task
    lastTask, State next, Scope scope, Object state, Boolean isCompleted)
    at Microsoft.AspNetCore.Mvc.Infrastructure.ResourceInvoker.<InvokeAsync>
    g__Awaited|17_0(ResourceInvoker invoker, Task task, IDisposable scope)
    at Microsoft.AspNetCore.Routing.EndpointMiddleware.<Invoke>
    g__AwaitRequestTask|6_0(Endpoint endpoint, Task requestTask,
    ILogger logger)
    at Microsoft.AspNetCore.Server.Kestrel.Core.Internal.Http.HttpProtocol.
    ProcessRequests[TContext](IHttpApplication`1 application)
```

In chapter 10, we will return to logging and see how to configure it and make it even more useful, but for now, we are happy with having all exceptions logged.

7.3.5   *Deploying to Kubernetes*

We have implemented robustness patterns in all the collaborations around the loyalty program microservice, but we haven't changed the collaboration styles—queries are still queries, commands are still commands, and events are still events. Moreover, the dependencies between the microservices are still the same: the loyalty program microservice still subscribes to events from the special offers microservice and still sends commands to the notifications microservice. This means that the deployment to Kubernetes does not have to change and is therefore exactly the same as we saw in chapter 5.

This concludes the implementation of robustness measures in collaborations around the loyalty program microservice. With these fairly simple measures in place, the collaborations are likely to be a good deal more robust under production load.

Summary

- Due to the amount of communication between microservices, you must expect some communication to fail. It's vital for the robustness of the system that your microservices handle such failures gracefully.
- You should design robustness into your microservices so that failures don't propagate through the system and eventually become errors.
- The client side of a collaboration is responsible for making communication robust in the face of failures.
- You should have good logs that are easy to access and search through when you need to investigate production problems. A central log microservice should receive all log messages and provide access to them.
- The most important strategies for making communications robust are the retry and circuit breaker patterns.
- Polly makes it easy to set up and use retry policies as well as circuit breakers.
- By default ASP.NET logs errors to standard out. The off-shelf logging products support gathering up these logs from all the microservices and centralizing them.

Writing tests
for microservices

8

This chapter covers

- Writing good automated tests
- Understanding the test pyramid and how it applies to microservices
- Testing microservices from the outside
- Writing fast, in-process tests for endpoints
- Using `Microsoft.AspNetCore.TestHost` for integration and unit tests

Up to this point, we've written a few microservices and set up collaborations between some of them. The implementations are fine, but we haven't written any tests for them. As we write more and more microservices, developing systems without good automated tests becomes unmanageable. In the first half of this chapter, I'll discuss what you need to test for each individual microservice. Then we'll dive into code, looking first at testing endpoints in isolation, and then at testing a complete micro-service as if you were sending it requests from another microservice, but in-process using the `TestServer` from the `Microsoft.AspNetCore.TestHost` library.

8.1   *What and how to test*

In chapter 1, you saw three characteristics of a microservice that make it good for continuous delivery:

- *Individually deployable*—As soon as any small, safe change has been made to a microservice, the microservice can be deployed to production. But how do you know a change is safe? This is where testing and particularly test automation come into the picture. Several other activities, like code reviews, static code analysis, and designing public APIs for backward compatibility, also play into determining that a change is safe, but testing is where much of your confidence will come from.
- *Replaceable*—You should strive to be able to replace the implementation of a microservice with another functionally equivalent implementation within the normal pace of work. Again, tests play an important role because a good set of tests lets you assess whether the new implementation really is equivalent to the old one.
- *Maintainable by a small team*—Microservices are sufficiently small and focused so that a team can maintain several of them. An advantage is that you can write tests that cover all parts of your microservices.

If you want to become confident about changes quickly and be able to replace a badly implemented microservice, testing has to be fast and repeatable. To make testing fast and repeatable, you must automate a significant part of it—and that's the focus of this chapter.

8.1.1   *The test pyramid: What to test in a microservices system*

The *test pyramid* shown in figure 8.1 is a tool you can use to guide which kinds of tests you should write and how many you should have of each kind. You can find variations of the test pyramid in different writings; all of them put tests on different levels, where the levels at the top of the pyramid are broad in scope and the tests at the bottom are narrow. The test pyramid illustrates that you should aim for having many narrowly focused tests (the ones at the wide bottom of the pyramid) and only a few broadly scoped tests (the ones at the narrow top).

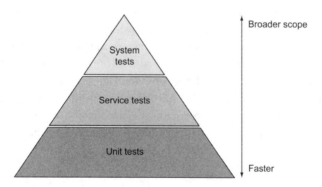

Figure 8.1   The test pyramid illustrates that you should have a few system-level tests, many service-level tests, and even more unit-level tests.

The version of the test pyramid that I use here has three levels:

- *System tests (top level)*—Tests that span the complete system of microservices and are usually implemented through the GUI.
- *Service tests (middle level)*—Tests that work against one, but only one, complete microservice.
- *Unit tests (bottom level)*—Tests that test one small piece of functionality in a microservice. Unit tests call code in the microservice under tests in process and usually involve only part of a microservice.

Note that when I use the term *unit test*, the word *unit* refers to a small piece of functionality. I define the scope of a unit test not in terms of any particular code construct, like a class or a method, but rather in terms of functionality. When we look at implementations of unit tests later, you'll see that unit tests can easily span all layers of a microservice, such as from an MVC controller, through a domain object, or down to a data access class.

Although the test pyramid tells you to have more tests as you move down the levels, exactly how many tests you should have on each level is situational. It depends on such factors as the size of the system, the complexity of the system, and the cost of failure.

8.1.2 System-level tests: Testing a complete microservice system end to end

The tests at the top of the pyramid have a very broad scope and therefore cover a lot of code with just a few tests. Because they have such a broad scope, they're also imprecise. When a system-level test breaks, it isn't immediately clear where the problem lies. The test can potentially use the entire system, so the issue could be anywhere.

An example of a system-level test is one that uses the web UI of the POS system we talked about in earlier chapters to add a number of items to an invoice, apply a discount code, and pay using a test credit card. If that test passes, it gives you confidence that invoices are created, that discounts can be applied, and that you can receive credit card payments. During such a system test, you might assert that the amount due on the invoice is as expected. If that assertion fails, any number of things could have caused the problem: you might be using the wrong price for one or more items, you might have applied the discount incorrectly, or you might have misinterpreted the invoice data. In other words, such a failure could be caused by at least a handful of different microservices. To figure out which one is the culprit, you need to investigate.

The specific way a system-level test fails can give some hints as to where the problem lies, but there's usually a lot of code that could be at fault. From the system test alone, it won't even be clear which microservice caused the failure. On the other hand, when system-level tests pass, they give you a good deal of confidence.

The second downside to system-level tests is that they tend to be slow. This again is the flip side of them involving the complete system: real HTTP requests are made, things are written to real data stores, and real event feeds are polled.

Considering that system-level tests, when successful, can give you good confidence, but that they're both slow and imprecise, my advice is to write system-level tests for the success path of the most important use cases. This should give you coverage for the success paths of all the most important parts of the system. You can, optionally, supplement this with some tests for the most common and important failure scenarios. Exactly how many system-level tests this amounts to is, as mentioned earlier, entirely situational. This advice applies equally to microservices, traditional SOA, and monoliths. There's nothing microservice-specific about system-level tests. For this reason, I won't show implementations of any system-level tests in this chapter.

8.1.3 Service-level tests: Testing a microservice from outside its process

The tests in the middle level of the test pyramid interact with one microservice as a whole and in isolation—the collaborators of the microservice under test are replaced with *microservice mocks*. Like system tests, these tests interact with the microservice under test from the outside. But unlike system-level tests, they interact directly with the public API of the microservice and make assertions about responses to the microservice, as well as the interactions the microservice has with other microservices, such as the commands the microservice under test sends to other microservices and the events it publishes.

> ### A microservice mock simulates a real microservice and records interactions
>
> A *microservice mock* can be used in place of a real microservice in service-level tests. It implements the same endpoints as the real microservice, but instead of using real business logic to implement the endpoints, the mock has dumbed-down endpoint implementations; usually, endpoints in a mock return hardcoded responses. Furthermore, a mock often records the requests made to the endpoints, so the test code can inspect the requests made during the test.
>
> This is similar to the mock objects widely used in tests for object-oriented code. But where mock objects replace a real object, a microservice mock replaces a real microservice.

Like system-level tests, service-level tests test scenarios rather than single requests. That is, they make a sequence of requests that together form a meaningful scenario. The requests made from the microservice under test to its mocked collaborators are real HTTP requests, and the responses are real HTTP responses.

For example, recall the loyalty program microservice from the example POS system. In chapter 5, you saw that it collaborated with a number of other microservices, as shown in figure 8.2, using all three collaboration styles: events, queries, and commands.

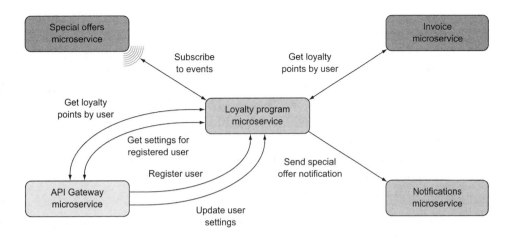

Figure 8.2   The loyalty program microservice collaborates with a number of other microservices through all three types of collaboration: events, queries, and commands.

To test a loyalty program in isolation, you can create mock versions of its collaborators. As shown in figure 8.3, when a loyalty program interacts with a mocked collaborator, it gets back a hardcoded response.

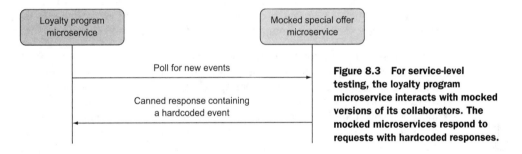

Figure 8.3   For service-level testing, the loyalty program microservice interacts with mocked versions of its collaborators. The mocked microservices respond to requests with hardcoded responses.

A service-level test for the loyalty program microservice could do the following:

1. Send a command to create a user.
2. Wait for the loyalty program microservice to query a mock special offer microservice for events and then receive a hardcoded event about a new special offer.
3. Record any commands sent to the notifications microservice and assert that a command for a notification to the new user about the new special offer was sent.

When a test like this passes, you can have confidence that important aspects of the loyalty program microservice work. When it fails, you know that the problem is within the loyalty program itself.

Service-level tests are much more precise than system-level tests because they cover only a single microservice: if such a test fails, the problem should lie within the microservice under test, assuming the test setup itself isn't buggy. Because microservices are small—they're replaceable, after all—knowing that a problem lies within a certain microservice is a lot more precise than what you get from system-level tests.

To call the endpoints implemented in our MVC controllers, we'll use the `Microsoft` `.AspNetCore.TestHost` library. This library lets you write tests that make calls to ASP.NET endpoints in memory. The calls go through ASP.NET in exactly the same way HTTP requests would, but without going through the network stack. To the code in our controllers, calls made through the `TestServer` from `Microsoft.AspNetCore.Mvc` `.Testing` look exactly like real HTTP requests. On the other hand, service-level tests are still relatively slow, because the microservice uses a real database and because it interacts with its mocked collaborators over HTTP.

Contract tests

As you know by now, there's a lot of collaboration between microservices in a microservices system. You implement the collaborations as requests from one microservice to another. If you aren't careful, changes in an endpoint can break the microservices that call that endpoint. This is where contract tests (https://martinfowler.com/bliki/ContractTest.html) come into the picture.

When any two microservices in the system collaborate, the one making requests to the other has some expectations about how the other will behave. That is, given a collaboration, the calling microservice expects the called microservice to implement a certain contract. A contract test is a test with the purpose of determining whether the called microservice implements the contract expected by the calling microservice.

Contract tests are written from the point of view of the caller and are there for the sake of the calling microservice: as long as the contract test passes, the assumptions the caller makes about the contract are still valid. Consequently, the contract tests are part of the caller's code base. They aren't part of the same code base as the endpoints they test. Contract tests shouldn't have any knowledge of how the microservices they test are implemented. This is where contract tests differ from service-level tests. With service-level tests, you isolate the microservice under test by providing it with mocked microservices in place of its collaborators. You don't want to do that for contract tests because the contract tests shouldn't know about the other collaborators of the microservice they test. In other words, contract tests run against the complete system.

Because contract tests are part of the code base of one microservice but test things in other microservices, and because they run against the complete system, it can be a good idea to run them against a QA or staging environment. Moreover, it's a good idea to have them run automatically every time the microservice under test is deployed. When a contract breaks, it's a strong indication that the collaboration between the microservice the contract test belongs to and the microservice under test is broken, too.

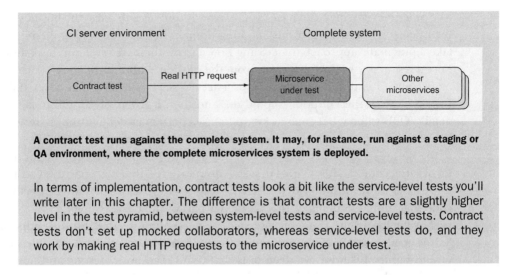

A contract test runs against the complete system. It may, for instance, run against a staging or QA environment, where the complete microservices system is deployed.

In terms of implementation, contract tests look a bit like the service-level tests you'll write later in this chapter. The difference is that contract tests are a slightly higher level in the test pyramid, between system-level tests and service-level tests. Contract tests don't set up mocked collaborators, whereas service-level tests do, and they work by making real HTTP requests to the microservice under test.

My recommendation regarding service-level tests is that you should write such tests for the success versions of all functionality the microservice under test offers. Such tests will naturally use all endpoints of the microservice as well as rely on any event subscriptions in the microservice. In other words, they will cover all success paths in the microservice. In general, I recommend writing service-level tests only for the most important failure scenarios. Again, the number of service-level tests needed and how many failure scenarios they should cover depends on the system and the cost of failure in that particular system.

8.1.4 *Unit-level tests: Testing endpoints from within the process*

The tests at the bottom of the test pyramid also deal with a single microservice, but these don't deal with the entire microservice; they interact with the parts of the microservice under test directly and in memory using an `HttpClient` created by the `TestServer` from the `Microsoft.AspNetCore.TestHost` library.

At the unit-test level, I'll show you two kinds of tests (see figure 8.4): one that uses a database and one that uses a mock in place of the database. I consider both unit tests, even though the first type uses a database, be it a fully fledged database or an in-memory database. Two things make a test a unit test: its scope is a small piece of functionality, and the test code and the production code in the microservice run in the same process.

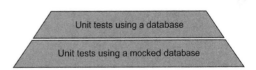

Figure 8.4 At the unit-test level, there are two kinds of tests: those that use a database and those that don't.

The narrow scope of a unit test makes it precise: when it fails, the problem lies in a small amount of code. A narrow scope also enables you to write tests that cover failure scenarios properly. Both types of unit tests are faster than service-level tests, but of course the tests that mock out databases are faster than those that use a database.

Sometimes you may also have even narrower unit tests that test the business logic in the microservices directly by instantiating domain objects and testing them directly. I take a pragmatic approach to deciding how narrow the narrowest unit tests should be. I use a test-first workflow that starts from the outside, with tests that use `TestServer` to make calls to endpoints in my microservices. I start with tests that cover the broad strokes of what the endpoint should do, and then I progressively add tests for more details. Only when it becomes awkward to test a particular detail through the endpoint handler do I begin to write narrower unit tests. For instance, covering a particular case in the business logic with tests that call through the endpoint handler might require a lot of setup code. That's a signal to switch down to a test that has a narrower scope—just those cases in the business logic. I'll write tests for those cases that work directly on the code that should implement that particular part of the business logic.

For the loyalty program microservice, we need unit tests that test the endpoint that lets us create users with a number of different inputs covering both possible valid and invalid inputs. Likewise, we need tests that try to read both existing and nonexistent users from the query endpoint that lets us read users. We need similar tests for the other endpoints in the microservice. The loyalty program is sufficiently simple that we don't need to switch down to tests that are narrower than the microservice's endpoints. So, the units tests I'll show you later all work by calling endpoint handlers through `TestServer`.

8.2 *Testing libraries: Microsoft.AspNetCore.TestHost and xUnit*

In this chapter, we'll use two new libraries:

- `Microsoft.AspNetCore.TestHost`
- xUnit

I'll give you a brief introduction to both, and then we'll implement tests for some of the microservices we wrote in earlier chapters.

8.2.1 *Meet Microsoft.AspNetCore.TestHost*

The `Microsoft.AspNetCore.TestHost` library is a companion to ASP.NET that makes it easy to test endpoints. With it, we configure a `TestHost` in much the same way we configure a web host in the production code. The `TestHost` uses the `TestServer`, which can create `HttpClient` objects for use in tests. An `HttpClient` created by `TestServer` is the same `HttpClient` we are used to working with in production code. It allows us to use methods like `GetAsync`, `PostAsync`, `PutAsync`, and `DeleteAsync` to call GET, POST, PUT, and DELETE endpoints in controllers, respectively. These calls go through the entire ASP.NET pipeline. This means that the dependency injection is set up and used as usual, middleware (which we will talk about in the next chapter) run as usual, MVC filters run as usual, and deserialization and serialization run as usual. In short, to the endpoint the call looks exactly like a real HTTP request, but it all happens in process, so it's a good deal faster than a real HTTP request going through the network stack would be. The return value of each method is an `HttpResponseMessage` just like we usually get from an `HttpClient`, and we can use it just like we otherwise would and inspect headers, status, and the response body.

The `Microsoft.AspNetCore.TestHost` library hooks into the normal configuration of ASP.NET application, so apart from the `TestServer` and the `HttpClients`, it creates everything with a `TestHost` the same as it would with a real host. Therefore, we can do all the usual configuration including, but not limited to

- Overriding registration in the dependency injection container, for instance, to provide mock objects in place of real ones
- Adding special hooks to the ASP.NET pipeline
- Configuring logging, for instance, to allow tests to inspect the contents of log messages

8.2.2 Meet xUnit

xUnit (https://xunit.net/) is a unit-test tool for .NET. It has a library part that allows you to write automated tests and a runner part that can run those tests. To write a test with xUnit, you create a method with a `Fact` attribute over it and put the code to perform the test there. The xUnit runner scans for methods with a `Fact` attribute and executes all of them. In addition, xUnit has an API for making assertions in tests. If an assertion fails, the xUnit runner picks up the failure and reports it back when it's finished running tests. The xUnit test runner can be run by `dotnet` and is therefore well suited for the projects you're building in this book.

Other .NET unit-test tools similar to xUnit—NUnit, for instance—are available and will also work for everything we will do in this chapter, so feel free to pick your own favorite.

8.2.3 xUnit and Microsoft.AspNetCore.TestHost working together

Putting `Microsoft.AspNetCore.TestHost` and xUnit together, you can write succinct tests for endpoints implemented in MVC controllers. In section 8.3.1, you'll set up a project for these unit tests and run them with `dotnet`; but for now, I want to give you a quick peek at how the tests will look. The following test calls the GET endpoint in `TestController` and makes the assertion that the response status code is "200 OK."

> **Listing 8.1 Simple controller test using xUnit and `Microsoft.AspNetCore.TestHost`**

```
namespace LoyaltyProgramUnitTests
{
    using System;
    using System.Net;
    using System.Net.Http;
    using System.Threading.Tasks;
    using Microsoft.AspNetCore.Builder;
    using Microsoft.AspNetCore.Hosting;
    using Microsoft.AspNetCore.Mvc;
    using Microsoft.AspNetCore.TestHost;
    using Microsoft.Extensions.Hosting;
    using Xunit;
```

```
public class TestController_should : IDisposable
{
  private readonly IHost host;
  private readonly HttpClient sut;

  public class TestController : ControllerBase
  {
    [HttpGet("/")]
    public OkResult Get() => Ok();          ◁──┐ Endpoint used
  }                                              in the test

  public TestController_should()
  {                                            Create an ASP.NET host
    this.host = new HostBuilder()     ◁──┐    for the test endpoint.
      .ConfigureWebHost(host =>
        host
          .ConfigureServices(x =>
            x.AddControllersByType(typeof(TestController)))    ◁──┐
          .Configure(x =>                                          Explicitly add the test
            x.UseRouting()                                         controller to the
              .UseEndpoints(opt => opt.MapControllers())))         service collection
          .UseTestServer())                                        using a custom
        .Start();                                                  extension method.
    this.sut = this.host.GetTestClient();
  }
```

Map all endpoints in the test controller. └─▷ (arrow to `.UseEndpoints(opt => opt.MapControllers())`)

```
  [Fact]
  public async Task respond_ok_to_request_to_root()
  {                                                Call the endpoint in
    var actual = await this.sut.GetAsync("/");  ◁─┘ the test controller.
    Assert.Equal(HttpStatusCode.OK, actual.StatusCode);  ◁──┐
  }                                                            Assert that the
                                                               call succeeded.
  public void Dispose()
  {
    this.host?.Dispose();     ◁──┐ Stop and dispose the ASP.NET
    this.sut?.Dispose();           host after the test is done.
  }
}
}
```

There are a few things to notice about this test:

- The test class, TestController_should, is IDisposable. The xUnit runner understands IDisposable and calls the Dispose method after running the Fact. In the dispose method, the host and sut are disposed, which makes sure that everything is cleaned up. If the host is not disposed, the test will hang until the test runner times out.

- In the TestController_should constructor we create a web host just like we do in the production code. This is where we can configure everything around the endpoint under test. In this test, we use a setup similar to that in the production code, except that we use the test server, which ensures that requests are done in process.

- During the configuration of the host, we use a custom extension method, `AddControllersByType`, which I will show next. By using `AddControllersByType`, we make sure that the host only has one controller: the `TestController`. Therefore, the test controls quite accurately which endpoints are available through the host.

Naming conventions

My tests follow these naming conventions:

- My tests work on an object called `sut` for *system under test*. In the previous test, `sut` is a `HttpClient` object that I use to make a call to an endpoint.
- I name my test classes after the thing they test—`TestController` in this example test—followed by _should.
- I name the `Fact` method after the scenario being tested and the expected result. I separate the words in `Fact` method names with underscores and try to make sure they form a sentence when combined with the name of the surrounding class. For instance, in this test, by concatenating the class name and the `Fact` method name and replacing underscores with spaces you get "TestController should respond okay to requests to root."

Whether you like these conventions is a matter of taste. I happen to like them, but they're in no way essential to writing good tests.

You can run the previous test with `dotnet test`; it will execute in memory and give you good coverage because the call to `sut.GetAsync("/")` executes the real ASP.NET pipeline, including the implementation of the endpoint in `TestController`. The string argument "/" is the relative URL to which the fake request is made. In section 8.3.1, we'll look at setting up a project for these unit tests and how to run them with `dotnet test`.

In the `TestController_should` constructor, we have used the custom extension method `AddControllersByType`, which works by overriding how MVC decides which types are controllers. This is done by creating a custom version of MVC's `ControllerFeatureProvider` and replacing MVC's default `ControllerFeatureProvider` with the custom one. MVC uses the `ControllerFeatureProvider` to decide which types are controllers, so by overriding it with a custom version we get to decide which types MVC sees as controllers and therefore which endpoints are part of the test. This is the implementation where the first part is the customer `ControllerFeatureProvider` and the second is the extension method, as shown in the following listing.

Listing 8.2   Extension method to control which controllers are part of the test

```
namespace LoyaltyProgramUnitTests
{
  using System;
  using System.Linq;
```

```
using System.Reflection;
using Microsoft.AspNetCore.Mvc.Controllers;
using Microsoft.Extensions.DependencyInjection;

public class FixedControllerProvider : ControllerFeatureProvider
{
  private readonly Type[] controllerTypes;

  public FixedControllerProvider(params Type[] controllerTypes)
  {
    this.controllerTypes = controllerTypes;
  }

  protected override bool IsController(TypeInfo typeInfo)
  {
    return this.controllerTypes.Contains(typeInfo);
  }
}

public static class MvcBuilderExtensions
{
  public static IMvcBuilder AddControllersByType(
      this IServiceCollection services,
      params Type[] controllerTypes)
      =>
    services
      .AddControllers()
      .ConfigureApplicationPartManager(mgr =>
      {
        mgr.FeatureProviders.Remove(
          mgr.FeatureProviders.First(f =>
            f is ControllerFeatureProvider));
        mgr.FeatureProviders.Add(
            new FixedControllerProvider(controllerTypes));
      });
}
}
```

Custom implementation of the controller provider

Override the method used to identify controllers.

The extension method

Make the service collection aware of controllers.

Get access to feature providers.

Remove the default controller provider feature.

Add a custom controller provider feature.

We will use this extension in later tests too as a convenient way to control the scope of a test.

For the rest of this chapter, we'll work at the code level and implement unit tests and service-level tests for the loyalty program microservice. When you implemented loyalty program in chapter 5, it didn't have an event feed, but for these examples, you'll add one that other microservices can subscribe to.

8.3   *Writing unit tests using Microsoft.AspNetCore.TestHost*

In this section, you'll implement some unit tests for the endpoints in the loyalty program microservice. In chapter 5, you saw that the loyalty program has three command and query endpoints:

- An HTTP GET endpoint at URLs of the form "/users/{userId}" that responds with a representation of the user
- An HTTP POST endpoint to "/users/" that expects a representation of a user in the body of the request and then registers that user in the loyalty program
- An HTTP PUT endpoint at URLs of the form /"users/{userId}" that expects a representation of a user in the body of the request and then updates an already registered user

Let's write tests for these endpoints. The loyalty program microservice has an event feed for which you'll also write a test. You won't write comprehensive tests for the endpoints and event feed in the loyalty program—only enough to see how tests against MVC endpoints are written. In the following subsections, you'll do the following:

- Set up a test project to house unit tests for the loyalty program microservice.
- Write tests that use Microsoft.AspNetCore.TestHost to test endpoints in the loyalty program and that let the code in the microservice use the real database. You'll write three such tests, one for each of these pieces of functionality:
  - A test that tries to read a user that doesn't exist
  - A test that creates a user and reads it back out
  - A test that modifies a user and reads it back out
- Write tests that also use Microsoft.AspNetCore.TestHost to test an endpoint but are limited in scope by a mocked database injected in the endpoint under test. These tests test the event feed in the microservice.

When you're finished, you'll have learned to write unit tests for MVC endpoints both with and without a real database.

8.3.1 Setting up a unit-test project

Before you can start writing tests, you need a project to house them. For that, create a new project next to the LoyaltyProgram project, and call it LoyaltyProgramUnit-Tests. You can create the test project with your IDE with the dotnet cli using the command dotnet new xunit -n LoyaltyProgramUnitTests. Your solution should look similar to this:

```
C:.
    Ch08.sln
    Dockerfile
    loyalty-program.yaml

──── EventConsumer
        EventConsumer.csproj
        Program.cs

──── LoyaltyProgram
    │   appsettings.Development.json
```

```
           appsettings.json
           LoyaltyProgram.csproj
           Program.cs
           Startup.cs

        ─── EventFeed
               EventFeedController.cs
               EventStore.cs
        ─── Users
               LoyaltyProgramSettings.cs
               LoyaltyProgramUser.cs
               UsersController.cs

  ─── LoyaltyProgramUnitTests
         LoyaltyProgramUnitTests.csproj
         UnitTest1.cs
```

You can now run the tiny test in UnitTest1.cs with `dotnet` like this:

```
PS> dotnet test
```

Once you have the initial tests running, add a dependency on `Microsoft.AspNet-Core.TestHost` so you can use the `TestServer` and `HttpClient`. Also add a dependency on `LoyaltyProgram` so you can begin testing it. The dependencies in the LoyaltyProgramUnitTests.csproj now look like this:

```
<ItemGroup>
  <PackageReference Include="Microsoft.AspNetCore.TestHost" Version="3.1.8"/>
  <PackageReference Include="Microsoft.NET.Test.Sdk" Version="16.5.0" />
  <PackageReference Include="xunit" Version="2.4.0" />
  <PackageReference Include="xunit.runner.visualstudio" Version="2.4.0" />
  <PackageReference Include="coverlet.collector" Version="1.2.0" />
</ItemGroup>

<ItemGroup>
  <ProjectReference Include="..\LoyaltyProgram\LoyaltyProgram.csproj" />
</ItemGroup>
```

The last line is the reference to the `LoyaltyProgram` project. Now we are ready to start writing tests.

8.3.2 *Using the TestServer and HttpClient to unit-test endpoints*

Now that you have a test project set up, you can begin adding tests to it. The first test you'll add is very simple: given that there are no registered users in the loyalty program microservice, a user expects to get back a response with a "404 Not Found" status code. Add a file called UsersEndpoints_should.cs to the `LoyaltyProgramUnit-Tests` project and put the following code in it.

```
namespace LoyaltyProgramUnitTests
{
```

```
using System;
using System.Net;
using System.Net.Http;
using System.Threading.Tasks;
using LoyaltyProgram;
using Microsoft.AspNetCore.Hosting;
using Microsoft.AspNetCore.TestHost;
using Microsoft.Extensions.Hosting;
using Xunit;

public class UsersEndpoints_should : IDisposable
{
  private readonly IHost host;                          Remember that sut stands
  private readonly HttpClient sut;     ◁──┘             for "system under test."

  public UsersEndpoints_should()
  {
    this.host = new HostBuilder()
      .ConfigureWebHost(x => x              Real LoyaltyProgram
        .UseStartup<Startup>()    ◁──┘      startup            Use the test server so
        .UseTestServer())                              ◁──┘    requests are in process.
      .Start();
    this.sut = this.host.GetTestClient();   ◁─┐   The host uses the test server
  }                                             to create a test HttpClient.

  [Fact]
  public async Task respond_not_fount_when_queried_for_unregistered_user()
  {
    var actual = await this.sut.GetAsync("/users/1000");      1((CO3-5))
    Assert.Equal(HttpStatusCode.NotFound, actual.StatusCode);
  }

  public void Dispose()
  {
    this.host?.Dispose();
    this.sut?.Dispose();
  }
}
```

The most interesting part of this test class is in the constructor, where you create a host and an HttpClient object. When xUnit runs, it creates an instance of Users-Endpoints_should and then calls a method with the Fact attribute on that instance. Unlike most other .NET test frameworks, xUnit creates a new, clean instance for each Fact method.

The host object in the previous listing is initialized with the real Startup class from LoyaltyProgram. This means the LoyaltyProgram application that the Http-Client calls into is wired up the same way it is when it runs on top of a real web server and receives real HTTP requests.

Let's move on to a test that registers a new user and then queries it to check that it was registered as it should be. Add the following test to the UsersEndpoints_should class.

Listing 8.4   Test for registering a user through the users endpoint

```
[Fact]
public async Task allow_to_register_new_user()
{
  var expected = new LoyaltyProgramUser(
    0,
    "Christian",
    0,
    new LoyaltyProgramSettings());

  var registrationResponse =                    Registers a new user
    await this.sut.PostAsync(          ⊲┘       through the POST endpoint
      "/users",
      new StringContent(
        JsonSerializer.Serialize(expected),
        Encoding.UTF8,                          Reads the new user from the body
        "application/json"));                   of the response from the POST
  var newUser =
    await JsonSerializer.DeserializeAsync<LoyaltyProgramUser>(
      await registrationResponse.Content.ReadAsStreamAsync(),   ⊲┘
      new JsonSerializerOptions
      {
        PropertyNameCaseInsensitive = true          Reads the new user
      });                                           through the GET endpoint

  var actual = await this.sut.GetAsync($"/users/{newUser?.Id}");   ⊲┘
  var actualUser =
    JsonSerializer.Deserialize<LoyaltyProgramUser>(
      await actual.Content.ReadAsStringAsync(),
      new JsonSerializerOptions
      {
        PropertyNameCaseInsensitive = true
      });

  Assert.Equal(HttpStatusCode.OK, actual.StatusCode);    Checks that the response
  Assert.Equal(expected.Name, actualUser?.Name);   ⊲┘   from the GET is correct
}
```

Here, you see another use of the `HttpClient`: we add a body to the `Post` via the second argument.

The last test you'll add registers a user and then modifies it via the PUT endpoint in the loyalty program microservice. Add it to `UsersEndpoints_should`, as shown next.

Listing 8.5   Test for modifying users through the users endpoint

```
[Fact]
public async Task allow_modifying_users()
{
  var expected = "jane";
  var user = new LoyaltyProgramUser(
    0, "Christian", 0, new LoyaltyProgramSettings());
```

```
var registrationResponse = await this.sut.PostAsync(          Registers
  "/users",                                                    a user
  new StringContent(
    JsonSerializer.Serialize(user),
    Encoding.UTF8,
    "application/json"));
var newUser = await
  JsonSerializer.DeserializeAsync<LoyaltyProgramUser>(
    await registrationResponse.Content.ReadAsStreamAsync(),
    new JsonSerializerOptions
    {
      PropertyNameCaseInsensitive = true
    })!;

var updatedUser = newUser! with {Name = expected};          Updates
var actual = await this.sut.PutAsync($"/users/{newUser.Id}", the user
  new StringContent(
    JsonSerializer.Serialize(updatedUser),
    Encoding.UTF8,
    "application/json"));
var actualUser = await
  JsonSerializer.DeserializeAsync<LoyaltyProgramUser>(
    await actual.Content.ReadAsStreamAsync(),
    new JsonSerializerOptions
    {
      PropertyNameCaseInsensitive = true
    });
                                                     Asserts that the
                                                     update was done
  Assert.Equal(HttpStatusCode.OK, actual.StatusCode);
  Assert.Equal(expected, actualUser?.Name);
}
```

There's nothing new in this code compared to what you've seen in the two previous tests, but I wanted to include it because it's a good illustration of the kind of unit tests I think you should write for the endpoints in your microservices: unit tests that focus on the behavior the endpoints provide rather than on testing just one endpoint in isolation.

8.3.3 Injecting mocks into endpoints

Now that you've tested the endpoints in UsersController, let's turn to testing the LoyaltyProgram event feed, a controller that depends on an IEventStore to store and read events. Here's the IEventStore interface.

> **Listing 8.6 IEventStore interface**

```
public interface IEventStore
{                                                      Stores events to
  Task RaiseEvent(string name, object content);        the event store
  Task<IEnumerable<EventFeedEvent>>
    GetEvents(int start, int end);        Reads events from
}                                         the event store
```

You saw an event feed in chapter 5, but I'll repeat it here, to remind you how it works.

Listing 8.7   Event feed

```
namespace LoyaltyProgram.EventFeed
{
  using System.Linq;
  using System.Threading.Tasks;
  using Microsoft.AspNetCore.Mvc;

  [Route(("/events"))]
  public class EventFeedController : ControllerBase
  {
    private readonly IEventStore eventStore;

    public EventFeedController(IEventStore eventStore)
    {
      this.eventStore = eventStore;
    }

    [HttpGet("")]
    public async Task<ActionResult<EventFeedEvent[]>>
      GetEvents([FromQuery] int start, [FromQuery] int end)
    {
      if (start < 0 || end < start)
        return BadRequest();

      return
        (await this.eventStore.GetEvents(start, end))
        .ToArray();
    }
  }
}
```

Gets the start and end value from the query string ⟵

Reads events "start" through "end" from the event store ⟵

As you can see, the event feed is a controller that responds to requests to /events with the events it reads from IEventStore. We want to write a test to check whether the event feed returns exactly the event from the IEventFeed. Toward that end, we want to control which events IEventStore returns. So, we'll create a fake implementation of IEventStore and use that in the test.

Listing 8.8   Fake IEventStore to use in tests

```
public class FakeEventStore : IEventStore
{
  public Task RaiseEvent(string name, object content) =>
    throw new System.NotImplementedException();

  public Task<IEnumerable<EventFeedEvent>>
    GetEvents(int start, int end)
  {
    if (start > 100)
      return Task.FromResult(
```

```
          Enumerable.Empty<EventFeedEvent>());

   return Task.FromResult(Enumerable          ◁──────┐ Returns a list of fake events
     .Range(start, end - start)                       │ when start is less than 100
     .Select(i =>
       new EventFeedEvent(
          i,
          DateTimeOffset.UtcNow,
          "some event",
          new object()))));
  }
}
```

With this fake implementation of an event store, you know it will return a list of events only if the start argument is less than 100. Otherwise, FakeEventStore will return an empty list of events. If you inject this IEventStore implementation into EventFeed-Controller, you'll know which events EventFeedController will get from the event store and therefore which events it should return.

We can take advantage of the fact that we create ASP.NET web hosts in our tests to take control of what's registered in the IServiceCollection. That allows us to register the FakeEventStore as the implementation of IEventStore so the FakeEvent-Store will be injected in the EventFeedController by ASP.NET. The complete setup of the web host for the test of the event feed looks like the following.

> **Listing 8.9 Using the fake event store while testing**

```
public EventFeed_should()
{
  this.host = new HostBuilder()
    .ConfigureWebHost(host =>          Configures what's          Registers FakeEventStore
      host                             registered in the          as the implementation of
        .ConfigureServices(x => x  ◁── service collection          IEventStore
          .AddScoped<IEventStore, FakeEventStore>()     ◁──
          .AddControllersByType(typeof(EventFeedController))          ◁─────┐
          .AddApplicationPart(typeof(EventFeedController).Assembly))
        .Configure(x =>
          x.UseRouting().UseEndpoints(opt => opt.MapControllers()))
        .UseTestServer())
    .Start();                                            Limits the host to
  this.sut = this.host.GetTestClient();                  using EventFeed-
}                                                        Controller only
```

With this code in the test's constructor, instances of EventFeedController will have FakeEventStore injected. We should add a Dispose method to the EventFeed_should class that disposes the host and sut exactly like we saw in previous unit tests.

Listing 8.10 shows how we can use the host to write two tests:

- A test that asserts events are returned from the feed when the start number in the request is less than 100
- A test that asserts no events are returned when the start number is greater than 100

Listing 8.10   Tests for the event feed, using the fake event store

```
[Fact]
public async Task return_events_when_from_event_store()
{
  var actual = await this.sut.GetAsync("/events?start=0&end=100");        ◁──┐

  Assert.Equal(HttpStatusCode.OK, actual.StatusCode);
  var eventFeedEvents =await
    JsonSerializer.DeserializeAsync<IEnumerable<EventFeedEvent>>(
      await actual.Content.ReadAsStreamAsync())
    ?? Enumerable.Empty<EventFeedEvent>();
  Assert.Equal(100, eventFeedEvents.Count());
}


[Fact]
public async Task return_empty_response_when_there_are_no_more_events()
{
  var actual = await this.sut.GetAsync("/events?start=200&end=300");      ◁──┐

  var eventFeedEvents = await
    JsonSerializer.DeserializeAsync<IEnumerable<EventFeedEvent>>(
      await actual.Content.ReadAsStreamAsync());
  Assert.Empty(eventFeedEvents);
}
```

> *Makes a request to /events with the query string start=0&end=100*

> *Makes a request to /events with the query string start=200&end=300*

Now that you have some unit tests in place, you can run them with dotnet test, as you saw earlier. When you do, xUnit will scan for classes with Fact methods and then execute each Fact method. The output from the tests shows a summary of how many tests ran, how many errors there were, how many tests failed, and how many were skipped:

```
> dotnet test
Test run for .\LoyaltyProgramUnitTests\bin\Debug\netcoreapp3.1\
  LoyaltyProgramUnitTests.dll(.NETCoreApp,Version=v3.1)
Microsoft (R) Test Execution Command Line Tool Version 16.6.0
Copyright (c) Microsoft Corporation.  All rights reserved.

Starting test execution, please wait...

A total of 1 test files matched the specified pattern.

Test Run Successful.
Total tests: 6
     Passed: 6
 Total time: 1,9937 Seconds
```

As you can see, six tests were run, and none of them failed. In other words, all tests passed.

Now that you have tests for EventFeedController and UsersController, you're off to a good start writing unit tests for endpoints in your microservices. In real life, these tests aren't sufficient; I'd write more tests for edge cases and error scenarios. But now you know how to write those tests using Microsoft.AspNetCore.TestHost.

8.4   *Writing service-level tests*

Let's move on to writing service-level tests for the entire loyalty program microservice. Service-level tests interact with a microservice from the outside and provide the microservice with mocked versions of its collaborators.

The loyalty program makes requests to two collaborators: the event feed in the special offers microservice and the API of the notifications microservice. The service-level tests for the loyalty program go through these steps:

1 Set up two endpoints in the same process as the test:
   - One that works as a mocked special-offer event feed
   - One that works as a mocked notification endpoint
2 Start the loyalty program microservice and configure it to use the mocked endpoints in place of the real collaborators. This means whenever the loyalty program needs to call one of its collaborators, it will call one of the mocked endpoints.
3 Execute a scenario against the loyalty program as a sequence of requests to the loyalty program endpoints.
4 Record any calls to the mocked endpoints.
5 Make assertions on the responses from the loyalty program and on the requests made to the mocked endpoints.

Figure 8.5 shows the runtime setup for the service-level tests for the loyalty program microservice.

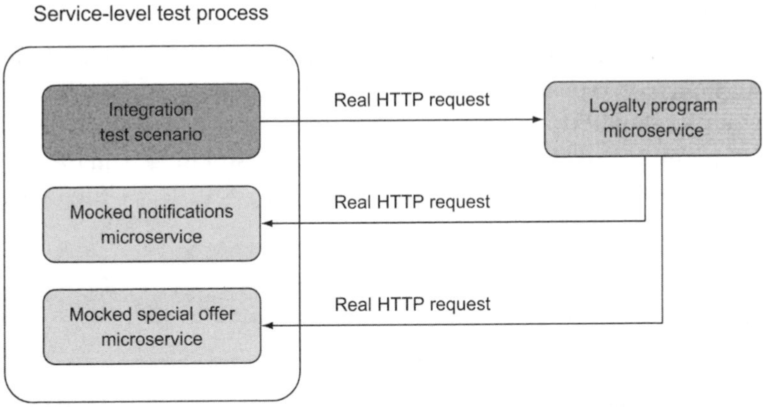

Figure 8.5   A service-level test executes a scenario against the API of the microservice under test but configures the microservice to use mocked endpoints running in the same process as the test, in place of real collaborators. When a service-level test runs, it makes requests to the microservice under test, which makes real HTTP requests back to mocked endpoints as needed. The test can inspect the responses from the microservice under test as well as the calls it makes to the mocked endpoints.

You'll follow these steps to create the test setup from figure 8.5:

1   Create a test project for the service-level tests.
2   Create the mocked endpoints for the special-offers event feed and the notification endpoint.
3   Start the loyalty program API in a test server. The event consumer will be called when needed by the tests.
4   Write test code that executes a test scenario against the loyalty program.

When that setup is in place, you'll write a test that uses it.

8.4.1   Creating a service-level test project

For the service-level tests, you'll create a new test project exactly like the unit-test project you created earlier. That is, create a project from the xUnit project template and add the `Microsoft.AspNetCore.TestHost` NuGet package. Just like the unit test project, the service-level test project is next to the production code, so you now have four folders in the loyalty program:

- LoyaltyProgram
- EventConsumer
- LoyaltyProgramServiceTests
- LoyaltyProgramUnitTests

These are the two projects that make up the loyalty program microservice—the MVC application and the event consumer—and the test projects that go along with the microservice.

8.4.2   Creating mocked endpoints

As shown in figure 8.5, you need to create mocked versions of the endpoints in the special offers microservice and the notifications microservice that the loyalty program microservice uses. You'll do so by writing two simple MVC controllers, each of which implements an endpoint that returns a hardcoded response. Listing 8.11 shows the mocked special-offers event feed endpoint, and listing 8.12 shows the mocked notifications endpoint.

Listing 8.11   Mock event feed returning hardcoded events

```
namespace LoyaltyProgramServiceTests.Mocks
{
  using Microsoft.AspNetCore.Mvc;

  public class SpecialOffersMock : ControllerBase
  {
    [HttpGet("/specialoffers/events")]
    public ActionResult<object[]> GetEvents(
      [FromQuery] int start,
      [FromQuery] int end)
    {
```

```
    return new[]                ◁──┐ Returns a
    {                              │ hardcoded response
      new
      {
        SequenceNumber = 1,
        Name = "baz",
        Content = new
        {
          OfferName = "foo",
          Description = "bar",
          Item = new {ProductName = "name"}
        }
      }
    };
  }
}
}
```

Listing 8.12 Mock endpoint that records when it was called

```
namespace LoyaltyProgramServiceTests.Mocks
{
  using Microsoft.AspNetCore.Mvc;

  public class NotificationsMock : ControllerBase
  {
    public static bool ReceivedNotification = false;   ◁──┐ Used later in the test
                                                          │ to make assertions on
    [HttpPost("/notify")]
    public OkResult Notify()
    {
      ReceivedNotification = true;
      return Ok();                 ◁──┐ Returns a
    }                                 │ hardcoded response
  }
}
```

The plan is to run these two controllers in the test process. To do that, we'll use an ASP.NET web host like you usually do in production code, and we will make the service-level test project use the web SDK by changing the first line of the Loyalty-ProgramServiceTests.csproj to reference the Microsoft.NET.Sdk.Web SDK. Last, we will add project references to the two production code projects in the loyalty program: the MVC application and the event consumer. The LoyaltyProgramServiceTests.csproj should now look like this.

Listing 8.13 Service-level tests project file

```
<Project Sdk="Microsoft.NET.Sdk.Web">   ◁──┐ Use the web SDK to allow
                                            │ listening for real HTTP requests.
  <PropertyGroup>
    <TargetFramework>net5.0</TargetFramework>
    <LangVersion>9</LangVersion>
```

```
        <WarningsAsErrors>true</WarningsAsErrors>
        <TreatWarningsAsErrors>true</TreatWarningsAsErrors>
        <Nullable>Enable</Nullable>
        <IsPackable>false</IsPackable>
    </PropertyGroup>

    <ItemGroup>
        <PackageReference Include="Microsoft.AspNetCore.TestHost"
                          Version="3.1.8" />
        <PackageReference Include="Microsoft.NET.Test.Sdk"
                          Version="16.5.0" />
        <PackageReference Include="xunit"
                          Version="2.4.0" />
        <PackageReference Include="xunit.runner.visualstudio"
                          Version="2.4.0" />
        <PackageReference Include="coverlet.collector"
                          Version="1.2.0" />
    </ItemGroup>

    <ItemGroup>
        <ProjectReference
          Include="..\LoyaltyProgram\LoyaltyProgram.csproj" />
        <ProjectReference
          Include="..\EventConsumer\EventConsumer.csproj" />
    </ItemGroup>

</Project>
```

Reference the MVC application of the service under test.

Reference the event consumer of the service under test.

Next, add a file called MocksHost.cs containing the following code, which starts an ASP.NET host in the test process.

Listing 8.14   Starting ASP.NET inside the test process

```
namespace LoyaltyProgramServiceTests.Mocks
{
  using System;
  using System.Threading;
  using Microsoft.AspNetCore.Builder;
  using Microsoft.AspNetCore.Hosting;
  using Microsoft.Extensions.DependencyInjection;
  using Microsoft.Extensions.Hosting;

  public class MocksHost : IDisposable
  {
    private readonly IHost hostForMocks;

    public MocksHost(int port)
    {
      this.hostForMocks =
        Host.CreateDefaultBuilder()                          Creates an
          .ConfigureWebHostDefaults(x => x                   ASP.NET host
            .ConfigureServices(services => services.AddControllers())
            .Configure(app =>
              app.UseRouting().UseEndpoints(opt => opt.MapControllers()))
```

Creates an ASP.NET host

Adds the mock controllers

```
            .UseUrls($"http://localhost:{port}"))          Lets the ASP.NET
            .Build();                                       application listen on port

        new Thread(() => this.hostForMocks.Run()).Start();   Starts the host in
    }                                                        a separate thread

    public void Dispose()
    {
      this.hostForMocks.Dispose();
    }
  }
}
```

This `MockHost` will be used as a utility in the test classes where we implement the service-level test. Next, we'll add such a test class.

8.4.3 *Executing the test scenario against the microservice under test*

We're now ready to write the test. It has three steps:

1 Make an HTTP request through the test host to register a user.
2 Run the event consumer. This simulates the Cron schedule calling the event consumer and makes the loyalty program's event consumer poll for events from special offers.
3 Assert that a request to the notifications endpoint was made.

For this, add a file called RegisterUserAndGetNotification.cs and add this code to it.

Listing 8.15 Service-level test using an outside loyalty program

```
namespace LoyaltyProgramServiceTests.Scenarios
{
  using System;
  using System.Net;
  using System.Net.Http;
  using System.Text;
  using System.Threading.Tasks;
  using LoyaltyProgram;
  using LoyaltyProgram.Users;
  using Microsoft.AspNetCore.Hosting;
  using Microsoft.AspNetCore.TestHost;
  using Microsoft.Extensions.Hosting;
  using Mocks;
  using Newtonsoft.Json;
  using Xunit;

  public class RegisterUserAndGetNotification : IDisposable
  {
    private static int mocksPort = 5050;
    private readonly MocksHost serviceMock;
    private readonly IHost loyaltyProgramHost;
    private readonly HttpClient sut;
```

```
public RegisterUserAndGetNotification()
{
  this.serviceMock = new MocksHost(mocksPort);          ◁──  Start the mocks
  this.loyaltyProgramHost = new HostBuilder()     ◁──        in process.
    .ConfigureWebHost(x => x                                 Start the loyalty program
      .UseStartup<Startup>()                                API in a test host.
      .UseTestServer())
    .Start();
  this.sut = this.loyaltyProgramHost.GetTestClient();
}

[Fact]
public async Task Scenario()
{
  await RegisterNewUser();          ◁──  The three high-level
  await RunConsumer();                   steps of the test
  AssertNotificationWasSent();
}

private async Task RegisterNewUser()
{
  var actual = await this.sut.PostAsync(      ◁──  Request to /users
    "/users",                                      to register a user.
    new StringContent(
      JsonSerializer.Serialize(
        new LoyaltyProgramUser(
          0, "Chr", 0, new LoyaltyProgramSettings())),
        Encoding.UTF8,
        "application/json"));

  Assert.Equal(HttpStatusCode.Created, actual.StatusCode);
}
                                              Run the event consumer once and
private Task RunConsumer() =>                 override the addresses for the special
  EventConsumer.ConsumeBatch(        ◁──      offers and notifications microservices.
    0,
    100,
    $"http://localhost:{mocksPort}/specialoffers",
    $"http://localhost:{mocksPort}"
  );

private void AssertNotificationWasSent() =>
  Assert.True(NotificationsMock.ReceivedNotification);          ◁──

public void Dispose()                                                Assert that the
{                                         Clean                      notification service mock
  this.serviceMock?.Dispose();     ◁──    up.                        received a request.
  this.sut?.Dispose();
  this.loyaltyProgramHost?.Dispose();
}
  }
}
```

This test shows how relatively easy and straightforward it is to write service-level tests for our microservices. With fewer than 100 of lines of code, the RegisterUserAndGet-Notification covers a lot of the code and functionality in the loyalty program: the user registration API is covered, the event consumer is covered, the interaction between the API and event consumer is covered, and the collaboration with the special offers and notifications microservices is covered. Moreover, with the `MocksHost` and the code for starting the loyalty program API in a test host in place, writing other scenarios covering even more of the microservice is quite straightforward.

You can run the service-level test in PowerShell or bash with `dotnet test` or in your IDE of choice. This test is relatively slow—about 400 ms on my laptop—which is why we need to strike a balance between the coverage and confidence service-level tests give and the speed and precision unit tests give.

Summary

- The test pyramid tells you to have few system-level tests that test the complete system, several service-level tests for each microservice, and many unit tests for each microservice.
- System-level tests are likely to be slow and are very imprecise.
- You should write system-level tests for important success scenarios to provide some test coverage for most of the system.
- Service-level tests are likely to be somewhat slow, but they're faster and more precise than system-level tests.
- You should write service-level tests for success scenarios and important failure scenarios for each microservice. This adds more test coverage to each microservice than just the system-level tests.
- You can use the process for writing service-level tests as the basis for writing contract tests that verify the assumption one microservice makes about the API and behavior of another microservice. In terms of the test pyramid, contract tests are between system-level tests and service-level tests.
- Unit tests are fast and should be kept fast. They're also precise because they target a specific, narrow piece of functionality.
- You should write unit tests for success and failure scenarios alike. Use them to cover edge cases that are harder to cover with higher-level tests.
- I recommend working in an outside-in fashion with each microservice: write service-level tests first and then begin writing unit tests when the service-level tests become awkward to work with.
- The `Microsoft.AspNetCore.TestHost` library is a powerful companion to ASP.NET that makes it easier to test endpoints in ASP.NET applications.
- You use the test host and `TestServer` from `Microsoft.AspNetCore.TestHost` to test endpoints through the familiar API of an `HttpClient` that lets you simulate HTTP requests. Calls through `HttpClient`s created by the `TestServer` look exactly like real HTTP requests to the endpoint MVC controllers.
- You can test endpoints in a test host with both real and mocked data stores.

- To write service-level tests:
  - Write mocked endpoints for the collaborators of the microservice under test as MVC controller and use a ASP.NET web host to host these in the test process.
  - Start up the API of the microservice under test in a test host. Use ASP.NET's configuration APIs to configure the microservice under test to call the mocked collaborators.
  - Write scenarios that interact with the microservice under test via requests going through the test host.
  - Simulate the event consumer Cron schedule by calling the event consumer directly when needed in the tests.
  - Make assertions both on the response from the microservice under test and on the requests it makes to its collaborators.
- You can use the xUnit test framework to write and run your automated tests.
- xUnit can be run with `dotnet` or in your IDE of choice.

Part 3

Handling cross-cutting concerns: Building a reusable microservice platform

In this part, you'll learn how to handle some important cross-cutting concerns. The cross-cutting concerns you'll handle include monitoring, logging, passing trace IDs along with requests between microservices, and security concerns around microservice-to-microservice requests. All these concerns make microservices behave well in production. With them in place, you can gain insight into the health of each microservice and trace business transactions across microservices. In chapter 9, we will leverage features of ASP.NET to help implement monitoring, logging, and tracing concerns.

In chapter 10, we survey different approaches to authentication and authorization and to securing microservices-to-microservice requests, as well as authentications and authorization. As an example, we will leverage Kubernetes to secure requests and to control which microservices are allowed to call each other.

You can implement such concerns in each microservice, or create reusable implementations to use in many microservices. Implementing concerns in each microservice obviously incurs some duplication of effort, but reusing an implementation creates coupling between microservices. How much you want to reuse is, in other words, a tradeoff between keeping microservices independent of each other and avoiding repeated effort. Where you land on this tradeoff is a decision you'll have to make in the context of your system.

Finally, chapter 11 shows how to build a platform that you can easily reuse in many microservices.

Cross-cutting concerns: Monitoring and logging

This chapter covers
- Monitoring in a microservice system
- Exploring structured logging
- Distributed tracing across microservices
- Logging unhandled exceptions

In this chapter, you'll start to learn how ASP.NET helps us tackle some important cross-cutting concerns: monitoring, logging, and tracing. All three are needed across all microservices, and they play an important role in making a microservice system operations friendly. Once your system is in production, you need to know whether all your microservices are up, which is why you need to monitor them. In addition, as discussed in chapter 7, you need good logging to be able to diagnose the system.

Here, you'll configure middleware in the context of one microservice. Then, in chapter 11, you'll take that configuration and put it into NuGet packages, ready to be reused easily across all your microservices.

9.1   *Monitoring needs in microservices*

When you deploy any server-side system into production, you need to be able to check the health of the system. You want to know whether it is up, whether it's experiencing failures or errors, and whether it's performing as well as it usually does. This is true of any system. With a traditional monolithic system, you'd most likely set up some monitoring and add logging to the system, as shown in figure 9.1. Logging is often done many places in the code base—where there's something important to log—and the messages are often stored in a database.

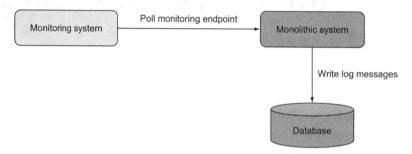

Figure 9.1   Traditionally, you set up monitoring around a system and add logging to the system code that logs messages to a database.

The situation for a system of microservices is similar. You have the same overarching need to monitor the health of the system in terms of availability, performance, throughput, and error rates. The difference is that a microservice system consists of many small pieces that run independently and are deployed independently, and you need to monitor all those small parts. In figure 9.2 that seems complicated, but it doesn't have to be if you stick to a few conventions that let you easily make your microservices monitoring friendly. We'll get to that in a bit.

In order to monitor a microservice, you add two endpoints that the monitoring system will poll. These tell when the microservice is ready to receive requests. One endpoint is used during startup and should fail until the microservice is fully booted and ready to receive requests, at which point it should succeed. The other endpoint is used once the microservice has started and should succeed until the microservice is not able to receive requests for some reason. These two endpoints fit into how Kubernetes supports monitoring, which we will discuss later in the chapter.

The first endpoint—at /health/startup—checks whether everything is ready for the microservice to receive requests, which could include things like checking database connections, warming a cache, or otherwise making sure the microservice has everything it needs (figure 9.3). While the microservice is still starting, the endpoint will indicate that the microservice is not yet ready to receive requests by responding with a 503 Service Unavailable status code like this:

```
HTTP/1.1 503 Service Unavailable

Unhealthy
```

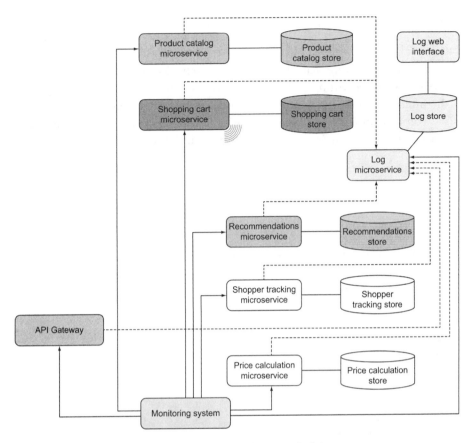

Figure 9.2 Each microservice is monitored by polling an endpoint.

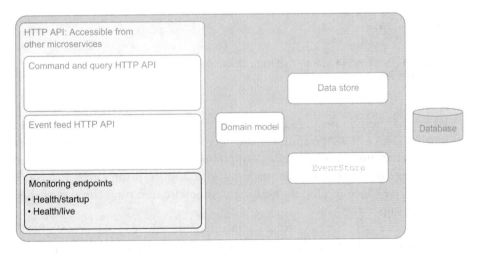

Figure 9.3 Every microservice should have two monitoring endpoints: one at /health/startup and one at /health/live. The monitoring system polls both endpoints. As long as both respond with a success response, the monitor considers the microservice to be up.

When everything is okay the endpoint responds with a simple 200 OK response:

```
HTTP/1.1 200 OK
```

The second endpoint—at /health/live—checks the internal health of the microservice and, if everything is okay, also responds with a 200 OK status code. What checking the internal health of a microservice entails differs from microservice to microservice.

You can implement both monitoring endpoints using the health check middleware that comes with ASP.NET, as illustrated in figure 9.4.

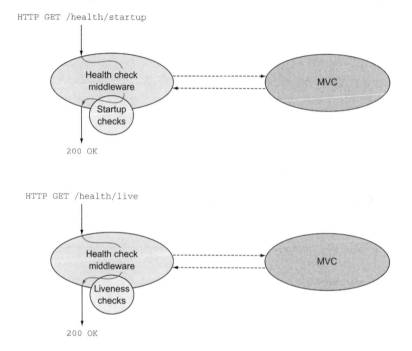

Figure 9.4   You can use ASP.NET's health check middleware to implement monitoring endpoints.

When a request to the /health/startup endpoint comes in, the health check middleware gives a 200 OK response if the microservice is ready to receive requests. When a request to the /health/live endpoint comes in, the health check middleware runs a health check and then responds with 200 OK if the check succeeded. Other requests pass through the monitoring middleware and onto the rest of the pipeline endpoint up in the MVC.

ASP.NET has a built-in health check middleware we can extend with health checks specific to our microservices to implement the two monitoring endpoints. Later in this chapter, we will implement health checks and configure Kubernetes to use them to monitor our microservice.

9.2 *Logging needs in microservices*

In addition to monitoring each individual microservice, you also need to send out log messages regarding failures, errors, performance, and whatever else you need insight into. As discussed in chapter 7, you can introduce a centralized logging microservice that receives log messages from all the other microservices, saves them (e.g., in a search engine), and provides easy access to them through dashboards and search UIs (see figure 9.5). Again, you want to be able to easily set up each microservice to send log messages to the logging microservice.

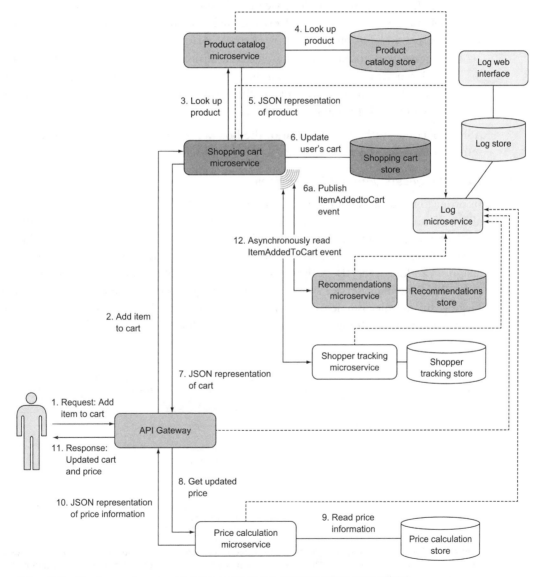

Figure 9.5   All microservices send log messages to the central logging microservice.

You also want each microservice to perform a base level of logging. All microservices should log HTTP requests, HTTP response status codes, and the processing time for each request. These logs provide insight into the microservice's health:

- The HTTP request log provides invaluable insight into what's going on in production when you need to debug problems. Request logs aren't enough for debugging, though. The microservice's business logic should also send log messages to the logging microservice about all unusual occurrences.
- The logged HTTP responses reveal whether requests to a microservice are failing. In particular, a microservice that responds often with status codes in the 500 range—used for server errors, such as unhandled exceptions—is most likely stressed or buggy.
- Logged request times can be used to establish a baseline for how well the microservice performs. Once the baseline is established, you can compare current request times to the baseline. If the request times increase significantly, the microservice is probably stressed.

ASP.NET comes with all of this out of the box; all we have to do is make sure it gets sent to the logging microservice.

9.2.1   *Tracing requests across microservices*

In order to make sense of the logs coming out of all the microservices, we need to be able to connect the ones that are related. To that end, we will use tracing across microservices and make sure all log messages include tracing information. As shown in figure 9.6, the first microservice to receive a request coming from outside the system will assign a random trace ID to the request, which will follow the request wherever it goes within the microservice system. The trace ID gets added to all HTTP requests as a header. In the microservices receiving such requests, the trace ID is taken from the header and used in all log messages, and is also included in further HTTP requests.

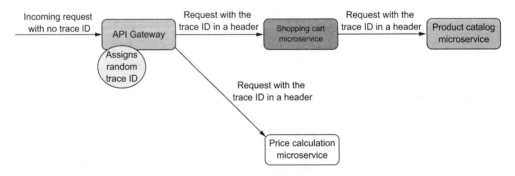

Figure 9.6   The API Gateway assigns a random trace ID to incoming requests. The trace ID is included in a header on outgoing requests. The other microservice takes the trace ID from the header and also includes it in any outgoing requests.

Propagating trace IDs throughout the system and including them in log messages enable us to follow—or *trace*—requests through the system. This provides context, which allows us to better troubleshoot issues.

The trace ID is sent from one microservice to another by using the `traceparent` header, as specified in the W3C trace context standard,[1] which specifies four fields that together form the `traceparent` header: version, trace ID, parent ID, and trace flags. The trace ID field is the one we are primarily interested in because it is meant to follow the request all the way through the system. The parent ID provides more local context and is allowed to change as the request moves through the system. The format of the `traceparent` header is:

```
"version"-"trace id"-"parent id"-"trace flags"
```

For instance, if the trace ID is cb32e1c31b369748bf45958f8a49e3e7 and the parent ID is 90757069a8f0ea4b, the trace parent header looks like this:

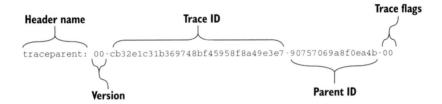

This means a request from the shopping cart microservice to the product catalog microservice could look like this:

```
HTTP GET /products?productIds=[1,2] HTTP/1.1
Accept: application/json
traceparent: 00-cb32e1c31b369748bf45958f8a49e3e7-90757069a8f0ea4b-00
```

This will tell the product catalog microservice that the trace ID is cb32e1c31b369748 bf45958f8a49e3e7 and that trace ID should be included in all log messages.

On top of propagating trace IDs in the HTTP requests, we should include them in events. Saving the trace ID along with events when the event is raised allows us to trace why an event was raised after the fact. This, again, is a strong troubleshooting tool.

ASP.NET implements the trace context standard, so out of the box ASP.NET will look for `traceparent` headers on incoming requests and propagate the trace ID to outgoing requests made with `HttpClient`. If there is no `traceparent` header on incoming requests, ASP.NET will assign a random one. We will see this in action shortly.

9.2.2 Structured logging with Serilog

Traditional logging libraries treat log messages as simple strings, possibly with an exception attached, but we'll use something better: a *structured logging* library named

---

[1] W3C, "Trace Context" https://www.w3.org/TR/trace-context/.

Serilog. The idea of structured logging is to allow log messages to contain structured data: a log message contains not only a flat message—like something went wrong—but also objects.

Serilog introduces a bit of syntax to log messages on top of .NET format strings. The extra syntax lets you give names to parameters and control whether a parameter's value should be converted to a string with a .ToString() call or whether the object should be included as a whole in the log message. Named parameters are enclosed in braces, for example, "{RequestTime}". You tell Serilog to include the entire value in the message by putting an @ in front of the name: "{@Request}". As with .NET format strings, you add formatting directives to parameters without a leading @.

For instance, you can use Serilog in conjunction with .NET's own logger to send a log message like this—assuming that log is an instance the .NET type Ilogger configured to use Serilog:

```
var simplifiedRequest = new
{
  Path = "/foo",
  Method = "GET",
  Protocol = "HTTP",
};

var requestTime = 200;

log.LogInformation(
  "Processed request: {@Request} in {RequestTime:000} ms.",
  simplifiedRequest,
  requestTime);
```

simplifiedRequest and requestTime are objects that are part of the message. Like other logging frameworks, Serilog lets you configure different *sinks* to which log messages are written. The sink you'll use here is the console sink. When the previous log message is written to the console, simplifiedRequest and requestTime are JSON serialized and inserted into the log message string. Serilog also adds some metadata, so the message written to the console looks like this:

```
2020-12-03 09:14:33 INF Processed request {"Path":"/
    foo", "Method":"GET", "Protocol":"HTTP"} in 200 ms.
```

As you can see, this preserves all the data from the original log message, because the complete simplifiedRequest object and requestTime are included in the message written to the console. This is nice, but it becomes even better when we ship the logs to a search engine like Elasticsearch. When you do that, the objects included in the log messages—like simplifiedRequest—are stored and indexed in the search engine. This means you can search for log messages based on values of particular properties of the objects included in the messages. For instance, you might search for log messages with a Request object that has a Path property with the value /foo. The previous message would be included, but a log message about a request to /bar wouldn't.

Preserving the structure of the data included in log messages means the web frontend of the logging microservice can present the log message in a structured way. The end results are logs that are easier to search and get an overview from, include more data, and that you can drill into as needed. One such frontend is Kibana, which works well with logs stored in Elasticsearch and provides powerful search and visualization tools.

As you'll see when you implement the logging later, you can configure Serilog to include extra data with every log message. One example of such extra information is the tracing information from the `traceparent` header covered in the previous section. Including that in every log message enables you to efficiently search for all log messages with a given trace ID. Since the trace IDs are propagated across services, this allows us to follow—or indeed, trace—the log messages related to a particular operation as they move through the system (e.g., as illustrated in figure 9.6, when a customer adds an item to a shopping cart and there is an incoming request to the API Gateway, which is assigned a trace ID). The trace ID follows the "add to shopping cart" operation as it moves to other services—the shopping cart, the product catalog, and the price calculation microservices. By searching for log messages with the trace ID assigned to that "add to shopping cart" operation, you can see all log information related to that particular instance of adding items to the shopping cart. You can see what the API Gateway did, what the shopping cart did, what the product catalog did, and what the price calculation microservice did. This is very powerful when debugging production issues.

For the remainder of this chapter, you'll be implementing monitoring and logging. You want to do this in all microservices, so you can work in the context of any one of the microservices you've already implemented. I'll use the shopping cart microservice as an example and build on top of the code from chapter 7, but the code fits just the same in the other microservices.

9.3 *Implementing the monitoring endpoints*

In this section, you'll use APS.NET's *health checks* support to implement the two monitoring endpoints we discussed earlier. The endpoints will behave as follows:

- `/health/live` responds to every request with a `200 OK` status, to indicate that the microservice is running and able to handle requests. Depending on the implementation of your microservices, you may want to add a deeper health check in this endpoint.
- `/health/startup` performs a basic health check and then responds with `200 OK` status if the health check succeeds. If the health check fails, it responds with `503 Service Unavailable`. The health check will query the shopping cart microservice database to check that a connection to the database can be established because the shopping cart microservice is ready to receive requests as soon as it is able to query its database.

The plan to implement the monitoring endpoints is as follows:

1 Add the /health/live endpoint to the ASP.NET pipeline.
2 Create the health check for the shopping cart database.
3 Add the /health/startup endpoint to the pipeline.

Let's get started.

9.3.1 Implementing the /health/live monitoring endpoint

To implement the /health/live endpoint, we take advantage of ASP.NET's health checks, which allows us to easily add monitoring endpoints. First we need to add a health check to the service collection. Next we will connect that health check to the /health/live endpoint. We will call the health check LivenessHealthCheck and add to the service collection by changing the ConfugreServices method in Startup to this.

Listing 9.1 Adding the `LivenessHealthCheck` to the service collection

```
public void ConfigureServices(IServiceCollection services)
{
    services.AddHealthChecks()                        Add facilities supporting
                                                      health checks.
        .AddCheck(
            "LivenessHealthCheck",                    Add the
            () => HealthCheckResult.Healthy(),        LivenessHealth-
            tags: new []{ "liveness"});               Check.
    services.AddControllers();
}
```

Give the health check a name. → "LivenessHealthCheck",

Implement the health check to always respond 200 OK.

Tag the health check to make it easier to find later.

This code simply adds a health check that always responds 200 OK to the service collection. Let's connect that to the /health/live endpoint by adding health/live as a health check to the APS.NET pipeline by changing the Configure method in Startup to this:

```
public void Configure(IApplicationBuilder app, IWebHostEnvironment env)
{
    app.UseHttpsRedirection();
    app.UseHealthChecks("/health/live",              Add /health/live as a
                                                     monitoring endpoint.
        new HealthCheckOptions
        {                                            Configure how to
                                                     perform the health
            Predicate = x => x.Tags.Contains("liveness")   check for /health/live.
        });
    app.UseRouting();
    app.UseEndpoints(endpoints => endpoints.MapControllers());
}
```

Use all health checks tagged with liveness.

This adds /health/live as an endpoint that accepts HTTP GET requests to the pipeline. When a requests to /health/live comes in, all health checks tagged with "liveness" in the service collection are performed, and if they all succeed, the response will be 200 OK. In this case, there is only one health check tagged with "liveness," but we could add more if need be. This gives a nice, modular way to combine different health checks into monitoring endpoints.

This is all we need to implement the /health/live endpoint. Now let's turn to the /health/startup endpoint, which follows the same pattern with just one extra piece added.

9.3.2 Implementing the /health/startup monitoring endpoint

With the liveness health check in place, we can turn to implementing the startup health check. This a little bit more involved since we will check if the microservice can reach the database in the startup health check. To do that, we will first implement the database check in a class implementing the ASP.NET interface IHealthCheck and then use that class to define another health check. The following listing shows the implementation of the database check.

Listing 9.2 Class implementing a database health check

```
namespace ShoppingCart
{
  using System.Data.SqlClient;
  using System.Threading;
  using System.Threading.Tasks;
  using Dapper;
  using Microsoft.Extensions.Diagnostics.HealthChecks;

  public class DbHealthCheck : IHealthCheck         ◁—— Implement IHealthCheck.
  {
    public async Task<HealthCheckResult> CheckHealthAsync(
      HealthCheckContext context,
      CancellationToken cancellationToken)
    {
      await using var conn =
        new SqlConnection(@"Data Source=localhost;
Initial Catalog=ShoppingCart;                       ◁—— Open database connection.
User Id=SA; Password=yourStrong(!)Password");

      var result = await conn.QuerySingleAsync<int>("SELECT 1");    ◁——┐
      return result == 1         ◁—— If the query result is 1, the   Perform
        ? HealthCheckResult.Healthy()   health check is successful.   simple
        : HealthCheckResult.Degraded();                              query.
    }
  }
}
```

This class implements the IHealthCheck interface, which defines just one method—CheckHealthAsync—which is called whenever the health check is executed. The return value from CheckHealthAsync indicates whether the check was successful.

The rest of the implementation of the /health/startup endpoint is similar to the implementation of the /health/live endpoint and consists of adding the health check to the service collection and using it in an endpoint in the pipeline. To implement that we change the `Startup` class to the following.

Listing 9.3   The full `Startup` class with both monitoring endpoints

```
public class Startup
{
    public void ConfigureServices(IServiceCollection services)
    {
        services.AddHealthChecks()          Use the DbHealthCheck class
            .AddCheck<DbHealthCheck>(        to implement a health check.
            nameof(DbHealthCheck),
            tags: new []{ "startup"})        Tag the health check
            .AddCheck(                       with "startup."
            "LivenessHealthCheck",
            () => HealthCheckResult.Healthy(),
            tags: new []{ "liveness"});
        services.AddControllers();
    }

    public void Configure(IApplicationBuilder app, IWebHostEnvironment env)
    {
        app.UseHttpsRedirection();
        app.UseHealthChecks(                 Add /health/startup as
            "/health/startup",               a health check endpoint.
            new HealthCheckOptions
            {
                Predicate = x => x.Tags.Contains("startup")   Use the new health
            });                                               check in /health/startup.
        app.UseHealthChecks(
            "/health/live",
            new HealthCheckOptions
            {
                Predicate = x => x.Tags.Contains("liveness")
            });
        app.UseRouting();
        app.UseEndpoints(endpoints => endpoints.MapControllers());
    }
}
```

With this in place, you can run the shopping cart microservice with `dotnet` and test the monitoring endpoints. A request to the `/health/live` endpoint looks like this:

```
GET https://localhost:5001/health/live
```

A successful response looks as follows:

```
HTTP/1.1 200 OK
Content-Type: text/plain

Healthy
```

Here's a request to the `/health/startup` endpoint:

```
GET https://localhost:5001/health/startup
```

And this is a successful response:

```
HTTP/1.1 200 OK
Content-Type: text/plain

Healthy
```

Finally, the following is a failure response:

```
HTTP/1.1 503 Service Unavailable
Content-Type: text/plain

Unhealthy
```

This concludes the implementation of the monitoring endpoints. Later, we will return to these endpoints and look at how to configure Kubernetes to use them.

9.4 *Implementing structured logging*

As discussed, having structured logs raises the value of the logs, mainly by making them more searchable. In this section we will configure the shopping cart to use Serilog to make the log output structured. There are three small steps to making the logs structured:

1. Adding the Serilog NuGet package and a helper package to the shopping cart microservice
2. Configuring the .NET logger to use Serilog behind the scenes
3. Changing the log output to a JSON format, which is more machine-friendly

Once these three steps are performed, we will have logs that lend themselves to being picked up from the Kubernetes logs and shipped to a logging product of your choice. (I will not show how to ship the logs, since that becomes more specific to the logging product you choose, and each vendor has the documentation needed to set up the log shipping.)

First, we will add two NuGet packages to the shopping cart microservice:

1. Serilog.Sinks.ColoredConsole: The library that allows us to do structured logging to the console
2. Serilog.AspNetCore: A helper package for using .NET's logging and Serilog together

Once these two packages have been added to the shopping cart microservice we can configure the .NET logger to use Serilog with the following code in Program.cs.

Listing 9.4 Using Serilog as the backend for the .NET logger

```
namespace ShoppingCart
{
  using Microsoft.AspNetCore.Hosting;
  using Microsoft.Extensions.Hosting;
  using Serilog;
```

```
using Serilog.Enrichers.Span;
using Serilog.Formatting.Json;

public class Program
{
  public static void Main(string[] args)
  {
    CreateHostBuilder(args).Build().Run();
  }

  private static IHostBuilder CreateHostBuilder(string[] args) =>
    Host.CreateDefaultBuilder(args)
      .UseSerilog((context, logger) =>
      {
        logger
          .Enrich.FromLogContext()
          .WriteTo.ColoredConsole();
      })
      .ConfigureWebHostDefaults(x => x.UseStartup<Startup>());
  }
}
```

> Direct all log messages to Serilog.

> Include the context in each log message.

> Output log messages to the console.

This integrates Serilog into the .NET logger. If you run the shopping cart, you can notice the logging output at startup is a bit different because Serilog formats the log messages differently:

```
PS > dotnet run
2020-12-03 10:24:34 INF Now listening on: "https://localhost:5001"
2020-12-03 10:24:34 INF Now listening on: "http://localhost:5000"
2020-12-03 10:24:34 INF Application started. Press Ctrl+C to shut down.
2020-12-03 10:24:34 INF Hosting environment: "Development"
2020-12-03 10:24:34 INF Content root path: "C:\\Users\\chors\\Documents\\
  horsdal3\\code\\Chapter10\\ShoppingCart"
```

This is not overly exciting, but if we log something from a controller in the shopping cart, we can start to see the value. To do that, we can take a dependency on `ILogger` in the `ShoppingCartController` and use the logger in one of the action methods. .NET already registers `ILogger` with the service collection, so it will be injected in the `ShoppingCartController` just like other dependencies. To take a dependency, we simply add `ILogger` as an argument to the constructor, as shown next.

Listing 9.5   Taking a dependency on `ILogger` to be able to log from controllers

```
public ShoppingCartController(
  IShoppingCartStore shoppingCartStore,
  IProductCatalogClient productCatalog,
  IEventStore eventStore,
  ILogger<ShoppingCartController> logger)
{
  this.shoppingCartStore = shoppingCartStore;
  this.productCatalog = productCatalog;
  this.eventStore = eventStore;
  this.logger = logger;
}
```

> Take a dependency on ILogger.

> Assign logger to a private field.

Then the logger can be used in, for example, the endpoint for adding items to the shopping cart, which you can see in the following listing.

Listing 9.6 Including structure in logs from controllers

```
[HttpPost("{userId:int}/items")]
public async Task<ShoppingCart> Post(int userId, [FromBody] int[]
    productIds)
{
  var shoppingCart = await shoppingCartStore.Get(userId);
  var shoppingCartItems = await
    this.productCatalog.GetShoppingCartItems(productIds);
  await shoppingCart.AddItems(shoppingCartItems, this.eventStore);
  await this.shoppingCartStore.Save(shoppingCart);
                                                          Log a structured
  this.logger.LogInformation(              ⟵──           message.
    "Successfully added products to shopping cart {@productIds},
      {@shoppingCart}", productIds, shoppingCart);

  return shoppingCart;
}
```

If we make an HTTP post to add items to the cart now, one of the log messages we will see in the console is as follows.

Listing 9.7 Structured log message including a shopping cart

```
2020-12-03 11:37:08 INF Successfully added products to shopping cart [1, 2],
{"userId":123,"items":[{"productCatalogueId":1,"productName":
"Basic t-shirt","description":"a quiet t-shirt","price":{"currency":
"eur","amount":40}},{"productCatalogueId":2,"productName":"Fancy shirt",
"description":"a loud t-shirt","price":{"currency":"eur","amount":50}}]}
```

This log message includes the whole shopping cart as JSON, which provides a lot more context to the message than the simple "Successfully added products to shopping cart" message. This is the strength of structured logging.

The last step we need is to make the log message a bit easier to consume in a log shipping pipeline. To that end, we format them as JSON logs. This makes the message a bit harder to read for humans, though, so I prefer to use the output we've seen so far in development and the JSON output in production, as shown in the following listing. This is done by telling Serilog to JSON format the output to the console when the environment is not "development."

Listing 9.8 Using JSON logs in production

```
private static IHostBuilder CreateHostBuilder(string[] args) =>
  Host.CreateDefaultBuilder(args)
    .UseSerilog((context, logger) =>
    {
      logger
```

```
    .Enrich.FromLogContext();
  if (context.HostingEnvironment.IsDevelopment())          Check the
    logger.WriteTo.ColoredConsole();                       environment.
  else
    logger.WriteTo.Console(new JsonFormatter());           JSON format
})                                                         in production
.ConfigureWebHostDefaults(x => x.UseStartup<Startup>());
```

NOTE The environment is controlled by the environment variable ASPNET-
CORE_ENVIRONMENT.

The JSON-formatted log messages created when we start the shopping cart microservice in production look like this:

```
{"Timestamp":"2020-12-03T12:00:41.5723302+01:00","Level":"Information",
  "MessageTemplate":"Now listening on: {address}","Properties":{"address":
  "https://localhost:5001","SourceContext":"Microsoft.Hosting.Lifetime"}}
{"Timestamp":"2020-12-03T12:00:41.5803748+01:00","Level":"Information",
  "MessageTemplate":"Now listening on: {address}","Properties":{"address":
  "http://localhost:5000","SourceContext":"Microsoft.Hosting.Lifetime"}}
{"Timestamp":"2020-12-03T12:00:41.5809434+01:00","Level":"Information",
  "MessageTemplate":"Application started. Press Ctrl+C to shut down.",
  "Properties":{"SourceContext":"Microsoft.Hosting.Lifetime"}}
{"Timestamp":"2020-12-03T12:00:41.5812286+01:00","Level":"Information",
  "MessageTemplate":"Hosting environment: {envName}","Properties":{
  "envName":"Production","SourceContext":"Microsoft.Hosting.Lifetime"}}
{"Timestamp":"2020-12-03T12:00:41.5815246+01:00","Level":"Information",
  "MessageTemplate":"Content root path: {contentRoot}","Properties":
{"contentRoot":"C:\\Users\\chors\\Documents\\horsdal3\\code\\Chapter10\\
  ShoppingCart","SourceContext":"Microsoft.Hosting.Lifetime"}}
```

Now that you've configured the log messages to be structured, let's enrich them with
tracing information.

9.4.1 Adding a trace ID to all log messages

Recall from chapter 7 and from earlier in this chapter that log messages become more
valuable if you can use them to trace how a user request moves through the microservice system. The user request might not be handled by a single microservice. Often,
several microservices will collaborate to fulfill the user request. Being able to trace
user requests across all those collaborating microservices is useful—and that's what a
trace ID can give you. As stated earlier, ASP.NET implements the trace context standard, so ASP.NET already assigns trace IDs to all requests. The trace ID is either reading it from the traceparent header or—if there is no traceparent header on the
request—by assigning a random trace ID. ASP.NET stores the trace ID and other tracing information in the type System.Diagnostics.Activity, where it can be accessed
through the property Activity.Current. All we have to do is add the trace ID to every
log message. We will use a convenient package, called Serilog.Enrichers.Span that
works with Serilog to do exactly that. First, we will install Serilog.Enrichers.Span
and then change the configuration of Serilog slightly so it becomes the following.

Listing 9.9 Configuring Serilog to include tracing information in all log messages

```
private static IHostBuilder CreateHostBuilder(string[] args) =>
  Host.CreateDefaultBuilder(args)
    .UseSerilog((context, logger) =>
    {
      logger
        .Enrich.FromLogContext()              Enrich all logs with
        .Enrich.WithSpan();          ◁──┘    trace information.
      if (context.HostingEnvironment.IsDevelopment())
        logger.WriteTo.ColoredConsole(
          outputTemplate: @"{Timestamp:yyyy-MM-dd HH:mm:ss}
{TraceId} {Level:u3} {Message}{NewLine}{Exception}"  ◁──┐  Include the trace ID in
        );                                                │  development log output.
      else
        logger.WriteTo.Console(new JsonFormatter());
    })
    .ConfigureWebHostDefaults(x => x.UseStartup<Startup>());
```

The important new part in the previous listing is the line `.Enrich.WithSpan();`, which configures Serilog to read the trace information from the `Activity.Current` and add it to every log message. In the JSON output used in production, all information on log messages is included by default. In the text output used in development, we need to override the default output format to add the trace ID, which is done by passing an output format that includes trace ID into the logger configuration.

Running the shopping cart microservice and making requests to it now produces log messages with trace information. In development, that looks like this:

```
2020-12-07 11:10:39 f2e604d90da6114a8d4a77daa57a7890 INF Request starting
  HTTP/1.1 POST https://localhost:5001/users/0/items application/json 9
2020-12-07 11:10:39 f2e604d90da6114a8d4a77daa57a7890 INF Executing endpoint
  '"ShoppingCart.Users.UsersController.Post (ShoppingCart)"'
2020-12-07 11:10:39 f2e604d90da6114a8d4a77daa57a7890 INF Route matched with
  "{action = \"Post\", controller = \"Users\"}". Executing controller action
  with signature "Task<Shoppingcart> Post(Int32, Int32[])" on controller
  "Shoppingcart.Users.UsersController" ("ShoppingCart").
2020-12-07 11:10:39 f2e604d90da6114a8d4a77daa57a7890 INF Successfully added
  products to shopping cart [1, 2], {"userId":123,"items":[{
  "productCatalogueId":1,"productName":"Basic t-shirt","description":
  "a quiet t-shirt","price":{"currency":"eur","amount":40}},{
  "productCatalogueId":2,"productName":"Fancy shirt","description":
  "a loud t-shirt","price":{"currency":"eur","amount":50}}]}
2020-12-07 11:10:39 f2e604d90da6114a8d4a77daa57a7890 INF Executed action
  "ShoppingCart.Users.UsersController.Post (ShoppingCart)" in 45.891ms
2020-12-07 11:10:39 f2e604d90da6114a8d4a77daa57a7890 INF Executed endpoint
  '"ShoppingCart.Users.UsersController.Post (ShoppingCart)"'
2020-12-07 11:10:39 f2e604d90da6114a8d4a77daa57a7890 INF Request finished
  HTTP/1.1 POST https://localhost:5001/users/0/items application/json 9
  - 200 0 - 193.4576ms
```

All these requests are tied together by the trace ID—f2e604d90da6114a8d4a77daa57a7890. The same request with the production configuration produces this log output:

"Protocol":"HTTP/1.1","Method":"POST","ContentType":"application/json",
 "ContentLength":9,"Scheme":"https","Host":"localhost:5001","PathBase":"",
 "Path":"/users/0/items","QueryString":"","HostingRequestStartingLog":
 "Request starting HTTP/1.1 POST https://localhost:5001/users/0/items
 application/json 9","EventId":{"Id":1,"Name":"RequestStarting"},
 "SourceContext":"Microsoft.AspNetCore.Hosting.Diagnostics","RequestId":
 "0HM4QJ9RN6M7Q:00000002","RequestPath":"/users/0/items","ConnectionId":
 "0HM4QJ9RN6M7Q","SpanId":"469950e2392d4a4b","TraceId":
 "7e413f37415aea4d8c4ff04924292ad2","ParentId":"0000000000000000"},
 "Renderings":{"HostingRequestStartingLog":[{"Format":"l","Rendering":
 "Request starting HTTP/1.1 POST https://localhost:5001/users/0/items
 application/json 9"}]}}}
{"Timestamp":"2020-12-07T11:25:49.4047774+01:00","Level":"Information",
 "MessageTemplate":"Executing endpoint '{EndpointName}'","Properties"
 :{"EndpointName":"ShoppingCart.Users.UsersController.Post (ShoppingCart)",
 "EventId":{"Name":"ExecutingEndpoint"},"SourceContext":
 "Microsoft.AspNetCore.Routing.EndpointMiddleware","RequestId":
 "0HM4QJ9RN6M7Q:00000002","RequestPath":"/users/0/items","ConnectionId":
 "0HM4QJ9RN6M7Q","SpanId":"469950e2392d4a4b","TraceId":
 "7e413f37415aea4d8c4ff04924292ad2","ParentId":"0000000000000000"}}
{"Timestamp":"2020-12-07T11:25:49.4527811+01:00","Level":"Information",
 "MessageTemplate":"Route matched with {RouteData}. Executing controller
 action with signature {MethodInfo} on controller {Controller} ({
  AssemblyName}).","Properties":{"RouteData":"{action = \"Post\",
  controller = \"Users\"}","MethodInfo":"Void Post(Int32, Int32[])",
  "Controller":"ShoppingCart.Users.UsersController","AssemblyName":
  "ShoppingCart","EventId":{"Id":3,"Name":"ControllerActionExecuting"},
  "SourceContext":"Microsoft.AspNetCore.Mvc.Infrastructure.
  ControllerActionInvoker","ActionId":"68aa2aa9-04a9-449d-ab84-
  cb196a437710","ActionName":"ShoppingCart.Users.UsersController.Post
  (ShoppingCart)","RequestId":"0HM4QJ9RN6M7Q:00000002","RequestPath":
  "/users/0/items","ConnectionId":"0HM4QJ9RN6M7Q","SpanId":
  "469950e2392d4a4b","TraceId":"7e413f37415aea4d8c4ff04924292ad2",
  "ParentId":"0000000000000000"}}
{"Timestamp":"2020-12-07T11:25:49.4982026+01:00","Level":"Information",
 "MessageTemplate":"Successfully added products to shopping cart
 {@productIds}, {@shoppingCart}","Properties":{"productIds":[1,2,3],
 "shoppingCart":{"userId":123,"items":[{"productCatalogueId":1,
 "productName":"Basic t-shirt","description":"a quiet t-shirt",
 "price":{"currency":"eur","amount":40}},{"productCatalogueId":2,
 "productName":"Fancy shirt","description":"a loud t-shirt",
 "price":{"currency":"eur","amount":50}}]}}"SourceContext":
 "ShoppingCart.Users.UsersController","ActionId":
 "68aa2aa9-04a9-449d-ab84-cb196a437710","ActionName":
 "ShoppingCart.Users.UsersController.Post (ShoppingCart)","RequestId":
 "0HM4QJ9RN6M7Q:00000002","RequestPath":"/users/0/items","ConnectionId":
 "0HM4QJ9RN6M7Q","SpanId":"469950e2392d4a4b","TraceId":
 "7e413f37415aea4d8c4ff04924292ad2","ParentId":"0000000000000000"}}
{"Timestamp":"2020-12-07T11:25:49.5054475+01:00","Level":"Information",
 "MessageTemplate":"Executed action {ActionName} in {
  ElapsedMilliseconds}ms","Properties":{"ActionName":
  "ShoppingCart.Users.UsersController.Post (ShoppingCart)",
  "ElapsedMilliseconds":45.7401,"EventId":{"Id":2,"Name":
  "ActionExecuted"},"SourceContext":"Microsoft.AspNetCore.Mvc.
  Infrastructure.ControllerActionInvoker","ActionId":"68aa2aa9-04a9-

```
            449d-ab84-cb196a437710","RequestId":"0HM4QJ9RN6M7Q:00000002",
            "RequestPath":"/users/0/items","ConnectionId":"0HM4QJ9RN6M7Q",
            "SpanId":"469950e2392d4a4b","TraceId":
            "7e413f37415aea4d8c4ff04924292ad2","ParentId":"0000000000000000"}}
{"Timestamp":"2020-12-07T11:25:49.5069173+01:00","Level":"Information",
    "MessageTemplate":"Executed endpoint '{EndpointName}'","Properties":
    {"EndpointName":"ShoppingCart.Users.UsersController.Post (ShoppingCart)",
    "EventId":{"Id":1,"Name":"ExecutedEndpoint"},"SourceContext":"Microsoft.
    AspNetCore.Routing.EndpointMiddleware","RequestId":
    "0HM4QJ9RN6M7Q:00000002","RequestPath":"/users/0/items","ConnectionId":
    "0HM4QJ9RN6M7Q","SpanId":"469950e2392d4a4b","TraceId":
    "7e413f37415aea4d8c4ff04924292ad2","ParentId":"0000000000000000"}}
{"Timestamp":"2020-12-07T11:25:49.5124936+01:00","Level":"Information",
    "MessageTemplate":"{HostingRequestFinishedLog:l}","Properties":
    {"ElapsedMilliseconds":165.5149,"StatusCode":200,"ContentType":null,
    "ContentLength":0,"Protocol":"HTTP/1.1","Method":"POST","Scheme":"https",
    "Host":"localhost:5001","PathBase":"","Path":"/users/0/
        items","QueryString":
    "","HostingRequestFinishedLog":"Request finished HTTP/1.1 POST
    https://localhost:5001/users/0/items application/json 9 - 200 0
    - 165.5149ms","EventId":{"Id":2,"Name":"RequestFinished"},"SourceContext":
    "Microsoft.AspNetCore.Hosting.Diagnostics","RequestId":
    "0HM4QJ9RN6M7Q:00000002","RequestPath":"/users/0/items","ConnectionId":
    "0HM4QJ9RN6M7Q","SpanId":"469950e2392d4a4b","TraceId":
    "7e413f37415aea4d8c4ff04924292ad2","ParentId":"0000000000000000"},
    "Renderings":{"HostingRequestFinishedLog":[{"Format":"l","Rendering":
    "Request finished HTTP/1.1 POST https://localhost:5001/users/0/items
    application/json 9 - 200 0 - 165.5149ms"}]}}
```

While this is a lot less readable for humans than the development logs, it does contain even more information, and when these logs are stored in a search engine and presented in a good UI, they become powerful. For now, notice that each log message includes the trace ID: `"TraceId":"7e413f37415aea4d8c4ff04924292ad2"`.

9.4.2 Trace ID is included in outgoing HTTP requests

Not only does ASP.NET read trace IDs from incoming `traceparent` headers, it also automatically adds `traceparent` headers to outgoing requests made with `HttpClient`, so we do not have to do anything extra to get `traceparent` headers that include the trace ID on outgoing requests. For instance, the requests the shopping cart microservice makes to the product catalog microservice already include `traceparent` headers, so the trace IDs are sent along to the product catalog microservice, meaning that we can trace requests across microservices in the logs.

9.4.3 Logging unhandled exceptions

As we discussed earlier, things fail from time to time. In these cases it is important to have logs that show how the failure occurred. MVC will catch any otherwise unhandled exception from controllers and log the exception message. Like any other log message, these logs will include a trace ID. This means we can trace what led to the unhandled exception. We can find the original user request and all other log messages made along the way up to the point the exception was thrown. This is another powerful component of logging.

9.5 *Implementing monitoring and logging in Kubernetes*

In the previous sections, I showed how to implement monitoring and logging in our microservices. In this section, we will see how to easily use the monitoring and the logging with Kubernetes.

> **NOTE** The way we have implemented monitoring endpoints, structured logging, and tracing is not bound to Kubernetes and works equally well in a variety of other environments

There are two parts we want to use with Kubernetes:

1 *Monitoring*—We will configure Kubernetes to use the startup and liveness endpoints to monitor the containers. When the liveness endpoint fails, Kubernetes will restart the container.
2 *Logging*—We will see how to get the logs from containers. The logs are JSON formatted and structured and contain trace information.

9.5.1 *Configure monitoring in Kubernetes*

Recall that we created two monitoring endpoints:

- Startup: The endpoint `/health/startup` fails until the container is fully booted and ready to process requests, at which point it succeeds,
- Liveness: The endpoint `/health/live` succeeds for as long as the container is healthy. When it fails the container cannot process requests and should be restarted.

Kubernetes allows us to configure *health probes*, which Kubernetes uses to decide the health of a container. Kubernetes supports both startup and liveness probes that correspond exactly to the startup and liveness endpoints we already created. We will extend the shopping cart microservice's Kubernetes manifest with the configuration for two health probes: a startup probe and a liveness probe. The full manifest becomes the following.

Listing 9.10   Kubernetes manifest with health probes

```
kind: Deployment
apiVersion: apps/v1
metadata:
  name: shopping-cart
spec:
  replicas: 1
  selector:
    matchLabels:
      app: shopping-cart
```

```
    template:
      metadata:
        labels:
          app: shopping-cart
      spec:
        containers:
          - name: shopping-cart
            image: shopping-cart
            imagePullPolicy: IfNotPresent
            ports:
              - containerPort: 80
            env:
              - name: STARTUPDLL
                value: "api/ShoppingCart.dll"      ◁──┐ Configure the
            livenessProbe:                              liveness probe.
              httpGet:
                path: /health/live              ◁──┐ Use /health/live
                port: 80                             to check liveness.
                periodSeconds: 30     ◁──┐ Probe every
            startupProbe:                   30 seconds.
              httpGet:
                path: /health/startup         ◁──┐ Use the /health/startup
                port: 80                           to check startup.
                initialDelaySeconds: 10
                periodSeconds: 10
    ---
    apiVersion: v1
    kind: Service
    metadata:
      name: shopping-cart
    spec:
      type: LoadBalancer
      ports:
        - name: shopping-cart
          port: 5001
          targetPort: 80
      selector:
        app: shopping-cart
```

Configure the startup probe.

Now, when we run `kubectl apply -f shopping-cart.yaml` to redeploy the shopping cart microservice, Kubernetes will use the startup and liveness probes to decide the health of the container. We can test if the container is running as expected with `kubectl get pods`, which should show that the shopping cart pod is running and has not been restarted with a line like this one:

```
NAME                              READY   STATUS    RESTARTS   AGE
shopping-cart-54ff7c4846-rvkcc    1/1     Running   0          8m3s
```

NOTE If you do not have SQL Server running in your Kubernetes cluster, the startup probe will fail, since the startup health check tries to connect to SQL Server. You can either deploy SQL Server to your Kubernetes cluster or remove the startup probe if you want to see the liveness probe succeed.

Furthermore, we can inspect the configuration with `kubectl describe deployment .apps/shopping-cart`, which will show the configuration of the probes along with the rest of the configuration of the shopping cart deployment.

We can also expect to see the calls to the monitoring endpoints in the logs. We can get the logs from Kubernetes with `kubectl logs`. To get all the logs for the shopping cart deployment, we can run this command to print the logs from the shopping cart deployment:

```
kubectl logs -f --tail=10 deployment.apps/shopping-cart
```

The `-f` tells `kubectl` to follow the logs, so as soon as the shopping cart microservice logs something, we will see it in the console. The `--tail=10` tells kubectl to start by printing the 10 latest logs. Once the shopping cart microservice is up and running, some of the log output looks like these two log messages stemming from one call to the liveness probe:

```
{"Timestamp":"2020-12-07T13:15:21.1589211+00:00","Level":"Information",
  "MessageTemplate":"{HostingRequestStartingLog:l}","Properties":
  {"Protocol":"HTTP/1.1","Method":"GET","ContentType":null,"ContentLength":
  null,"Scheme":"http","Host":"10.1.0.22:80","PathBase":"","Path":
  "/health/live","QueryString":"","HostingRequestStartingLog":
  "Request starting HTTP/1.1 GET http://10.1.0.22:80/health/live - -",
  "EventId":{"Id":1,"Name":"RequestStarting"},"SourceContext":
  "Microsoft.AspNetCore.Hosting.Diagnostics","RequestId":
  "0HM4QLU8CA0OI:00000002","RequestPath":"/health/live","ConnectionId":
  "0HM4QLU8CA0OI","SpanId":"a2c71b41ba089b44","TraceId":
  "ca68d09e29e61e4d92d363cb3bfa4827","ParentId":"0000000000000000"},
  "Renderings":{"HostingRequestStartingLog":[{"Format":"l","Rendering":
  "Request starting HTTP/1.1 GET http://10.1.0.22:80/health/live - -"}]}}
{"Timestamp":"2020-12-07T13:15:21.1591769+00:00","Level":"Information",
  "MessageTemplate":"{HostingRequestFinishedLog:l}","Properties":
  {"ElapsedMilliseconds":0.3009,"StatusCode":200,"ContentType":"text/plain",
  "ContentLength":null,"Protocol":"HTTP/1.1","Method":"GET","Scheme":"http",
  "Host":"10.1.0.22:80","PathBase":"","Path":"/health/live","QueryString":
  "","HostingRequestFinishedLog":"Request finished HTTP/1.1
  GET http://10.1.0.22:80/health/live - - - 200 - text/plain 0.3009ms",
  "EventId":{"Id":2,"Name":"RequestFinished"},"SourceContext":
  "Microsoft.AspNetCore.Hosting.Diagnostics","RequestId":
  "0HM4QLU8CA0OI:00000002","RequestPath":"/health/live","ConnectionId":
  "0HM4QLU8CA0OI","SpanId":"a2c71b41ba089b44","TraceId":
  "ca68d09e29e61e4d92d363cb3bfa4827","ParentId":"0000000000000000"},
  "Renderings":{"HostingRequestFinishedLog":[{"Format":"l","Rendering":
  "Request finished HTTP/1.1 GET http://10.1.0.22:80/health/live - -
  - 200 - text/plain 0.3009ms"}]}}
```

This is exactly how we output these log messages from the microservice; they're JSON, they're structured, and they contain tracing information.

In this chapter, you created two monitoring endpoints in the shopping cart microservice, but they do not use any of the microservice's business logic. They may as well have been written in any other microservice. You also configured Kubernetes to use the new endpoints. Again, this would be exactly the same in other microservices. The same is true for the logging work you have done in this chapter. It is the same for all the microservices. In chapter 12, you'll extract the common pieces of code from the shopping cart and package them in NuGet packages, ready to be reused across many microservices.

Summary

- Microservice systems need monitoring and logging just like any other server-side systems.
- Every microservice should be monitored and sending log messages.
- Because of the number of microservices in a system, setting up monitoring and logging needs to be easy.
- Trace IDs make it easier to trace a request across several microservices.
- ASP.NET implements the trace context standard and therefore uses the `trace-parent` HTTP header to propagate trace IDs.
- You can use ASP.NET's health check middleware to create two monitoring endpoints: one for startup and one for liveness.
- Structured logging is a good way to include valuable information in log messages and make that data searchable.
- Serilog is a library for doing structured logging.
- ASP.NET stores trace information in `Activity.Current`.
- You can configure Serilog to include trace information from `Activity.Current` in all log messages
- The `HttpClient` will include a `traceparent` header with every outgoing HTTP request, making sure trace IDs are sent to other microservices.
- Kubernetes supports health probes that fit well with our monitoring endpoints.
- Kubernetes allows us to easily access the logs from our containers.
- To get the full benefit of the logs all log messages should be shipped to a central logging microservice with good search and visualization capabilities.

Securing microservice-to-microservice communication

This chapter covers

- Where to perform user authentication and authorization in a microservice system
- Deciding on the level of trust in your microservice system
- Limiting microservice-to-microservice requests
- Using an API Gateway to authenticate users
- Using Kubernetes network policies to limit microservice-to-microservice requests

Up to this point in the book, we've ignored security; but for most systems, security is an important concern that needs careful attention. This chapter discusses how to address security concerns in a microservice system. In a monolith, the monolith completes user authentication and authorization—there is, after all, only the monolith to do those things. In a microservice system, several microservices are involved in answering most user requests; the question is this: which ones are responsible for authentication, and which ones are responsible for authorization? You must also ask how much the microservices can trust each other:

- If one microservice authenticates a user, can other microservices trust that user?
- Are all microservices allowed to call each other?

The answers vary from system to system. The first part of this chapter discusses how to address these questions. The second part of the chapter outlines an implementation of one possible answer to the first question and shows a full implementation of an answer to the second question.

10.1 Microservice security concerns

Security is an important concern for almost any server-side system. It's also a very broad topic, much of which is outside the scope of this book. We'll concentrate on two areas of security that are relevant to developers of microservice systems:

1. Authentication and authorization
2. How to limit communication between microservices

Most systems have some functionality that's only accessible to logged-in users. Think about the point-of-sale system discussed in earlier chapters. In chapters 4 and 5, we talked about adding a loyalty program that allows registered users to receive special offers via email, based on their interests. If users are interested in golf, they'll be notified about good deals on golf balls. If users want to edit their interests—they may have given up golf and taken up quilting, instead—they need to be logged in. Otherwise, one user could edit another user's interests, resulting in their being notified about the wrong offers. Making sure a user really is who they claim to be is a matter of *authentication*. Deciding what the user is allowed to do—for instance, that they can edit their own interests but not anyone else's—is a matter of *authorization*.

Authentication and authorization are concerns that your systems will probably have regardless of whether you build them with microservices. The difference is that the granular nature of a microservice system begs the question: which microservices handle authentication and authorization? The following two sections address that question.

Data in motion vs. data at rest

Systems handle data. That data is most often essential to the systems, but it's also often essential to users. The data may be sensitive, such as users' home addresses, credit card numbers, or medical records. Even if the data isn't sensitive, it can still be valuable to the system—the product catalog of an e-commerce site isn't sensitive, but it's worth a lot to the business behind the site. The data your systems handle is important and needs to be handled safely. Broadly speaking, we can place data handling in one of two categories:

- *Data in motion*—When data is moved from one part of a system to another, it's said to be in motion. For instance, when collaborating microservices exchange data via commands, queries, or events, the data they exchange is in motion.

- *Data at rest*—When data is stored for later use, it's said to be at rest. For instance, when the microservice that owns a piece of data stores it in its database, that piece of data is at rest.

It's important that data be kept safe in both situations. This chapter concentrates on data in motion, because this is where a microservice system differs from systems with other architectures. The techniques for securing data at rest are the same in a microservice system as in a monolithic or traditional SOA system.

10.1.1 *Authenticating users at the edge*

Authentication is about verifying that users are who they claim to be. In the context of a microservice system, that means verifying that requests are made on behalf of the users they appear to be from. Let's look at the example in figure 10.1, which shows part of the point-of-sale system from chapters 4 and 5—the part centered around the loyalty program microservice.

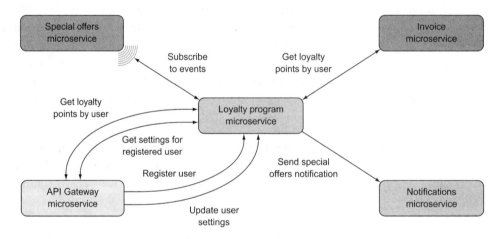

Figure 10.1   The loyalty program microservice in the point-of-sale system

If you add to the loyalty program a web frontend where registered users can edit their interests—for example, remove their interest in golf and add quilting instead—you get something like figure 10.2. You want users to be allowed to edit only their own interests, not the interests of others. Therefore, you require users to be logged in to be able to edit interests. In figure 10.2, you must authenticate the request to update user settings. The obvious place to perform the authentication is in the API Gateway microservice, which is the microservice that receives the request to update the user settings from the client. That request is made on behalf of a user, and you must verify that clients are allowed to make requests on behalf of users. You do so by making sure the user is logged in.

Figure 10.3 adds a login microservice to the system. The new microservice is responsible for handling the login process, but the API Gateway is still responsible for making sure only requests from logged-in users are accepted. Users are redirected to log in if they aren't already logged in. The login decides how the user can log in and leads the user through the process. Users can log in various ways, including the following:

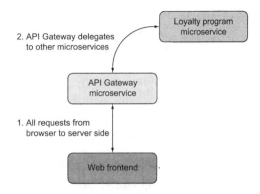

Figure 10.2 The web frontend for users of the loyalty program communicates only with the API Gateway.

- With a simple username and password
- With multifactor authentication
- Via an external system, such as active directory
- Via social identity providers like Facebook, Twitter, Google, and so on

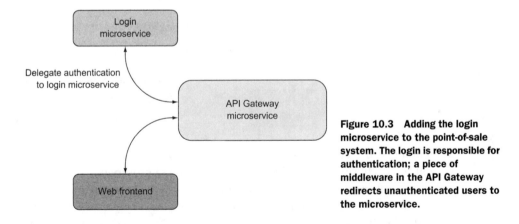

Figure 10.3 Adding the login microservice to the point-of-sale system. The login is responsible for authentication; a piece of middleware in the API Gateway redirects unauthenticated users to the microservice.

Whatever the login mechanism, the login microservice handles the login and gives the API Gateway proof of the user's identity in the form of an access token the API Gateway can verify. This can, for instance, be achieved with the OpenId Connect protocol.

Notice that user authentication is at the edge of the system—that is, it's done by the microservice that receives the request from the client. This is the general pattern; user authentication is done at the edge of the system.

The API Gateway microservice and the login microservice are examples of services that implement a technical capability. Furthermore, both are technical capabilities that are very similar across many different systems: in domain-driven design terms they are examples of *generic subdomains*—which means that they are prime candidates to be implemented by off-the-shelf products. The login microservice could be implemented by any identity provider, including products like Azure AD, AWS Cognito, Duende Identity Servcer, and Auth0. Likewise the API Gateway could be implemented by Azure API Management, AWS API Gateway, Traefik, and Istio.

10.1.2 *Authorizing users in microservices*

We've established that authentication is initiated at the edge of the system—by the API Gateway. When the request has been authenticated, you know who the user is, but you don't know whether the user is allowed to make the request. That's a question of authorization. The user is authorized to update only their own interests. If a client sends a request on behalf of user A that attempts to update the interests of user B, the system should reject the request.

In a microservice system, the microservice at the edge—the one that initiates authentication—often isn't the microservice that performs the action the request is about. Figure 10.4 shows the loyalty program again. The API Gateway microservice gets requests from the client, but the loyalty program microservice is responsible for keeping track of user interests. Therefore, the loyalty program updates users' interests.

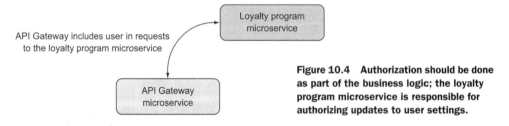

API Gateway includes user in requests
to the loyalty program microservice

Figure 10.4   Authorization should be done as part of the business logic; the loyalty program microservice is responsible for authorizing updates to user settings.

Remember from chapter 4 that microservices are primarily scoped to business capabilities—a business capability is handled by one microservice. That includes authorization, because authorization is part of the capability's business rules. This is in line with letting the loyalty program microservice decide whether a user is allowed to update interests. For this to work, the user identity needs to be passed along from microservice to microservice. In the loyalty program, the API Gateway microservice must include the user identity in the requests it sends to the loyalty program. The user identity can be included in the request to the loyalty program in several ways, depending on the level of trust you want between the API Gateway and the other microservices. If trust is low, the user identity can be passed in the form of a signed identity token that the loyalty program can validate or—if trust is higher—the user identity can be passed in clear text in a custom HTTP header. In both cases, the API Gateway authenticates the user and the loyalty program authorizes the user based on the user identity.

10.1.3 *How much should microservices trust each other?*

Microservices collaborate to deliver functionality to end users, assuming all microservices work toward delivering that end user functionality, but how can you be sure this is the case? Couldn't an attacker take control of a microservice and make it behave maliciously? Yes, that's possible. The question then becomes this: can one microservice trust another microservice? The answer to this question, unfortunately, is that it depends. It depends, for instance, on what threats the system faces and what the consequences of a successful attack would be. It can also depend on other factors, such as organizational structure and compliance with regulations.

At the highest level of trust between microservices, all microservices completely trust every request and every response from any other microservice. The microservices you've built so far in this book have, implicitly, had this high level of trust.

The principle of *defense in depth* suggests that this may not be a good idea. If an attacker can compromise just one microservice and have it make requests to other microservices, they will have full access to everything in the system. For a particular system, you may or may not be okay with that situation. If you aren't, you can limit which microservices can collaborate.

For instance, referring to figure 10.1, API Gateway and invoice are allowed to make calls to loyalty program, but notifications and special offers are not. On the other hand, only the loyalty program is allowed to make calls to notifications; the other microservices aren't. This limits the scope of what an attacker can do if they compromise one microservice.

> ### Defense in depth
>
> Defense in depth is an approach to security that uses several defense mechanisms in combination. The idea is to employ a layering strategy: if an attacker is able to get past the first line of defense, they meet the next line of defense. For example, even though a microservice at the edge of a system may authenticate and authorize all incoming requests, it shouldn't have administrative rights to the server it runs on. Even if an attacker circumvents the authorization and tricks a microservice into executing uploaded code, the attacker still doesn't have full control over the server— they're limited by what the operating system allows the microservice to do.

Even when you limit which microservices may collaborate, there's still an implicit trust that whatever one microservice sends to another is legitimate. If you use HTTPS instead of HTTP between microservices, you get transport-level encryption and thereby protection against an attacker tampering with requests going from one microservice to another.

As you can see, the level of trust between microservices will vary from system to system. You can choose from a range of trust levels. In the following sections, you'll implement a level of trust that follows the principles outlined so far in the chapter, but this isn't the only way to go about implementing these security principles.

10.2   Implementing secure microservice-to-microservice communication

For the remainder of this chapter, we'll look at implementing examples of the security around the loyalty program. The security requirements are as follows:

1 Authenticate users in the API Gateway.
2 Allow microservices to access the user identity.
3 Limit which microservices may collaborate.

The first two requirements can be fulfilled by an API Gateway. I will not go into the details of this, but only mention that you can use Azure API Management for this. The third requirement can be fulfilled using Kubernetes network policies, which we discuss with examples next.

10.2.1   Accessing the user identity in the loyalty program

In the loyalty program microservice, we will assume that the API Gateway is configured to perform user authentication and that the user identity is passed from the API Gateway to the loyalty program microservice as an identity token as illustrated in figure 10.5

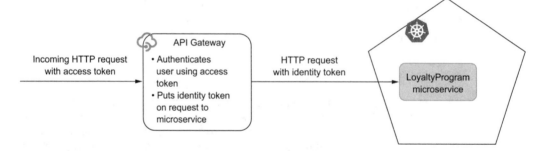

Figure 10.5   The API Gateway implemented in Azure API Management authenticates users and passes an identity token to the loyalty program microservice in Kubernetes.

In the following sections, you'll learn how to use the identity token in the loyalty program by

- Validating the token using ASP.NET authentication middleware
- Authorizing in MVC controllers

The first step is to add authentication middleware. We do this in the Startup class by adding authentication to the service collection. I will only outline the solution here since the details depend on the exact API Gateway configuration, which is beyond the scope of this chapter.

In the loyalty program, we can change the ConfgureServices method in Startup to the following.

Listing 10.1   Configuration to use JWT bearer tokens by default

```
public void ConfigureServices(IServiceCollection services)
{
  services.AddAuthentication(JwtBearerDefaults.AuthenticationScheme)
    .AddJwtBearer(x => x.TokenValidationParameters =
      new TokenValidationParameters
      {
        ValidAudience = ...,
        ValidIssuer = ...,
        IssuerSigningKey = ...,
      });
  services.AddControllers();
}
```

Add middleware to read and validate the identity token.

Configuration omitted since it depends on the API Gateway configuration

This outlines how to add middleware that reads and validates a JWT from the Authorization headers of incoming requests. This fits with an API Gateway configured to pass the user identity in a JWT in the Authorization header.

The next step is to make the user identity available for controllers, which is done by adding authorization to the pipeline in the Startup class, shown next.

Listing 10.2   Using authorization middleware to make identities available to controllers

```
public void Configure(IApplicationBuilder app, IWebHostEnvironment env)
{
  app.UseHttpsRedirection();
  app.UseRouting();
  app.UseAuthorization();
  app.UseEndpoints(endpoints => endpoints.MapControllers());
}
```

Add authorization middleware to the pipeline.

This means that the controllers can now demand that an identity token be present in the request using the Authorize attribute and can access the user identity through the User property on ControllerBase. For instance, to protect the PUT endpoint used to update existing users, we can add the Authorize attribute to the UpdateUser method in the UsersController:

```
[HttpPut("{userId:int}")]
[Authorize(AuthenticationSchemes =
    JwtBearerDefaults.AuthenticationScheme)]
public LoyaltyProgramUser UpdateUser(
  int userId,
  [FromBody] LoyaltyProgramUser user) =>
  return RegisteredUsers[userId] = user;
```

Only allow calls with a valid JWT.

This ensures that all requests to the PUT endpoint that updates users have a valid JWT token. But we still cannot be sure that the correct user is updated because simply using the user ID is passed in as part of the path: if this user ID is different from the user ID in JWT, one user can update another user. To guard against that, we have to compare it with the user ID in JWT. The values—or *claims*—in the JWT are available through the User property on the ControllerBase class, which the UsersController inherits from. The User property is a ClaimsPrincipal object, which has a collection of claims that contain all the claims from the JWT. Using this knowledge we can make sure that users are only authorized to update their own information.

Listing 10.3   Inspecting the claims on the user

```
[HttpPut("{userId:int}")]
[Authorize(AuthenticationSchemes = JwtBearerDefaults.AuthenticationScheme)]
public ActionResult<LoyaltyProgramUser> UpdateUser(
  int userId,
  [FromBody] LoyaltyProgramUser user)                    Find the user ID in the
{                                                        collection of claims.
  var hasUserId = int.TryParse(
    this.User.Claims.FirstOrDefault(c => c.Type == "userid")?.Value,   ◁──
    out var userIdFromToken);
  if (!hasUserId || userId != userIdFromToken)                  ◁──  Check that the token has
    return Unauthorized();                                           a user ID that matches
                                          Return an                  the user ID in the path.
  return RegisteredUsers[userId] = user;  unauthorized
}                                         response if the user
                                          IDs do not match.
```

Parse the user ID into userIdFrom-Token.

This concludes the implementation of the authorization in the PUT endpoint in the loyalty program. We chose a solution where the API Gateway passes a JWT with the identity of the user to the loyalty program microservice. If the level of trust is higher, we might choose to send the identity from the API Gateway to the loyalty program as plain text instead.

With authorization in place, we now turn our attention to limiting which microservices are allowed to communicate.

10.2.2 *Limiting which microservices can communicate*

Recall from figure 10.1 that one of the loyalty program's collaborators is the special offers microservice. Figure 10.6 zooms in on this collaboration.

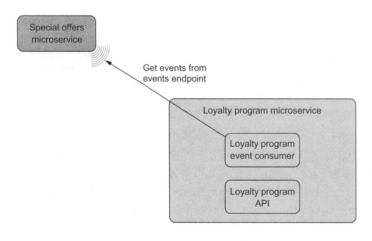

Figure 10.6   The loyalty program has an API and an event consumer; the event consumer uses the events endpoint in special offers to get events.

The loyalty program is deployed to Kubernetes as two containers: a loyalty program API container and a loyalty program event consumer container. The loyalty program event consumer is responsible for fetching and handling events from the special offers microservice. Therefore only the loyalty program event consumer container needs to be allowed to make requests to the special offers microservice.

We will use a network policy in Kubernetes to limit access to special offers so only the loyalty program event consumer is allowed to call endpoints in special offers. Neither the loyalty program API or any other microservice will be allowed to call endpoints in special offers. If there are other microservices outside the ones depicted in figure 10.1 that need access to special offers, the network policy can be extended to allow such access selectively.

Enabling network policies in Kubernetes

Network policies will unfortunately not work in the Kubernetes cluster we created in chapter 3 because the cluster needs a *network controller* that supports network policies. A network controller cannot be installed after the cluster is created, so we will have to create a new one with a network controller. In AKS, we can use a network plugin called `azure`, which will set up a network controller that supports network policies. In order to do so, we also need a slightly more involved network setup for the AKS cluster. The code download for this chapter contains a PowerShell script that creates an AKS cluster with a network controller and network policies enabled.

Docker Desktop does not support network controllers, so we cannot use network policies in it. In addition, network policies will have no effect in a Kubernetes cluster without a network controller; they will not produce any error, but they will not limit the traffic, either.

Back in chapter 5, we deployed the special offers microservice to Kubernetes using this manifest file.

Listing 10.4 Special offers microservice Kubernetes manifest from chapter 5

```
kind: Deployment
apiVersion: apps/v1
metadata:
  name: special-offers
spec:
  replicas: 1
  selector:
    matchLabels:
      app: special-offers
  template:
    metadata:
      labels:
        app: special-offers
    spec:
```

```
    containers:
      - name: special-offers
        image: your_unique_registry_name.azurecr.io/
          special-offers:1.0.0
        imagePullPolicy: IfNotPresent
        ports:
          - containerPort: 80
---
apiVersion: v1
kind: Service
metadata:
  name: special-offers
spec:
  type: LoadBalancer
  ports:
    - name: special-offers
      port: 5002
      targetPort: 80
  selector:
    app: special-offers
```

> **Create a pod with the special offers container.**

> **Create a load balancer that exposes special offers.**

This creates a pod with the special offers container and a load balancer that exposes special offers outside Kubernetes. We need to change this in two ways to get the limitation of the access to the special offers microservice we want. First, we will change the service section so that it does not expose special offers outside Kubernetes. Second, we will add a network policy.

The first change is simple. We only have to remove the line `type: LoadBalancer`. This means that we are no longer creating a load balancer, but we will still create the service.

The second change—introducing a network policy—adds another section to the manifest that specifies only the loyalty program event consumer is allowed to access special offers. The final special offers manifest in the `special-offers.yaml` looks like this.

> Listing 10.5   **Modified manifest for special offers with a network policy**

```
kind: Deployment
apiVersion: apps/v1
metadata:
  name: special-offers
spec:
  replicas: 1
  selector:
    matchLabels:
      app: special-offers-pod
  template:
    metadata:
      labels:
        app: special-offers-pod
    spec:
      containers:
```

> **The deployment creates the pod with the special offers container.**

```
        - name: special-offers
          image: your_unique_registry_name.azurecr.io/
            special-offers:1.0.0
          imagePullPolicy: IfNotPresent
          ports:
            - containerPort: 80
---
apiVersion: v1                          The service is no
kind: Service                           longer a load balancer.
metadata:
  name: special-offers
spec:
  selector:
    app: special-offers-pod
  ports:
    - port: 5002
      targetPort: 80
---
apiVersion: networking.k8s.io/v1        A network
kind: NetworkPolicy                     policy
metadata:
  name: special-offers-network-policy
spec:
  podSelector:
    matchLabels:                        The network policy applies
      app: special-offers-pod           to the special offers pod.
  policyTypes:
  - Ingress                             The policy controls incoming
  ingress:                              traffic to the special offers pod.
    - from:
      - podSelector:
          matchLabels:                  Allow only the loyalty
            app: loyalty-program-consumer   program consumer.
```

This will ensure that only the loyalty program event consumer can make calls to special offers. The network policy works by defining which pods it applies to—the special offers pod—and by defining which pod can call containers in pods protected by the policy. The policies allow pods with the label app: loyalty-program-consumer to call into special offers, but no other pods. The only pod with that label is the loyalty program event consumer.

To confirm that the loyalty program event consumer is indeed able to make calls to special offers we can inspect the logs from the event consumer using this command

```
kubectl logs -lapp=loyalty-program-consumer --all-containers
```

which will show the logs from the last few invocations of the loyalty program event consumer.

This concludes the implementation of the security requirements. You've fulfilled these requirements by leaning on Azure API Management to play the role of API Gateway and perform authentication, by using ASP.NET's support for JWTs, enabling the business logic in controllers to perform authorization, and by relying on Kubernetes network policies to limit which microservices can communicate.

Summary

- Users should be authenticated at the edge of the system. That is, the microservice that first receives a user request should initiate authentication.
- Authorization should happen in the microservice system in the microservice that owns whatever data or action the request is for. The principle is that authorization is part of the business rules belonging to a business capability. Because microservices are—as you saw in chapter 4—designed around business capabilities, it follows that a microservice responsible for a business capability should also be responsible for any authorization related to that business capability.
- The principle of security in-depth requires that you consider the level of trust you can accept between microservices. In some systems, it may be acceptable for microservices to trust requests from other microservices. In other systems, it may not.
- There's a tradeoff between the convenience of having a high degree of trust between microservices and the security that follows from a lower degree of trust.
- You can introduce a login microservice that's responsible for all authentication, including both end user authentication and authentication of calls from one microservice to another.
- You use Kubernetes network policies to control which microservices can collaborate by configuring scopes and which microservices receive which scopes.
- You can set up the login microservice using a number of different off-the-shelf products.
- You can use an identity token to pass the user identity around in a more secure way than including a user ID as plain text.
- You can read the identity token from incoming requests and use the claims in it to perform authorization in controller actions.

Building a reusable
microservice platform

A microservice system can include many microservices. You'll create new ones frequently, either because you're adding capabilities to the system or because you're replacing existing microservices. You want to be able to create them quickly but include all the code that makes them behave well in production—that is, the infrastructure code you've created in the previous couple of chapters. In this chapter, you'll start to create a platform—consisting of NuGet packages—that enables you to quickly create new, well-behaved microservices.

11.1 *Creating a new microservice should be quick and easy*

In chapter 1, I listed a number of characteristics of microservices, including this one: *a microservice is responsible for a single capability*. I explained that this characteristic is a variation of the single responsibility principle. Taking this seriously drives you toward having many microservices. And as the system evolves, you'll create new microservices fairly often when the system needs new end user functionality and as your understanding of the domain grows over time.

As discussed in chapter 4, you aren't likely to get the scoping of all microservices right the first time; and, when in doubt, you should create slightly bigger microservices. This also leads to the need to create new microservices along the way: when you gain a better understanding of the domain, the responsibilities of the different capabilities become clearer, and you'll sometimes discover that one microservice should be split in two.

Another characteristic of microservices from chapter 1 is as follows: *a microservice is replaceable*. The point is that a microservice can be completely rewritten quickly if its implementation becomes unsuitable. The code may get out of hand, or the design and technology choices you make early on may not be suitable for a growing load on the microservice; whatever the reason, you'll sometimes need to replace an existing microservice with a new one.

The bottom line is that when you work with a microservice system, you'll often need to create new microservices. If you don't, your system's services will slowly but surely become bigger, and its service boundaries will become less clear, meaning you'll lose the flexibility and speed of development that a microservice system provides. You need a way to make it both quick and easy to create new microservices so you won't be reluctant to do so.

11.2 *Handling cross-cutting concerns*

When we look at a single microservice, we see a number of components. For instance, chapter 2 broke the shopping cart microservice down into the components shown in figure 11.1.

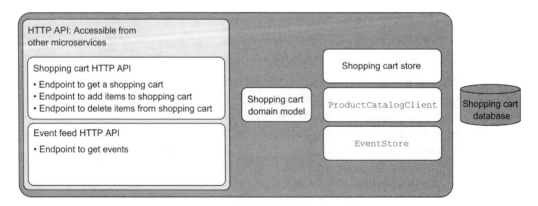

Figure 11.1 The view of the shopping cart microservice you've seen in earlier chapters shows a small number of components that together implement the shopping microservice behavior.

None of these components address the cross-cutting concerns such as monitoring, logging, standardized ways of handling database connections, security, and so on. Furthermore, none of these components are good candidates for places to implement those cross-cutting concerns. Why? Because all the components in figure 11.1 implement things specific to the shopping cart microservice. In contrast, cross-cutting concerns aren't specific to any one microservice. Therefore, we need to implement them in components separate from those in figure 11.1. Looking at the shopping cart from a different angle, in figure 11.2, you see that it gets HTTP requests through a web server, handles them using its various components, and returns responses to the web server, which then sends them back to the caller.

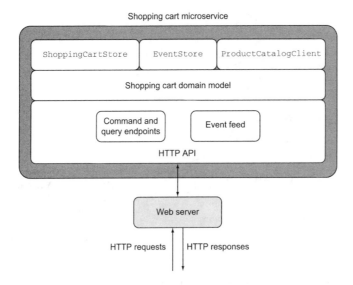

Figure 11.2   The shopping cart microservice takes in HTTP requests through a web server.

As I just mentioned, we want to keep the code for cross-cutting concerns separated from the components in figure 11.1. Furthermore, cross-cutting concerns apply to the microservice as a whole. This means a good place for the code that handles cross-cutting concerns is between the web server and the endpoint handlers in our MVC controller (see figure 11.3).

The pieces of code between the web server and the endpoint handlers form a pipeline: every request flows through each piece in turn before reaching the endpoint handler in the MVC controller. Likewise, the response from the endpoint handler flows back through the same pipeline before reaching the web server, which sends the response back to the caller. In this chapter, you'll use ASP.NET middleware to implement such a pipeline; each piece of the pipeline is called *middleware.* As you have seen

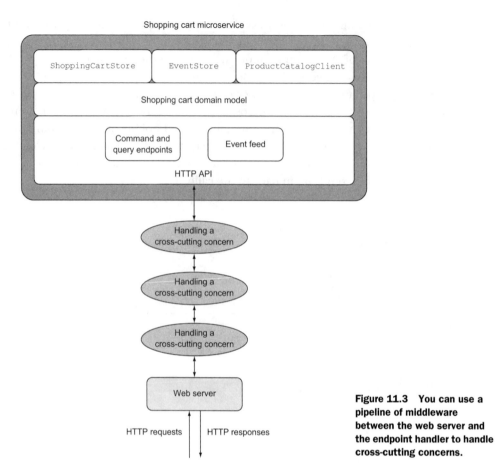

Figure 11.3 **You can use a pipeline of middleware between the web server and the endpoint handler to handle cross-cutting concerns.**

in previous chapters, ASP.NET supports many of the cross-cutting concerns out of the box—request logging and monitoring endpoints, for instance—often using middleware under the hood. As you move into concerns that are more specific to your environment, middleware can turn out to be very helpful. Later in this chapter, I give you an introduction to writing and testing your own middleware, but first let's take a look at gathering these cross-cutting concerns in a reusable microservice platform.

11.3 *Creating a reusable microservice platform*

Chapters 9 and 10 explained that microservices must be well-behaved citizens in the production environment. They need to provide insight into their health through logging, they should allowing monitoring, and they need to follow the security standards you decide on for the system. Thus, creating a new microservice involves more than just creating a new, empty ASP.NET project.

That's why I recommend building a standard microservice platform to use across your ASP.NET-based microservices in a microservices system. As shown in figure 11.4,

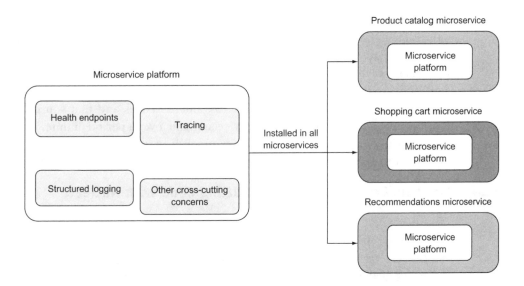

Figure 11.4 The microservice platform is a collection of implementations of technical concerns that cut across all microservices. The platform is installed in—and thus becomes part of—every microservice.

the platform is installed in every microservice. Later in this chapter, you'll create a first iteration of such a platform, including the following:

- Monitoring endpoints that fit into Kubernetes
- Logging configuration that streamlines structured logging and tracing

These are the platform areas I've chosen to cover for this book, but they aren't necessarily the things you'll need in a microservice platform for your system. I've tried to include common components. In particular, I think such platforms should include the monitoring, tracing, and structured logging bits. They don't have to be in the exact form used in this book; you may, for instance, prefer a different tracing standard or another logging framework. Depending on the approach you choose to use for security between microservices, you may also have an opportunity to make security easier by putting cross-cutting security code in the platform. Furthermore, you should consider including policies related to technologies you use in many microservices— for example, handling database connections.

The other side of the coin is this: should you include more in your microservice platform? There's no overarching answer, but you should be cautious about adding items; every time you include something in the platform, it becomes a little bigger and heavier. In addition, when you add something that all microservices are expected to include, what happens if they aren't running the same version of the platform? Can other microservices handle that? Can the infrastructure around your microservice system handle that? If the platform grows into something that must be in sync across all microservices, but it changes often, it becomes a serious bottleneck instead of an enabler. First, the platform must be updated in the code base of each microservice, and then each microservice must be deployed. If there are many microservices, that's a lot of work; and each time a new microservice is created, it becomes even more work.

Ideally, your microservice platform will hit the sweet spot of including only technical concerns that really do cut across microservices and that you can update incrementally—that is, in one microservice at a time over a period of time. This makes the barrier to creating a new microservice much lower: you need less-detailed knowledge about the cross-cutting technical concerns, and less effort is required.

11.4 Packaging and sharing cross-cutting code with NuGet

Using NuGet for your platform

NuGet is a package format as well as a group of tools for installing those packages. Until this point in the book, you've only installed existing NuGet packages; all of them have been publicly available in the package feed on nuget.org. But NuGet isn't limited to installing publicly available packages. As you'll see in section 11.4, you can install packages from your private package feed. And you can also create your own NuGet packages—as you'll also see in section 11.4.1—and put them in your private NuGet feed.

We'll now turn our attention to the code required to build a small platform you can reuse across microservices. You've already built the functionality that goes into this small platform, but you've done so in one microservice at a time. Now, you'll extract the code from the microservices in which you created it and put it in packages you can easily install and use in new microservices. You'll use NuGet because it will give you easy-to-create packages that your microservice can install and use. You're already using many NuGet packages in your microservices, so it's part of your workflow; the packages in the reusable microservice platform will fit right in. Once we have this small platform in place, we will return to middleware as a tool for you to build more cross-cutting concerns into the platform to make it fit right into your specific system and organization. You'll build the platform from the following pieces:

- The health checks from chapter 9
- The tracing from chapter 9
- The structured logging from chapter 9

As shown in figure 11.5, the platform will consist of the following NuGet packages:

- `MicroserviceNET.Logging`—The structured logging and tracing
- `MicroserviceNET.Monitoring`—The health checks

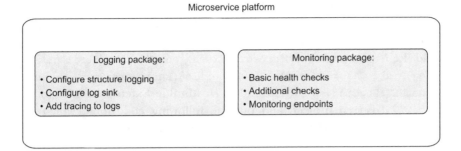

Figure 11.5   The microservice platform contains two packages, and each package contains code for a few technical cross-cutting concerns.

Your microservices will only have to add the `MicroserviceNET.Platform` package and a little startup code to use and configure the microservice platform. Does it seem like overkill to create NuGet packages for this? Maybe. ASP.NET already makes the monitoring and logging concerns pretty easy, so there isn't going to be much code in these packages at first. But these packages are only a starting point; as your system grows and your experience with operating it grows, you are likely to discover pieces and more details that you will want to standardize across your microservices. You could, if it is relevant for your particular system and environment, standardize how personal identifiable information is redacted from logs; how secrets (like database credentials) are handled; how events are fed into your data lake; how output caching is handled; how connection to database, queues, and other technologies are handled; and much more. It is certainly not necessary to standardize on all these things in all microservice systems, but most microservice systems will have their own list of cross-cutting concerns that do need some standardization and are good candidates for addition to the microservice platform. In the following sections, you'll create each of the two NuGet packages.

11.4.1 Creating a logging package

In this section, you'll create the MicroserviceNET.Logging NuGet package by doing the following:

1 Extract the structured logging and tracing configuration created in chapter 9 from the shopping cart microservice to a class library called `MicroserviceNET.Logging`.
2 Add a convenience method that makes it easy to add the monitoring and logging middleware to an ASP.NET pipeline.
3 Create a NuGet package from the MicroserviceNET.Logging library.

The first step is to create a .NET class library and call it `MicroserviceNET.Logging`. You can do that with your IDE or with `dotnet`. Then, add the logging and tracing configuration code from chapter 9 and the NuGet packages used by that code to the `MicroserviceNET.Logging` library. I'll repeat the code here, but for an explanation of the code, refer to chapter 9.

Add the NuGet packages `Microsoft.Extensions.Hosting`, `Serilog.AspNetCore`, `Serilog.Sinks.ColoredConsole`, and `Serilog.Enrichers.Span` to the `MicroservicesNET.Logging` library. Then add a HostBuilderExtensions.cs file to the `MicroserviceNET.Logging` project, and put the following code in it, which configures Serilog as the logger and enriches all logs with trace information.

Listing 11.1   Logger configuration from chapter 9

```
namespace MicroserviceNET.Logging
{
  using Microsoft.Extensions.Hosting;
  using Serilog;
  using Serilog.Enrichers.Span;
  using Serilog.Formatting.Json;

  public static class HostBuilderExtensions       Configure Serilog
  {                                                as the logger.
    public static IHostBuilder UseLogging(this IHostBuilder builder) =>
      builder.UseSerilog((context, logger) =>
      {
        logger                     Enrich logs
          .Enrich.FromLogContext()  with metadata.    Enrich logs with
          .Enrich.WithSpan();                          trace information.
        if (context.HostingEnvironment.IsDevelopment())
          logger.WriteTo.ColoredConsole(
            outputTemplate: "{Timestamp:yyyy-MM-dd HH:mm:ss} {TraceId} {
              Level:u3} {Message}{NewLine}{Exception}");
        else
          logger.WriteTo.Console(new JsonFormatter());     JSON format logs
      });                                                  in production
  }
}
```

This is all the code you need in the `MicroserviceNET.Logging` project. This lifts the logging configuration code out of the shopping cart microservice and places it in a convenient extension method called `UseLogging` that we can call from the Program.cs file of each microservice that uses the platform.

Listing 11.2   Using `UseLogging` in a Program.cs

```
using Microsoft.AspNetCore.Hosting;
using Microsoft.Extensions.Hosting;
using MicroserviceNET.Logging

CreateHostBuilder(args).Build().Run();

static IHostBuilder CreateHostBuilder(string[] args) =>
  Host.CreateDefaultBuilder(args)                    Adds standardized
    .UseLogging()                                    logging configuration
```

```
.ConfigureWebHostDefaults(
    webBuilder => { webBuilder.UseStartup<Startup>(); });
```

To create a NuGet package from the `MicroserviceNET.Logging` library, you can use dotnet. Go to the project folder—the one where the MicroserviceNET.Logging .csprof file is located—and run this command:

```
PS> dotnet pack --configuration Release
```

This creates a NuGet package called `MicroserviceNET.Logging.1.0.0.nupkg` in bin/ Release. The package contains the code of the `MicroserviceNET.Logging` project compiled to an assembly. Furthermore, the package requires the three Serilog packages and the `Microsoft.Extensions.Hosting` package that we installed in `Micro-serviceNET.Logging`, which means that whenever this package is installed in a project, so are those four packages.

This package is ready to be installed and used in as many microservices as you want.

11.4.2 Creating a package with monitoring endpoints

In this section, we will create another NuGet package in the same way. This will contain the health check code for monitoring endpoints that Kubernetes expects. There are three steps to creating the new package:

- Create a new class library called `MicroserviceNET.Monitoring`.
- Add the health check code from chapter 9.
- Build the package with `dotnet pack`.

Once you have created a new class library called `MicroserviceNET.Monitoring`, you should add these NuGet packages to it, since they are used by the health check code:

- `Microsoft.Extensions.DependencyInjection`
- `Microsoft.Extensions.Diagnostics.HealthChecks`
- `Microsoft.AspNetCore.Http.Abstractions`
- `Microsoft.AspNetCore.Diagnostics.HealthChecks`

There are two steps to adding health checks. First, they are added to the service collection and then to the application builder. The first part we put in a new file in the `MicroserviceNET.Monitoring` library called ServiceCollectionExtensions.cs. We lift the code for adding health checks to the service collection from the shopping cart code from chapter 9 and supplement with a couple of convenience methods for adding more health checks.

> **Listing 11.3 Convenient extension methods for adding health checks**

```
namespace MicroserviceNET.Monitoring
{
  using Microsoft.Extensions.DependencyInjection;
  using Microsoft.Extensions.Diagnostics.HealthChecks;

  public static class ServiceCollectionExtensions
  {
```

```
    private const string Liveness = "liveness";
    private const string Startup = "startup";

    public static IServiceCollection AddBasicHealthChecks(
      this IServiceCollection services)
    {
      services.AddHealthChecks()
        .AddCheck("BasicStasrtupHealthCheck",
          () => HealthCheckResult.Healthy(), tags: new[] {Startup})
        .AddCheck("BasicLivenessHealthCheck",
          () => HealthCheckResult.Healthy(), tags: new[] {Liveness});

      return services;
    }

    public static IServiceCollection AddAdditionStartupHealthChecks<T>(
      this IServiceCollection services)   where T : class, IHealthCheck
    {
      services.AddHealthChecks().AddCheck<T>(nameof(T), tags: new[] {
        Startup});
      return services;
    }

    public static IServiceCollection AddAdditionLivenessHealthChecks<T>(
      this IServiceCollection services)   where T : class, IHealthCheck
    {
      services.AddHealthChecks().AddCheck<T>(nameof(T), tags: new[] {
        Liveness});
      return services;
    }
  }
}
```

Annotations:
- **Add a basic startup check and a basic liveness check.**
- **Tag with startup for later use.**
- **Tag with liveness for later use.**
- **Allow adding more startup checks.**
- **Allow adding more liveness checks.**

This simply registers very basic—empty—health checks for startup and liveness. The checks are tagged with either startup or liveness, which will be used when we add the health checks to the application builder. There are two more methods—`AddAddition-StartupHealthChecks` and `AddAdditionLivenessHealthChecks`—that make it easy to register additional checks and have them added to either the startup or liveness health endpoint.

The second step is to add the health checks to the application builder. We add another file to the library. Call it `ApplicationBuilderExtensions` and fill in the following code.

Listing 11.4   Convenient extension method for adding health endpoints

```
namespace MicroserviceNET.Monitoring
{
  using Microsoft.AspNetCore.Builder;
  using Microsoft.AspNetCore.Diagnostics.HealthChecks;

  public static class ApplicationBuilderExtensions
  {
```

```
        public static IApplicationBuilder
          UseKubernetesHealthChecks(this IApplicationBuilder app) =>
          app
            .UseHealthChecks("/health/startup",          ◁──┐ Add the startup endpoint that
              new HealthCheckOptions                         │ we use in Kubernetes manifests.
              {
                Predicate = x => x.Tags.Contains("startup")
              })
            .UseHealthChecks("/health/live",             ◁──┐ Add the liveness endpoint that
              new HealthCheckOptions                         │ we use in Kubernetes manifests.
              {
                Predicate = x => x.Tags.Contains("liveness") ◁──┐ Add all health checks
              });                                                │ tagged with liveness.
        }
      }
```

Add all health checks tagged with startup. ──▷ *(points to the Predicate = x => x.Tags.Contains("startup") line)*

The tags on the health checks are used to determine which endpoint they belong to. This ensures that the basic health check, as well any additional health checks, are added to the startup and liveness endpoints.

Now we are ready to build the NuGet package with the dotnet pack and start using the MicroserviceNET.Monitoring package. It will help us make sure that all the microservices that use it expose the same monitoring endpoints.

There is one decision to make, though, before we build the NuGet package. In chapter 9, we also created a DbHealthCheck that ran during startup and checked that a database connection could be established. If this is relevant for almost all your microservices, you can add it to MicroserviceNET.Monitoring, too. If it is only relevant for some microservices, we enter a gray area: if enough microservices use an SQL Server database, we can add another NuGet package to our microservice platform and add the DbHealthCheck to that. The microservices can then pull in this third package.

As a reminder, I'll repeat the code for the DbHealthCheck, renamed to MsSql-StartupHealthCheck to make the usage more explicit.

> **Listing 11.5 Startup health check that uses an SQL Server database**

```
namespace MicroserviceNET.Monitoring
{
  using System.Data.SqlClient;
  using System.Net.Http;
  using System.Threading;
  using System.Threading.Tasks;
  using Dapper;
  using Microsoft.Extensions.Diagnostics.HealthChecks;
  using Microsoft.Extensions.Logging;

  public class MsSqlStartupHealthCheck : IHealthCheck     ◁──┐ New name indicated
  {                                                           │ as MS SQL server
    private readonly HttpClient httpClient;

    public MsSqlStartupHealthCheck(ILoggerFactory logger)
    {
```

```
        this.httpClient = new HttpClient();
    }

    public async Task<HealthCheckResult> CheckHealthAsync(
      HealthCheckContext context,
      CancellationToken cancellationToken)
    {
        await using var conn = new SqlConnection(...);
        var result = await conn.QuerySingleAsync<int>("SELECT 1");
        return result == 1
          ? HealthCheckResult.Healthy()
          : HealthCheckResult.Degraded();
    }
  }
}
```

> **Make query to check if database is available.**

> **Use query result to determine health.**

Notice that `MsSqlStartupHealthCheck` implements `IHealthChecks`, which means it fits right into the `AddAdditionStartupHealthChecks` created. A microservice can use the `MicroserviceNET.Monitoring` package and the `MsSqlStartupHealthCheck`.

Listing 11.6 Registering health checks using the microservice platform

```
public class Startup
  {
    public void ConfigureServices(IServiceCollection services)
    {
      services
        .AddBasicHealthChecks()
        .AddAdditionStartupHealthChecks<MsSqlStartupHealthCheck>();
    }
  }
```

The microservice can expose these checks in the standardized monitoring endpoints by leveraging the application builder extension created.

Listing 11.7 Adding the standardized monitoring endpoints

```
public void Configure(IApplicationBuilder app)
    {
      app.UseRouting();
      app.UseKubernetesHealthChecks();
      app.UseEndpoints(endpoints => endpoints.MapControllers());
    }
```

> **Add the monitoring endpoints.**

We have created a first iteration of a microservice platform that helps standardize our microservice log, trace, and expose monitoring endpoints. To use the platform, the microservices need to install two NuGet packages—`MicroserviceNET.Logging` and `MicroserviceNET.Monitoring`—and use the host builder extension in Program.cs to set up the logging and extensions on service collection and application builder to set up the monitoring endpoints in the `Startup` class.

You are likely to identify more cross-cutting concerns that make sense to implement in the platform while you develop your microservice system. Some of these can likely fit nicely in the middleware pipeline in ASP.NET, which is the topic of the next section.

11.5 *The ASP.NET pipeline*

We touched very briefly on middleware in chapter 1, but now it's time for a closer look. ASP.NET allows us to put pieces of middleware that are executed for every request. Each request flows through each piece of middleware in turn. Together the pieces of middleware form a pipeline that the request flows through.

The set up in figure 11.6 is a pipeline with one piece of middleware. ASP.NET defines the interface used to communicate between each part of the pipeline. This is a uniform interface that all parts of the pipeline implement: each piece of middleware implements the interface. By having one uniform interface, you can compose a pipeline as you like. You can put more middleware into it, you can take pieces out, or you can swap them around. Because they all use the same interface, they can be rearranged as needed.

When the request and the response pass through the middleware, the middleware can read them and even change them. The interface used between the pieces of middleware is the `RequestDelegate` defined by ASP.NET:

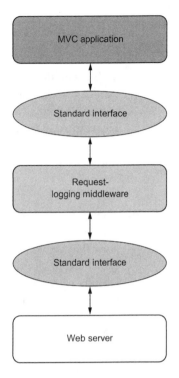

Figure 11.6   A pipeline is built from middleware that communicates through a uniform standard interface.

```
public delegate Task RequestDelegate(HttpContext context);
```

This delegate allows middleware to inspect and change the `HttpContext` and—as long as the middleware knows the next piece of middleware—pass it on to the next piece of middleware in the pipeline, just like figures 11.3 and 11.6 illustrate.

The `RequestDelegate` is a delegate type we can choose to implement with a lambda function, which is a lightweight way of implementing middleware. There's one slight complication, though: the middleware is supposed to be part of a pipeline of middleware, so it needs to know the next piece of middleware in the pipeline. We solve that with a small layer of indirection: we create a lambda that takes the next piece of middleware and returns a lambda that implements `RequestDelegate`. Let's look at that in code:

```
next =>          ◁──┤ The next piece
  ctx =>              of middleware        ◁──┤ The inner lambda
  {                                            is the middleware.
```

```
    System.Console.WriteLine("Got request");
    return next(ctx);
}
```

Let's break down this code snippet. First, the type of next is RequestDelegate and is expected to be the next piece of middleware in the pipeline. Second, the type of ctx is HttpContext. That means that the inner lambda takes an HttpContext as argument and returns a Task:

```
ctx =>                              The type of ctx
                                    is HttpContext.
  {
    System.Console.WriteLine("Got request");      next is a RequestDelegate,
    return next(ctx);                             so it returns a Task.
  }
```

Now that we've established that the inner lambda implements RequestDelegate, we can see how the outer lambda can be used to build up a pipeline. Calling the outer lambda with a piece of middleware creates a pipeline with two pieces of middleware: the middleware in the inner lambda first and the middleware passed in second:

```
RequestDelegate secondMiddleware = ...                   A piece of middleware
var fisrtMiddleware = next =>        The middleware from  from somewhere
  ctx =>                             the previous listings
  {
    System.Console.WriteLine("Got request");
    return next(ctx);                            The pipeline also implements
  }                                                      RequestDelegate.

RequestDelegate pipeline = firstMiddleware(secondMiddleware);
```

The fact that the pipeline itself is also a RequestDelegate allows for building longer pipelines and for combining them. During startup ASP.NET will build the pipeline, so it is ready to process HTTP requests as they come in.

The HttpContext contains everything related to the HTTP request and response. On the request side, this includes all request headers, the request path, and the request body. Likewise, on the response side, the HttpContext includes response headers, status code, and the response body. With access to all that, middleware can do anything to the HTTP request and response.

The RequestDelegate is a simple type, but enables a powerful concept. The middleware pipeline is both flexible and powerful, and I find it very useful. Next, I will discuss when to use ASP.NET middleware and when to use features of MVC.

11.5.1 *What belongs in middleware?*

ASP.NET gives you a way to build a pipeline of middleware that each request flows through. The different parts of the pipeline can react to the request and write to the response. Likewise, MVC lets you handle requests and write responses. With MVC, you primarily handle requests in methods in controllers, but you can also add code that's executed before and after the controller method. You do that by adding *MVC filters* to the MVC configuration. But what belongs where?

To decide what to implement in middleware and what to implement in MVC filters, you can follow a few simple rules of thumb:

- Code that addresses a cross-cutting concern and is meant to be used across many microservices belongs in middleware. These reusable pieces of code should have few dependencies so they don't enforce too many technology choices on the microservices in which they're used. Therefore, you want to keep them independent of MVC.
- Code that addresses a domain or business rule of a single microservice belongs in the application code behind an MVC controller. This type of code doesn't depend on HTTP, and therefore doesn't need to depend on ASP.NET or MVC. Putting it in a separate component—for example, a domain model—enables you to keep the implementation of business and domain rules clean and readable.
- Code that handles HTTP requests and responses in a way that's specific to a particular endpoint belongs in an MVC controller. This code interprets the incoming HTTP requests and then hands off control to the domain model. At the same time, that interpretation is tightly coupled to HTTP and to the specifics of the endpoint, making the controller the right place for it.
- Code that addresses a concern that cuts across all endpoints in a microservice, but not across several microservices, usually belongs in middleware, but not always. The more technical the concern is, the more I lean toward middleware; and the more domain or business logic there is in the concern, the more I lean toward MVC controllers or, in rare cases, an MVC filter.

I've introduced middleware and discussed what it's used for. Now we will turn to writing and testing middleware.

11.6 Writing middleware

We'll look at two ways to write middleware and hook them into the ASP.NET pipeline:

- *As a lambda*— You've seen this style earlier in this chapter, and we will build on that in the next section
- *As a class that has a method that implements the middleware signature*—You'll see this style right after we've taken another look at the lambda style.

The two styles are equivalent, and you can easily change between them. Which to choose for a particular piece of middleware is a matter of taste.

11.6.1 Middleware as lambdas

You've already seen middleware implemented with a lambda function. In this section, I'll show you how to add lambda-based middleware to the ASP.NET pipeline in a Startup.cs file.

This is the lambda middleware you've seen a few times before:

```
next =>                          next is a
  ctx =>                         RequestDelegate.
  {                                        The inner lambda is a RequestDelegate
    System.Console.WriteLine("Got request");   and takes in an HttpContext.
    return next(ctx);
  }
```

In Startup.cs, we can add middleware to the pipeline by calling the Use method on the application builder:

```
public class Startup
{
  public void Configure(IApplicationBuilder app)
  {                                         Use adds a piece of
    app.Use(next => ctx =>                  middleware to the pipeline.
    {
      Console.WriteLine("Got request in lambda middleware");
      return next(ctx);
    })
    ...
  }
}
```

That's all we need to do to add a piece of middleware to the pipeline. Now every incoming request runs through our little piece of middleware.

11.6.2 Middleware classes

Writing middleware as lambda functions works, but it becomes somewhat difficult when the middleware is more complex. In such cases, it's nicer to use a class to implement the middleware.

To use a class to implement middleware, you can create a class that has a method whose signature is a RequestDelegate.

Listing 11.8   Middleware implemented in a class

```
public class ConsoleMiddleware
{
  private readonly RequestDelegate next;

  public ConsoleMiddleware(RequestDelegate next)
  {                                         Holds onto next
    this.next = next;                       when instantiated
  }
                                            Has the RequestDelegate
  public Task Invoke(HttpContext ctx)       signature
  {
    Console.WriteLine("Got request in class middleware");
    return this.next(ctx);
  }
}
```

Middleware in this style takes in the next piece of middleware in the constructor and stores it in a private variable such that it can be called as needed in the `Invoke` method, which implements the middleware's behavior. To add this kind of middleware to the ASP.NET pipeline, you instantiate it and then use the `Invoke` method as a delegate:

```
app.Use(next => new ConsoleMiddleware(next).Invoke);
```

Or, we can use the more convenient extension method `UseMiddleware`, which essentially does the same thing by using reflection to find the `Invoke` method:

```
app.UseMiddleware<ConsoleMiddleware>()
```

Calling `UseMiddleware` is the preferred way to add class-based middleware. It's preferred because it's easier to read, but also because it allows us to use dependency injection: any dependencies in the middleware class's constructor, other than `next`, will be resolved from the service collection, just like dependencies in our MVC controllers. That opens the door to doing even more with middleware.

Now you know how to implement middleware as lambdas as well as classes. Next, let's look at testing middleware.

11.7 Testing middleware and pipelines

Testing ASP.NET middleware is straightforward: you create an `HttpContext` for the cases you want to test, and then you call the middleware, passing in that `HttpContext`.

> **NOTE** As detailed in chapter 8, you can create test projects from Visual Studio or using `dotnet`. These projects use xUnit, and that's also the test framework used here.

There's one small issue to overcome: in order to call middleware, you first need to provide it with a value for `next`. You get around that by passing in a `RequestDelegate` that does nothing:

```
RequestDelegate noOp = _ => Task.CompletedTask;
```

noOp is short for "no operation."

You'll use no-operation middleware in tests as a stub to provide to middleware under test.

With this in place, you can write tests for your middleware. Suppose you want to test the following class-based middleware that handles a redirect from `oldpath` to `newpath`.

Listing 11.9 An example piece of middleware

```
namespace Middleware
{
  public class RedirectingMiddleware
  {
    private readonly RequestDelegate next;
```

```
  public RedirectingMiddleware(RequestDelegate next)
  {
    this.next = next;
  }

  public Task Invoke(HttpContext ctx)
  {
    if (ctx.Request.Path.Value.TrimEnd('/') == "/oldpath")
    {
      ctx.Response.Redirect("/newpath", permanent: true);
      return Task.CompletedTask;
    }

    return this.next(ctx);
  }
}
}
```

If the request path is oldpath, it responds with a redirect. Otherwise, it calls the rest of the pipeline.

You can write a test for this middleware tests that oldpath is in fact redirected to newpath.

Listing 11.10   Test that invokes middleware directly

```
namespace MiddlewareTests
{
  using System.Threading.Tasks;
  using Microsoft.AspNetCore.Http;
  using Middleware;
  using Xunit;

  public class RedirectingMiddleware_should
  {
    private readonly RedirectingMiddleware sut;

    public RedirectingMiddleware_should()
    {
      this.sut = new RedirectingMiddleware(_ => Task.CompletedTask);
    }

    [Fact]
    public async Task redirect_oldpath_to_newpath()
    {
      var ctx = new DefaultHttpContext
      {
        Request = {Path = "/oldpath"}
      };

      await this.sut.Invoke(ctx);

      Assert.Equal(StatusCodes.Status301MovedPermanently,
        ctx.Response.StatusCode);
      Assert.Equal("/newpath", ctx.Response.Headers["Location"]);
    }
  }
}
```

Creates middleware with no-op as next

Sets up the HttpContext for this test

Invokes the middleware under test

Asserts on the contents of the HttpContext

The pattern of this test is to do the following:

1 Set up an `HttpContext` environment that mimics the scenario you want to test. This is done using the `DefaultHttpContext` type.

2 Create the middleware under test and pass in a no-op as the next piece of middleware. This terminates the pipeline, so calls to invoke on the middleware under test will also terminate.

3 Call the middleware with the `HttpContext` set up at the beginning of the test.

4 Make assertions on the contents of the `HttpContext` or other things that the middleware under test is expected to work on. If, for instance, the middleware under test creates a response that should be part of the `HttpContext`, and therefore accessible through the `HttpContext.Response` property.

You can use the same pattern to create more tests—for other paths than `oldpath`. See the following example:

```
[Fact]
public async Task not_redirect_other_paths()
{
  var ctx = new DefaultHttpContext
  {
    Request = {Path = "/otherpath"}
  };

  await this.sut.Invoke(ctx);

  Assert.NotEqual(
    StatusCodes.Status301MovedPermanently,
    ctx.Response.StatusCode);
  Assert.DoesNotContain("Location", ctx.Response.Headers);
}
```

This test follows the exact pattern as the previous test and is generally how you test middleware.

To test a longer pipeline of several pieces of middleware, you build the pipeline by passing one into the other as next, just as you passed noOp into your middleware. Once the pipeline is built, the rest is just like the previous middleware tests. You compose the pieces of middleware to form a pipeline that you can pass an `HttpContext` to and make an assertion of the result running the whole pipeline.

Now that you've learned how to write and test ASP.NET middleware, you're ready to use middleware to address cross-cutting concerns in the particular context of your project. Starting with a fairly simple microservice platform covering structured logging, tracing, and monitoring, you can extend it further with other cross-cutting concerns along the way. That way you can ensure that you can continue creating new microservices efficiently while also addressing cross-cutting concerns to make your life easier from an operational perspective.

Summary

- Because you'll often be building new microservices in a microservice system, you need to be able to quickly and easily build a new one from scratch.
- To meet cross-cutting requirements for monitoring, logging, and security, there are a number of things that all microservices in a system need to do. Exactly which things differ from system to system.
- You should develop a reusable microservice platform for your microservice system. With such a platform, it's simple to create new microservices that behave as they're supposed to in terms of logging, monitoring, and other cross-cutting concerns.
- A reusable microservices platform should address only cross-cutting technical concerns.
- A reusable microservices platform shouldn't address domain logic, because this differs between microservices.
- NuGet is a good format for distributing a microservice platform.
- You use the `dotnet pack` command to create a NuGet package.
- You can create NuGet packages to do the following:
  - Standardize monitoring endpoints to microservices
  - Standardize structured logging
  - Standardize tracing
  - Enforce any other technology-specific policies your system has
- You can build NuGet packages from libraries.
- You can use your own custom NuGet packages in your microservices.
- You can leverage ASP.NET middleware for cross-cutting concerns.
- You can easily write tests for ASP.NET middleware.

Part 4

Building applications

This part of the book adds a finishing touch to the picture: how to create applications for end users. You've learned how to break down a system into microservices and how to create those microservices. In chapter 12, you'll put a GUI on top of your microservices so end users can take full advantage of their functionality.

Creating applications over microservices

This chapter covers

- Building an end user application on top of a microservice system
- Understanding the composite application, API Gateway, and backend for frontend design patterns
- Using server-side and client-side rendering in web applications

So far, we've concentrated on implementing business capabilities in microservices and exposing those capabilities through HTTP APIs. But end users don't use HTTP APIs—they use web apps, mobile apps, desktop applications, smart TVs, VR headsets, and other applications on devices with interfaces geared toward humans. To give end users access to all the capabilities of microservices, we need to implement applications on top of microservices. This chapter is about doing that: we'll move from looking at designing single microservices to bringing all the microservices together in an architecture that supports building applications for end users.

We'll start with a broad, nontechnical discussion of how to approach building applications on top of a microservice system. Then we'll go into three specific architectural patterns for implementing applications: the *composite application, the API Gateway,* and the *backend for frontend* patterns.

12.1   End user applications for microservice systems: One or many applications?

There are several ways to go about building end user–oriented applications both from a user perspective and a technical perspective. We'll begin with the user perspective and look at a range of ways to surface the functionality in your microservices to end users in applications: from general-purpose applications that provide all the functionality of the system to a collection of small, specialized applications, each of which offers only a few capabilities. These two ways of surfacing functionality represent each end of a spectrum, as illustrated in figure 12.1.

Figure 12.1   A wide spectrum of application types can be built on top of a microservice system, ranging from general-purpose applications to very specialized applications.

Between the two extremes lie many other options for building applications that cover bigger or smaller parts of the microservice system's functionality. Where on the spectrum the applications for a particular microservice system should fall depends on the context of that particular system: its end users, its functionality, and so on.

Both ends of the spectrum have merit. The next two sections discuss them to give you a feel for the breadth of ways your microservice systems can provide functionality. The choice of where on the spectrum to land impacts how your application(s) should be built and which design pattern you should use.

12.1.1   General-purpose applications

A microservice system can provide a great deal of functionality. Consider, for instance, a line-of-business system for an insurance company. The system drives business processes, including selling policies, setting prices, and handling claims made by customers. Users include the following:

- Salespeople who call and solicit potential customers
- Actuaries who set policy prices and evaluate business risks based on estimated future claims and income
- Appraisers who evaluate goods that customers want to insure and about which customers make claims

- Claims adjusters who investigate and settle customer claims
- IT staff who oversee users and permissions

You implement all the different business capabilities of the insurance system in different microservices, but you may also decide to implement a common application that covers all functionality and is used by all users. This can be thought of as a *general-purpose application*. It can be any type of application—for example, a web or desktop application.

Various reasons may drive a decision to implement a general-purpose application that surfaces all functionality in the system. For example, some users in the insurance system may have more than one function, such as claims adjusters who also do appraisals. There may also be overlap between the functionalities needed by different types of users.

By managing their permissions, you can still limit what each user can do in a general-purpose application. But they all use the same application, and it provides all the system's functionality.

12.1.2 *Specialized applications*

Another option for building applications on top of a microservices system is to build lots of small, specialized applications. This is in some ways the opposite of the general-purpose application approach: you have many highly specialized applications, each of which surfaces only a little of the functionality of the entire system. Continuing with the example of a line-of-business application for an insurance company, you may have separate specialized applications for the following:

- Browsing the catalog of policies offered by the company
- Creating offers for potential customers
- Creating an insurance policy for a customer
- Creating reports about currently active insurance policies
- Creating forecasts about the cost of future claims
- Registering and investigating claims
- Appraising insured goods
- Settling claims

With this approach, users must use more than one application. That may sound like a bad user experience at first, but is it really? If you choose to implement the applications as web apps, they can easily link to each other, creating a cohesive experience even though the functionality is spread over many small applications. And the philosophy of doing one thing and doing it well can lead to very good applications for each piece of functionality. For instance, Facebook has an Android app called Selfies for Messenger, to do just one thing: take selfies and send them with Facebook Messenger. The app streamlines that single functionality.

Although I've mentioned only general-purpose applications and specialized applications, these aren't the only two possibilities. There's a spectrum of options (shown again in figure 12.2), ranging from one big application that provides all functionality in the system to a long list of single-capability applications. Other possibilities include the following:

- Splitting the large, all-in-one application into two applications, with administrative functionalities in the first and all other functionality in the second
- Joining some of the single-capability applications into slightly larger applications that cover all the functionalities required by one type of user

Single-functionality applications

All functionality in one application

Figure 12.2   A wide spectrum of types of applications can be built on top of microservices.

In the case of the insurance company, one middle-ground approach would be to create an application for each type of user. Salespeople would get a sales application with all the functionality they need, from canvassing for leads to signing a deal. Likewise, actuaries, appraisers, claims adjusters, and IT staff get applications tailored to their usage.

Although this approach avoids the complexities of big, general-purpose applications as well as those of a vast number of single-purpose applications, it does have its own issues: functionality will probably be duplicated between applications, some users play more than one role, and so on. There's no one right way; you need to decide where in the spectrum you fall, based on user-experience concerns rather than technical concerns.

Now, let's turn to the more technical side of things and look at three technical patterns for building applications on top of microservices.

12.2   *Patterns for building applications over microservices*

This section discusses the composite application, the API Gateway, and the backend for frontend design patterns. I'll explain each pattern in turn and also discuss their pros and cons. Then I'll turn to the question of when to use each one.

12.2.1   *Composite applications: Integrating at the frontend*

The first pattern for building applications over microservices is the *composite application*. A composite application is made up of functionality drawn from several places—in the case of microservices, from different microservices—by communicating with each one directly. In this pattern, each microservice provides both functionality and a UI for the functionality. Microservices may communicate with each other to perform their tasks; the composite application doesn't care.

Figure 12.3 returns to the insurance example, with a general-purpose application that includes all the system's functionality. The insurance system is built using microservices, so to provide all the system's functionality through the application, the application needs to draw on the business capabilities of many microservices. There are more microservices in the system than are shown in the figure, and the application won't draw directly from all of them. The application composes these functionalities into one application—thus the term *composite application*.

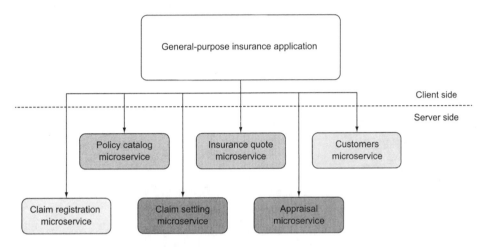

Figure 12.3 A composite general-purpose application uses many different microservices, each of which provides both functionality and a UI for that functionality.

When you build a general-purpose application in front of a microservice system as a composite application, the microservices provide functionality and also a UI to go with the functionality. As a consequence, the UI of the application is a composite of smaller UIs drawn from different microservices. Figure 12.4 shows an example structure for the insurance application's UI: it consists of four sections, each drawn from a microservice that provides both functionality and a UI.

How UI composition is achieved depends on the technology used to build the client. In the case of a desktop Windows Presentation Foundation (WPF) application, you could, for instance, use Managed Extensibility Framework (MEF; http://mng.bz/ 6NKA) to dynamically load components into the application, each of which could have its own piece of the UI. In the case of a web application, the UI can be built by loading HTML fragments and JavaScript bundles from the microservices into the main application and adding them to the DOM with JavaScript. In both cases, microservices provide both the functionality and the UI.

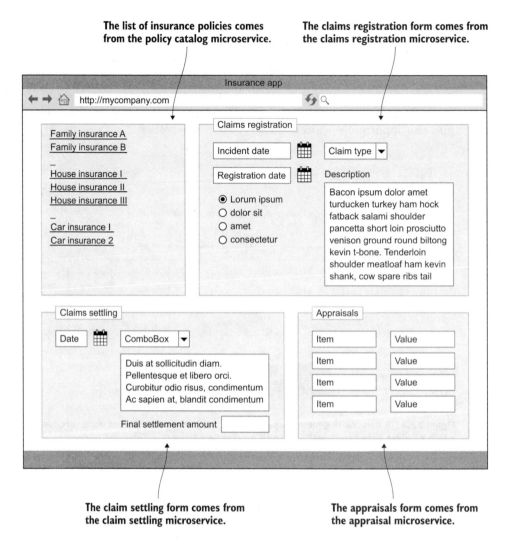

The list of insurance policies comes from the policy catalog microservice.

The claims registration form comes from the claims registration microservice.

The claim settling form comes from the claim settling microservice.

The appraisals form comes from the appraisal microservice.

Figure 12.4   A composite application takes UI components from different microservices and uses them to form a cohesive, composite UI.

Composite applications aren't all general-purpose applications; they can be smaller applications as well. For instance, if the insurance application has one application per user type, each application must provide functionality that belongs to different business capabilities and therefore to different microservices. It follows that each per-user-type application can be built as a composite application.

ADVANTAGES

When you're building composite applications, the UI is split into smaller parts according to business capabilities, just as functionality is distributed across microservices following business capabilities. That means the UI for each business capability is implemented close to the code for the capability and is deployed along with that code. Because the composite application draws the UI for the capability from the microservice, the application is updated every time a microservice UI is updated. This means the agility you gain by splitting the system into small, focused microservices applies to the application UI, too.

DISADVANTAGES

A composite application is responsible for integrating all the functionality implemented throughout the system of microservices. This can be a complex task: there are potentially many business capabilities in a microservice system, and the application's UI may not be split along quite the same lines, leading to pages or screens that include UIs from several different microservices but that need to feel like a single screen to the end user.

This kind of complexity can mean that the composite application has intimate knowledge of how the microservices work and, in particular, how their UIs work. If the composite application begins to make too many assumptions about the microservices' UIs, it becomes sensitive to changes in each microservice, and thus the application as a whole may break because of GUI changes in a single microservice. If you wind up in that situation, you lose the agility that's one of the major advantages of using a composite application.

Composite applications can work very well—but only if you can avoid implementing complex integrations.

12.2.2 API Gateway

The second pattern for building applications over microservices is the *API Gateway*. An API Gateway is a microservice with a public HTTP API that covers all the system's functionality but doesn't implement any of the functionality itself. Instead, the API Gateway delegates everything to other microservices. In effect, an API Gateway acts like an adapter between applications and the system of microservices.

When you build applications in front of a microservice system that uses an API Gateway, the applications are shielded from knowing anything about how the system functionality is split across microservices, or even that the system uses microservices. The application only needs to know about one microservice: the API Gateway.

Throughout this book, you've seen the example of a shopping cart in an e-commerce system, including an API Gateway. Figure 12.5 shows a request to add an item to a user's shopping cart coming in from the application to the API Gateway, which delegates to other microservices to serve the request. The role of the API Gateway in this case is to provide a single entry point for applications and thus simplify the system interface so that applications don't have to interact directly with several microservices.

You can build any kind of application in front of an API Gateway, from a general-purpose application that uses everything the API Gateway has to offer to specialized, single-capability applications that use only a fraction of the API Gateway, to everything in between.

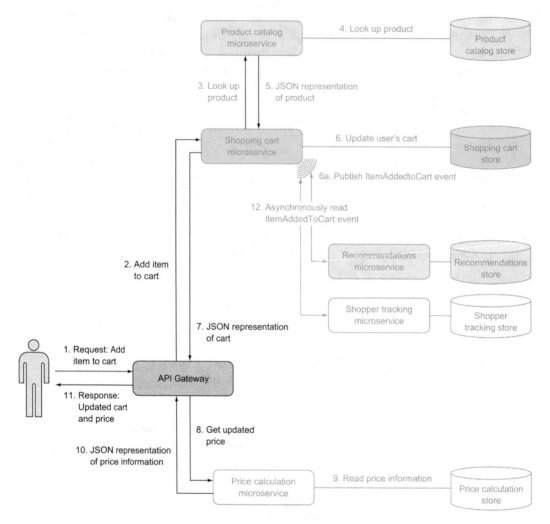

Figure 12.5   An API Gateway is the single entry point for applications. Any request from an application goes to the API Gateway, which delegates to the rest of the microservice system to fulfill the request.

ADVANTAGES

The main benefit of the API Gateway pattern is that it decouples applications nicely from the way the system is decomposed into microservices and hides that completely from applications. In cases where several applications have overlapping functionality or where some applications are built by third parties, using the API Gateway pattern facilitates the following:

- Maintaining a low barrier to entry for building applications
- Keeping the public API stable
- Keeping the public API backward compatible

Using an API Gateway means application developers need to look at only one API in order to get started. You can concentrate on keeping the API stable and backward compatible while other microservices evolve.

DISADVANTAGES

The main disadvantage of the API Gateway pattern is that the API Gateway itself can grow into a large codebase and display all the disadvantages of a monolith. This is especially true if you succumb to the temptation to implement business logic in the API Gateway, which may draw on many other microservices to serve a single request. Because it's combining the data from several microservices anyway, it's tempting to apply a few business rules to the data as well. Doing so may be quick in the short run, but it pushes the API Gateway down the path toward becoming a monolith.

In conclusion, the API Gateway pattern is very useful and often the right way to go. But keep a keen eye on the size of the API Gateway and be ready to react if it becomes so large that it's difficult to work with.

12.2.3 Backend for frontend (BFF) pattern

The third and final pattern for building applications over microservices that we'll look at is the *backend for frontend* (BFF) pattern. The BFF pattern is relevant when you need to build more than one application for a microservice system—for instance, the insurance system may have a web application for the most common functionality, an iOS app that appraisers can use on the road, and a specialized desktop application for actuarial tasks. A BFF is a microservice akin to an API Gateway, but it's specialized for one application. If you use this pattern for the applications in the insurance system, you'll have a BFF for the web app, a BFF for the iOS app, and a BFF for the actuarial desktop application (see figure 12.6).

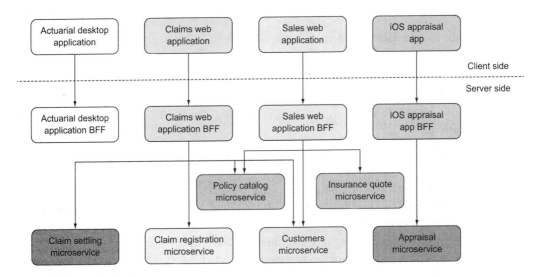

Figure 12.6 BFFs are used by a single application.

The point of a BFF is to support the single application built on top of it. That means the application and BFF are tightly coupled: the BFF exposes the functionality the application needs, and it does so in a way that makes writing the application as easy as possible.

ADVANTAGES

With the BFF pattern, each application gets to use an API that's tailored exactly to its needs. With an API Gateway, there's a risk of it becoming bloated as you add more and more functionality to it over time. With a BFF, this is less of a risk, because the BFF doesn't have to cover everything in the system, only the functionality needed by the application it serves.

It's fairly easy to know when something can be removed from a BFF: when no active version of the application it serves uses that functionality. Compare this to an API Gateway with several applications in front: something can be removed from the API Gateway only when no version of any of the applications uses it. All in all, BFFs offer a way to both simplify application development and keep the server-side focused and well factored.

DISADVANTAGES

In cases where you have several applications that provide similar or overlapping functionality to end users—such as having both an iOS app and an Android app targeted at the same type of end user—the BFF pattern leads to duplicating code among several BFFs. This comes with the usual disadvantages of duplication: duplicated effort every time there are changes to the duplicated parts, and a tendency for the duplicated parts to drift away from each other over time and end up working slightly differently in different applications.

The BFF pattern can strike a good balance between placing the burden of integration on the application and creating an API Gateway that may grow too large over time.

12.2.4   *When to use each pattern*

Now that you know about the three patterns for building end user applications for a microservice system, the inevitable question is which one to choose. All three patterns have merit and are useful, so I won't recommend one over the other. But when you're about to build an application, you must make a choice. I base that choice on the following questions:

- *How much intelligence do you want to put into the application?*

  For a line-of-business application that's only used within the company firewall and only on company machines, you may opt to build a desktop application with a lot of intelligence. In that case, the composite application pattern is the obvious choice.

  For a public-facing e-commerce application meant to run in any browser, with the risk of somebody trying to hack the app, you may shy away from putting intelligence into the application, making the composite application pattern less attractive.

- *Is there more than one application? If so, how different are the applications?*

  If you haven't put much intelligence in the application, and if there's only one application, or if all applications provide similar functionality—maybe even in similar ways—an API Gateway is probably a good choice.

  If there are several applications, and they provide different sets of functionality, the BFF pattern is a good option. With an API Gateway or with BFFs, the intelligence is on the backend. The API Gateway works well as long as it's cohesive—that is, as long as the set of all endpoints exposed by the API Gateway has a certain consistency in terms of how applications should use them and how they're structured.

  If some endpoints follow a remote procedure call (RPC) style and others follow a representation state transfer (REST) style, they're inconsistent, and cohesion in the API Gateway codebase will probably be low. In such cases, you should consider the BFF pattern. With BFFs, you can have some applications that work with an RPC-style API in one BFF and other apps that use a REST API in another, without compromising cohesion. Each BFF can be cohesive and consistent by itself, but you don't need consistency among BFFs in terms of API style.

- *How big is the system?*

  With a large system—in terms of the amount of functionality it exposes—an API Gateway can become an unmanageable codebase that exposes many of the disadvantages of monoliths. With large systems, using a number of BFFs is probably a better choice than one big API Gateway. On the other hand, if the system isn't that big, an API Gateway can be simpler than BFFs.

It's worth noting that you don't need to make the same choice for all applications. You may start with an API Gateway and build a few applications on it, but then decide that a new application with an innovative approach to doing things doesn't fit the API Gateway's way of doing things and give the new application a BFF. Likewise, you may have internal-facing applications that use the composite application pattern, while at the same time having external-facing apps that go through an API Gateway or BFFs.

12.2.5 *Client-side or server-side rendering?*

I've talked about three patterns for building applications over microservices: composite applications, API Gateway, and BFF. If you build web apps using these patterns, there's another question to address: should you use server-side or client-side rendering? That is, should you generate ready-to-go HTML on the server—using, for instance, Razor (http://mng.bz/6m4R) or Blazor server-side (http://mng.bz/o8ZD)—or should you render the HTML in a JavaScript application, using one of the many application frameworks such as Angular (https://angular.io/), Vue.js (https://vuejs.org/), React (https://reactjs.org/), or Blazor client-side (http://mng.bz/nrZd)?

  This, again, is a question that doesn't have one clear answer but depends entirely on the application you want to build. How dynamic is the application? Is it more concerned with working with data or with showing and entering data? The more dynamic the app is, and the more its workflow is about working with and manipulating data, the more I lean toward client-side rendering; whereas the more static the app is, and the more the workflow is about viewing and entering data, the more I lean toward server-side rendering. The main point, though, is that the choice between client- and server-side rendering is about the application you want to build, not the fact that you've chosen to use a microservice architecture on the server side.

All three patterns support both server-and client-side rendering. More than that, they support mixing server- and client-side rendering such that some parts of an application are server side–rendered and others are client side–rendered. For instance, the catalog of policies in the insurance system is static and read-only in most situations; it probably makes sense to render it on the server side. On the other hand, the valuation calculator is a more dynamic component that lets users play around with parameters before saving a final result; it's probably well suited for client-side rendering in a JavaScript application. The two can coexist in the same application:

- If you're building a composite application, it can draw in the server side–rendered catalog of policies as well as the JavaScript app for the valuation calculator. The microservice responsible for the policy catalog will provide the server side–generated UI for the policy catalog, whereas the microservice in charge of valuations will provide the valuation calculator JavaScript application.
- If you're using an API Gateway, it can contain endpoints that return HTML and others that return data—for example, in the form of JSON. It can even contain endpoints that can return either HTML or JSON data, based on the `Accept` header in the request. So again, an app can contain a server side–rendered policy catalog along with a client side–rendered valuation calculator.
- If you're using BFFs, you have the same possibilities for having endpoints return HTML, data, or both. In addition, BFFs give you the opportunity to make different decisions for different applications: in one BFF, the policy catalog can be server side–rendered, but in another it may be client side–rendered.

The choice between server- and client-side rendering of a web UI isn't impacted by the fact that the server side uses microservices. All the patterns we've looked at for building applications over microservices support both server- and client-side rendering.

12.3   *Example: A shopping cart and a product list*

Let's look at a concrete example and see the code required to implement a couple of pieces of functionality in one application. This example uses one application pattern and doesn't show the other two in detail; it will show you how to bring together functionality from a number of different microservices in an application, which is also at the core of the other two patterns.

The remainder of this chapter picks up the example of the shopping cart on an e-commerce website from earlier chapters. First I'll recap the example, then I'll show you a small UI for the shopping cart and a product list, and finally you'll implement them.

On the e-commerce website, users can browse products and add them to the shopping cart. When a user adds a product to their cart, the process shown in figure 12.7 is triggered. A number of things happen:

1. The item is added to the shopping cart.
2. A new total is calculated for the contents of the cart.
3. The recommendation and shopper tracking microservices are notified of the change to the shopping cart through the event feed on the shopping cart microservice.

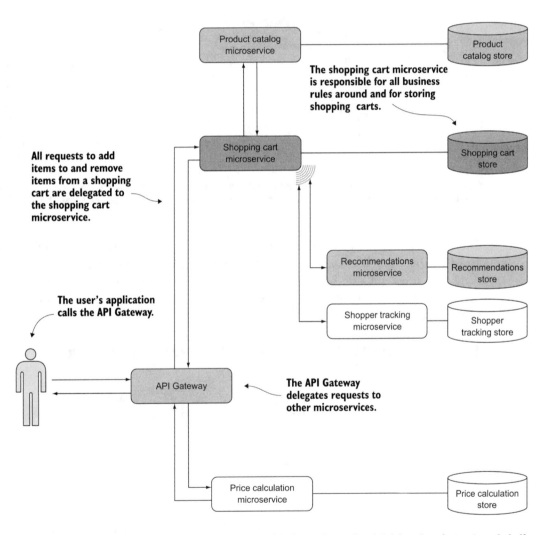

Figure 12.7   The shopping cart microservice is responsible for storing and maintaining shopping carts on behalf of users, but the API Gateway makes that functionality (along with other pieces of functionality) available to end users to use in a web app.

In the following sections, you'll implement part of this process as well as a simple product list that allows users to add items to their carts. Figure 12.8 shows the part of the system that you'll implement.

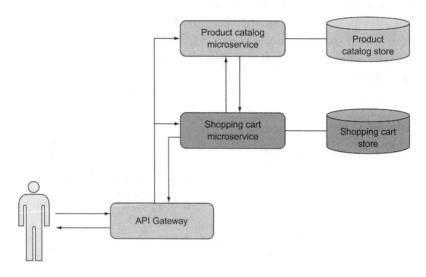

Figure 12.8   This example focuses on the API Gateway, the product catalog microservice, and the shopping cart microservice. You'll implement part of an application based on those three.

This will be enough to give users the page shown in figure 12.9, which lets users see a list of products and add them to their shopping cart. When a user adds a product to their cart, the right side of the page—the part showing the contents of the cart—updates and shows the new contents. The page also allows the user to remove products from the cart.

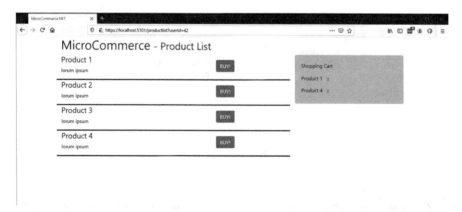

Figure 12.9   The part of the e-commerce application that you'll implement shows a list of products and lets users add and remove products from their shopping cart.

To implement this UI, you'll perform the following steps:

1   Reuse the product catalog and shopping cart microservices from chapter 5.
2   Create an API Gateway.
3   Create the product list from figure 12.9:
    – Create an endpoint in the API Gateway for fetching a page with the product list.
    – Make the new endpoint read the list of products from the product catalog.
    – Create a view with the list of products and return it from the new endpoint.
4   Add the shopping cart from figure 12.9 to the web page:
    – Make the API Gateway get the current state of the shopping cart from the shopping cart.
    – Add the shopping cart to the web page.
5   Create an endpoint in the API Gateway for adding products to the shopping cart:
    – Add a POST endpoint for adding products to the shopping cart in the API Gateway.
    – Call the shopping cart from the API Gateway to add the new product.
    – Update the view the user sees to reflect that a product was added to the shopping cart.
6   Create an endpoint in the API Gateway to remove products from the shopping cart.

You'll use the product catalog microservice and the shopping cart microservice from chapter 5 just as they are in the new API Gateway. You could, at this point, add the microservice platform from chapter 11 to these microservices, but for the sake of brevity you'll skip that step. The only thing you'll do in these microservices is run them on different ports when you run them at the same time on your development machine. You specify these ports in command line.

> **NOTE**   To keep the scope of this example tenable, I've cut some corners. Most notably, you won't implement a login system. Instead, you'll trust the user ID in the URL. Never do that in production. In chapter 10, we discussed how to deal with security in general, including authenticating end users, and how you should obtain the user ID.

12.3.1   Creating an API Gateway

Create a new project for the API Gateway the same way you've created projects many times before. Call the new project ApiGateway. Then, add the microservice platform you developed in chapter 11 as a NuGet package to the new project. The project file should look like the following.

Listing 12.1 Dependencies in the API Gateway

```
<Project Sdk="Microsoft.NET.Sdk.Web">

  <PropertyGroup>
   <TargetFramework>net5.0</TargetFramework>
  </PropertyGroup>
                                          The next two lines add
                                          the microservice platform.
  <ItemGroup>
   <PackageReference Include="MicroserviceNET.Logging" Version="1.0.0" />
   <PackageReference Include="MicroserviceNET.Monitoring" Version="1.0.0" />
  </ItemGroup>

</Project>
```

Next, change Progam.cs to initialize the logging from the microservice platform.

Listing 12.2 Using the logging from the microservice platform

```
using ApiGateway;
using MicroserviceNET.Logging;
using Microsoft.AspNetCore.Hosting;
using Microsoft.Extensions.Hosting;

CreateHostBuilder(args).Build().Run();

static IHostBuilder CreateHostBuilder(string[] args) =>
  Host.CreateDefaultBuilder(args)
    .UseLogging()                                    Use default logging from the
    .ConfigureWebHostDefaults(webBuilder =>          microservice platform.
    {
      webBuilder.UseStartup<Startup>();
    });
```

Then, change the Startup.cs file in this new project to do the same initialization of the MVC you've seen before, as well as the initialization of the microservice platform monitoring.

Listing 12.3 Initializing Nancy and the microservice platform

```
namespace ApiGateway
{
  using MicroserviceNET.Monitoring;
  using Microsoft.AspNetCore.Builder;
  using Microsoft.AspNetCore.Hosting;
  using Microsoft.Extensions.DependencyInjection;

  public class Startup
  {
    public void ConfigureServices(IServiceCollection services)
    {
      services.AddBasicHealthChecks();               Add default health endpoint
                                                     implementations.
```

```
        services.AddControllers();
    }

    public void Configure(IApplicationBuilder app, IWebHostEnvironment env)
    {
        app.UseRouting();
        app.UseKubernetesHealthChecks();          Use default health endpoints at the paths
        app.UseEndpoints(endpoints => endpoints.MapControllers());
    }
  }
}
```

Use default health endpoints at the paths
the Kubernetes deployments expect.

Now you have an empty project, ready for the implementation of the API Gateway.

12.3.2 *Creating the product list GUI*

The next step is to create the part of the application that lists products. Add a new MVC controller called ProductListController to a folder called ProductList in the API Gateway, and add a /productlist endpoint to that module. The ProductList-Controller will contain all the endpoints that serve the application to end users: it will have endpoints that give end users a web GUI and also endpoints used by the JavaScript in that web GUI.

To keep it simple at first, let's begin with an endpoint that does nothing. Then you'll add a GUI based on a hardcoded list of products, and finally you'll retrieve the real list of products from the product catalog microservice.

The ProductListController will serve the web frontend to end users, but start with the following endpoint that always responds with an empty 501 Not Implemented.

Listing 12.4 Placeholder endpoint implementation in the API Gateway

```
namespace ApiGateway.ProductList
{
    using Microsoft.AspNetCore.Mvc;
    using System.Threading.Tasks;

    public class ProductListController : Controller
    {
        [HttpGet("/productlist")]
        public async Task<IActionResult> ProductList([FromQuery] int userId)
            => StatusCode(501);                      Return the 501 Not
    }                                                Implemented status code.
}
```

The next step is to add a GUI that shows the product list. So far, you've returned data—for example, in the form of JSON—from all endpoints. Now, you'll return a GUI, in the form of server side–generated HTML using the Razor view engine, which allows us to dynamically generate HTML on the server side. To use Razor, you need to change the way you configure MVC slightly in the ConfigureServices method in the Startup class.

Listing 12.5 Adding the types necessary to use Razor views

```
public void ConfigureServices(IServiceCollection services)
    {
      services.AddBasicHealthChecks();
      services.AddControllersWithViews();    ◁─┐  Convenience method for adding
    }                                             controller and Razor view in one
```

To make the /productlist endpoint return a view, change it, as shown next. It returns a view called productlist and passes a hardcoded list of products into the view as a model object.

Listing 12.6 Hardcoded endpoint implementation in the API Gateway

```
namespace ApiGateway.ProductList
{
  using Microsoft.AspNetCore.Mvc;
  using System.Threading.Tasks;

  public class ProductListController : Controller
  {
    [HttpGet("/productlist")]
    public async Task<IActionResult> ProductList([FromQuery] int userId)
    {
      var products = new[]          ◁─┐  Hardcoded list of products
      {
        new Product(1, "T-shirt", "Really nice t-shirt"),
        new Product(2, "Hoodie", "The coolest hoodie ever"),
        new Product(3, "Jeans", "Perfect jeans"),
      };
      return View(new ProductListViewModel(products));   ◁─┐  Use a view called
    }                                                         ProductList and pass the
  }                                                           product list into the view.
                                                              (The ProductList view is
  public record Product(int ProductId,                        shown in listing 12.7.)
    string ProductName, string Description);
  public record ProductListViewModel(Product[] Products);
}
```

Listing 12.6 uses an MVC feature you haven't used before: View(new ProductListViewModel(products));. This is how you return a view from an MVC controller. The argument is a model object that will be passed to the view and that can be used while rendering the view. By convention the name of the view is equal to the name of the action method—ProductList in this case. This convention can be overridden by passing in a view name as the first parameter to View(...), but here the convention is fine.

To implement the ProductList view, create a new file called ProductList.cshtml next to ProductListController.cs in the ProductList folder. The file extension .cshtml tells ASP.NET that this a Razor view. The Productlist.cshtml file contains a simple view that iterates over the list of products in the model object and builds an HTML list from the products. To give the page just a little bit of structure, you import the Bootstrap CSS framework (http://getbootstrap.com), and add a few Bootstrap CSS classes here and there.

Listing 12.7 Simple product list view

```
@model ApiGateway.ProductList.ProductListViewModel

<!DOCTYPE html>
<html>

<head>
    <link rel="stylesheet" href="https://cdn.jsdelivr.net/npm/
        bootstrap@4.6.0/dist/css/bootstrap.min.css" integrity="
        sha384-B0vP5xmATw1+K9KRQjQERJvTumQW0nPEzvF6L/
        Z6nronJ3oUOFUFpCjEUQouq2+l" crossorigin="anonymous">     Imports
                                                                  Bootstrap
                                                                  and uses it
                                                                  for all styling
    <title>MicroCommerce.NET</title>        Adds a heading
</head>                                      to the page
<body>
<div class="container">
    <div class="page-header">
        <h1>MicroCommerce <small>- Product List</small></h1>
    </div>
    <div class="row">
        <div class="col-md-8">                        Iterates over all products
            @foreach (var product in Model.Products)   in the product list
            {
                <div class="row" style="border-bottom-style: solid">
                    <div class="col-md-8">
                        <h4>@product.ProductName</h4>       Writes out the
                        <p>@product.Description</p>         name of each product
                    </div>
                    <div class="col-md-4">
                        <p></p>
                        <button class="btn btn-primary" type="button">
                        BUY!</button>         Adds a placeholder BUY! button for each
                    </div>                    product. The button doesn't work yet.
                </div>
            }             End of the iteration
        </div>            over products
    </div>
</div>
</body>
</html>
```

(margin note on left: "Adds a row for each product")

If you run this, it will fail with a runtime error because ASP.NET cannot locate the ProductList.cshtml file. This is because ASP.NET expects view files to be in certain locations by default, but we put it right next to the controller, which is not one of the places ASP.NET expects. But, as I have mentioned in previous chapters, I like to group files by what they are about in terms of the domain—the product list in this case. To fix this, we need to add a bit of code to the `ConfigureService` in the `Startup` class.

Listing 12.8   Configuring ASP.NET to find views in the same folders as controller

```
public void ConfigureServices(IServiceCollection services)
    {
      services.AddBasicHealthChecks();
      services.AddControllersWithViews();
      services.Configure<RazorViewEngineOptions>(x =>
        x.ViewLocationFormats.Add("{1}/{0}.cshtml"));
    }
```

> Configure where ASP.NET looks for view files.

This configures ASP.NET to look for view files named after actions in folders named after the controller. For instance, the view returned by the `ProductList` action in the `ProductListController` should be in `ProductList/ProductList.cshtml`, which is exactly where it is. With this in place, the `/productlist` endpoint works and returns a product list view with the three hardcoded products.

This code renders a product list, but the products are hardcoded in the API Gateway. They should be fetched from the product catalog microservice. To perform that, change the `/productlist` endpoint in the `ProductListController` to make an HTTP request to the product catalog to get the list of products. To do that, you will need an `HttpClient`, so first we will configure that in the `Startup`. For now, we will assume that the product catalog runs on localhost port 5001.

Listing 12.9   Configuring `HttpClient` for calling the product catalog

```
public void ConfigureServices(IServiceCollection services)
{
  services.AddBasicHealthChecks();
  services.AddControllersWithViews();
  services.Configure<RazorViewEngineOptions>(x =>
    x.ViewLocationFormats.Add("{1}/{0}.cshtml"));
  services.AddHttpClient(
    "ProductCatalogClient",
    client => client.BaseAddress = new Uri("https://localhost:5001"))
    .AddTransientHttpErrorPolicy(p =>
      p.WaitAndRetryAsync(
        3,
        attempt => TimeSpan.FromMilliseconds(100 * Math.Pow(2, attempt))))
}
```

> Point the HttpClient at the product catalog.

> Configure a retry strategy.

Now we can turn to the `ProductListController` again and use the `HttpClient` we just configured to get products from the product catalog.

Listing 12.10   Finished endpoint implementation in the API Gateway

```
namespace ApiGateway.ProductList
{
  using System.Net.Http;
  using System.Net.Http.Json;
  using System.Text.Json;
  using System.Threading.Tasks;
```

```
using Microsoft.AspNetCore.Mvc;

public class ProductListController : Controller                      Get
{                                                            IHttpClientFactory
  private readonly HttpClient productCatalogClient;              injected.

  public ProductListController(IHttpClientFactory httpClientFactory)   ◁──┘
  {
    this.productCatalogClient =
      httpClientFactory.CreateClient("ProductCatalogClient");       ◁──┐
  }
                                              Use the IHttpCLientFactory to create
  [HttpGet("/productlist")]                      the product catalog HttpClient.
  public async Task<IActionResult> ProductList([FromQuery] int userId)
  {
    var products = await GetProductsFromCatalog();
    return View(new ProductListViewModel(products ));
  }

  private async Task<Product[]> GetProductsFromCatalog()
  {
    var response = await
      this.productCatalogClient.GetAsync(           Use the product catalog HttpClient
        "/products?productIds=1,2,3,4");    ◁──┘  to call the product catalog.
    response.EnsureSuccessStatusCode();
    var content = await response.Content.ReadAsStreamAsync();
    var products =
      await JsonSerializer.DeserializeAsync<Product[]>(           ◁──┐
        content,
        new JsonSerializerOptions {PropertyNameCaseInsensitive = true});
    return products;
  }                                          Deserialize products from the
}                                             product catalog response.
...
}
```

Now that the list of products is fetched from the product catalog microservice, the view shows the correct products (see figure 12.10).

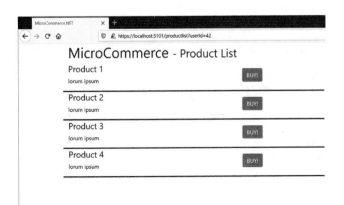

Figure 12.10 When you've fetched the list of products from the product catalog microservice, you can see them in the GUI.

12.3.3 Creating the shopping cart GUI

The next bit of GUI you want to add is the contents of the shopping cart. To do this, first extend the /productlist endpoint to call not only the product catalog microservice but also the shopping cart microservice, which means first we add another Http-Client to the IServiceCollection, assuming the shopping cart runs on localhost port 5201.

Listing 12.11   Adding shopping cart HttpClient to the service collection

```
public void ConfigureServices(IServiceCollection services)
{
  services.AddBasicHealthChecks();
  services.AddControllersWithViews();
  services.Configure<RazorViewEngineOptions>(x =>
    x.ViewLocationFormats.Add("{1}/{0}.cshtml"));
  services.AddHttpClient(
    "ProductCatalogClient",
    client => client.BaseAddress = new Uri("https://localhost:5001"))
    .AddTransientHttpErrorPolicy(p =>
    p.WaitAndRetryAsync(
      3,
      attempt => TimeSpan.FromMilliseconds(100 * Math.Pow(2, attempt))));
  services.AddHttpClient(
    "ShoppingCartClient",
    client => client.BaseAddress = new Uri("https://localhost:5201"));
}
```
> Add another HttpClient.

Use the new HttpClient to get the contents of the shopping cart.

Listing 12.12   Extending /productlist to fetch the shopping cart

```
namespace ApiGateway.ProductList
{
  using System.Net.Http;
  using System.Net.Http.Json;
  using System.Text.Json;
  using System.Threading.Tasks;
  using Microsoft.AspNetCore.Mvc;

  public class ProductListController : Controller
  {
    private readonly HttpClient productCatalogClient;
    private readonly HttpClient shoppingCartClient;

    public ProductListController(IHttpClientFactory httpClientFactory)
    {
      this.productCatalogClient =
        httpClientFactory.CreateClient("ProductCatalogClient");
      this.shoppingCartClient =
        httpClientFactory.CreateClient("ShoppingCartClient");
    }
```
> Get the shopping cart HttpClient.

```
[HttpGet("/productlist")]
public async Task<IActionResult> ProductList([FromQuery] int userId)
{
  var products = await GetProductsFromCatalog();
  var cartProducts = await GetProductsFromCart(userId);
  return View(new ProductListViewModel(
    products,
    cartProducts
  ));
}
private async Task<Product[]> GetProductsFromCart(int userId)
{
  var response = await
    this.shoppingCartClient.GetAsync($"/shoppingcart/{userId}");
  response.EnsureSuccessStatusCode();
  var content = await response.Content.ReadAsStreamAsync();
  var cart =
    await JsonSerializer.DeserializeAsync<ShoppingCart>(
      content,
      new JsonSerializerOptions {PropertyNameCaseInsensitive = true});
  return cart.Items;
}
private async Task<Product[]> GetProductsFromCatalog()
{
  var response = await
    this.productCatalogClient.GetAsync("/products?productIds=1,2,3,4");
  response.EnsureSuccessStatusCode();
  var content = await response.Content.ReadAsStreamAsync();
  var products =
    await JsonSerializer.DeserializeAsync<Product[]>(
      content,
      new JsonSerializerOptions {PropertyNameCaseInsensitive = true});
  return products;
}
}

public record Product(int ProductId, string ProductName,
  string Description);
public record ShoppingCart(int UserId, Product[] Items);
public record ProductListViewModel(
  Product[] Products,
  Product[] CartProducts);

}
```

Get the shopping cart for the user.

Deserialize the shopping cart from the response.

Add the shopping cart model.

Next, extend the view to render the contents of the shopping cart on the right side of the page.

Listing 12.13 Extending the view to include the shopping cart

```
@model ApiGateway.ProductList.ProductListViewModel

<!DOCTYPE html>
<html>
```

```html
<head>
    <link rel="stylesheet" href="https://cdn.jsdelivr.net/npm/
        bootstrap@4.6.0/dist/css/bootstrap.min.css" integrity="
        sha384-B0vP5xmATw1+K9KRQjQERJvTumQW0nPEzvF6L/
        Z6nronJ3oUOFUFpCjEUQouq2+1" crossorigin="anonymous">
    <title>MicroCommerce.NET</title>
</head>
<body>
<div class="container">
    <div class="page-header">
        <h1>MicroCommerce <small>- Product List</small></h1>
    </div>
    <div class="row">
        <div class="col-md-8">
            @foreach (var product in Model.Products)
            {
                <div class="row" style="border-bottom-style: solid">
                    <div class="col-md-8">
                        <h4>@product.ProductName</h4>
                        <p>@product.Description</p>
                    </div>
                    <div class="col-md-4">
                        <p></p>
                        <button class="btn btn-primary" type="button">
                        BUY!
                        </button>
                    </div>
                </div>
            }
        </div>
        <div class="col-md-4">                      ◁—┘  Adds a column on the right
            <div class="card bg-warning">                 for the shopping cart
                <div class="card-body">                          Iterates over the
                <div class="card-title">Shopping Cart</div>      products in the
                    @foreach(var product in Model.CartProducts)    shopping cart
                    {                                        ◁—
                        <div class="card-text">                Writes the name
                            @product.ProductName    ◁—┘  of each product
                            <button class="btn btn-link">X</button>   ◁—┐
                        </div>
                    }
                </div>                                       Placeholder button for
            </div>                                           removing products
        </div>                                               from the cart
    </div>
</div>
</body>
</html>
```

This view iterates over the products in the shopping cart and shows them all. With both the product list and the shopping cart, the view looks like figure 12.11.

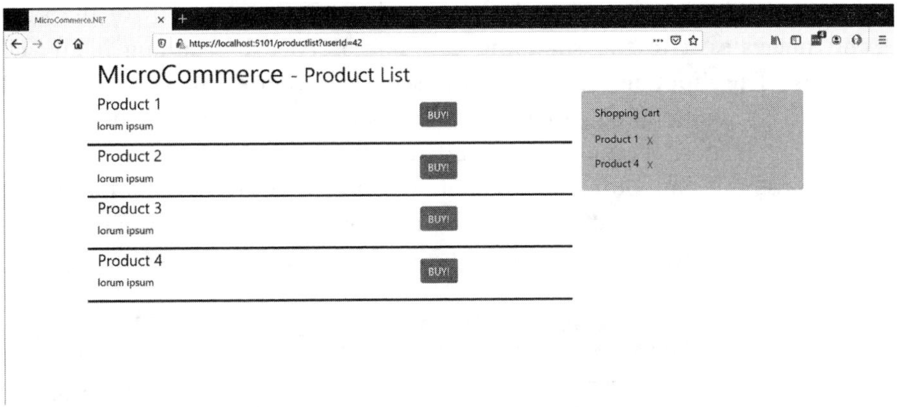

Figure 12.11 Now that you've built the first part of the application, it can show a list of products and an empty shopping cart.

You have the complete application GUI but no functionality. The BUY! buttons don't work, nor do the Xs in the shopping cart. You'll change this in the next two sections, where you'll add some behavior to the application.

12.3.4 Letting users add products to the shopping cart

The first piece of behavior you'll add will make the BUY! button in the product list work. You'll do two things:

1. Add an endpoint to `ProductListController` that allows the application to add a product to the shopping cart. This endpoint in the API Gateway is thin and delegates to the shopping cart microservice.
2. Add an `OnClick` function to the BUY! button that calls the new endpoint in `ProductListController`.

The following listing shows the endpoint in `GatewayModule` that lets the application add a product to the shopping cart.

Listing 12.14 Endpoint to add a product to the shopping cart

```
[HttpPost("/shoppingcart/{userId}")]              ←┐ New
public async Task<OkResult> AddToCart(             ┘ endpoint
    int userId,
    [FromBody] int productId)          ←┐ Reads a product ID from
{                                        ┘ the body of the request
    var response =
        await this.shoppingCartClient.PostAsJsonAsync(   ←┐ Uses HttpClient to
            $"/shoppingcart/{userId}/items",              ┘ call shopping cart
            new[] {productId});
    response.EnsureSuccessStatusCode();
    return Ok();
}
```

This endpoint receives some data—a product ID—in the body of the POST request and delegates it to the shopping cart microservice by sending it an HTTP POST request. The shopping cart—as you've seen in earlier chapters—handles adding the product to the shopping cart, storing the updated shopping cart, and raising an event that notifies subscribers about the update.

To use this endpoint from the application, you need to add a bit of JavaScript to the view: a function that calls the new endpoint and replaces the current page with the page returned from the endpoint.

Listing 12.15 Calling the endpoint to add a product to the shopping cart

```
async function buy(productId){                                            Function that should be
    const params = new URLSearchParams(location.search);                  used by the BUY button
    const rawResponse =
        await fetch('/shoppingcart/' + params.get('userId'), {
            method: 'POST',                                               Call the new
            headers: {                                                    endpoint in the
                'Accept': 'application/json',                             ProductListController.
                'Content-Type': 'application/json'
            },
            body: JSON.stringify(productId)
        });                                              Refresh
    window.location.reload(true);                        the page.
}
```

This function adds a product to the shopping cart. It should be called whenever the user clicks one of the BUY! buttons, so add an `onclick` handler to the BUY! button by changing the line in the view that renders the button for each product in the product list, as follows:

```
<html>
...
            <button class="btn btn-primary" type="button"
            onclick="buy(@Current.ProductId);">        Calls the buy function with
            BUY!                                        the product ID for the current
            </button>                                   product in the iteration over
...                                                     the list of products
</html>
```

That's all you need to do to make the BUY! buttons work.

12.3.5 *Letting users remove products from the shopping cart*

The last bit you need to implement will let users remove products from their shopping cart. Similar to the previous section, that means adding an endpoint to ProductList-Controller and adding an `onclick` handler to the X buttons in the shopping cart part of the application. Add a DELETE endpoint that again mainly delegates to the shopping cart microservice.

Listing 12.16   Endpoint to remove a product from the shopping cart

```
[HttpDelete("/shoppingcart/{userId}")]
public async Task<OkResult> RemoveFromCart(
  int userId,
  [FromBody] int productId)
{
  var request = new HttpRequestMessage(
    HttpMethod.Delete,
    $"/shoppingcart/{userId}/items");
  request.Content =
    new StringContent(JsonSerializer.Serialize(new[] {productId}));
  var response = await this.shoppingCartClient.SendAsync(request);
  response.EnsureSuccessStatusCode();
  return Ok();
}
```

Prepare the request to remove the product from the cart.

Add body to the DELETE request.

Send request to the shopping cart.

To use this endpoint, add another JavaScript function to the view, which is very similar to the previous JavaScript function except this one calls the DELETE endpoint.

Listing 12.17   Calling the endpoint to remove a product from the shopping cart

```
async function removeFromCart(productId){
    const params = new URLSearchParams(location.search);
    const rawResponse =
      await fetch('/shoppingcart/' + params.get('userId'), {
        method: 'DELETE',
        headers: {
            'Accept': 'application/json',
            'Content-Type': 'application/json'
        },
        body: JSON.stringify(productId)
    });
    window.location.reload(true);
}
```

Next, use this JavaScript function from the X button in the shopping cart part of the view:

```
<html>
...
        <button class="btn btn-link" onclick="removeFromBasket">X</button>
...
</html>
```

With this code in place, the example application works! The user can add products to and remove them from their shopping cart.

Summary

- There's a spectrum of possible kinds of applications to build on top of a micro-service system, from general-purpose applications covering all the functionality in the system to small, single-capability applications.

- Applications over microservices can be built as composite applications that draw in functionality and GUI components from various microservices and combine them together to form a complete application.
- The composite application pattern allows microservices to stay decoupled, but the composite application itself can become complex.
- Applications over microservices can be built using the API Gateway pattern, which puts one general-purpose API in front of all the microservices. That API Gateway is the only microservice the application uses directly, but it delegates all requests to other microservices in which the business capabilities are implemented.
- The API Gateway pattern can simplify application development and decouple applications from the server-side architecture.
- An API Gateway can grow bigger over time because it needs to expose all functionality. This is especially true if several applications use the API Gateway because it needs to support all scenarios in all applications architecture.
- Applications over microservices can be built with the backend for frontend (BFF) pattern. A BFF is a microservice that acts like an API Gateway, but for only one application.
- BFFs are less prone to growing bigger than API Gateways are.
- BFFs are tailored to the single application using them and should therefore make that application as simple to implement as possible.
- When you build web applications over microservices, you're free to use server-side rendering, client-side rendering, or a mix.
- All three patterns—composite application, API Gateway, and BFF—support server-side rendering, client-side rendering, and mixes of the two.
- The implementation of an API Gateway is very thin: all the endpoints you added to the example API Gateway delegate to other microservices.

appendix
Development
environment setup

This appendix describes how to set up a development environment for working with the code you write throughout this book. The development environment has five parts:

- *An IDE*— You can choose between using Visual Studio 2019 or newer, Visual Studio Code (VS Code for short), or JetBrains Rider. Visual Studio is Windows-only, whereas Visual Studio Code and JetBrains Rider both work on Windows, Mac, and Linux.
- *dotnet cli*—You need the dotnet command-line tool to build create, build, and run .NET projects from the command line.
- *REST client*—You need a tool for making HTTP requests. There are many such tools, including cURL, Fiddler, and Postman; I tend to use the REST client plug-in for Visual Studio Code, which I find easy to use, works on Windows, Mac, and Linux, and is compatible with the built-in HTTP request tools in JetBrains' IDEs.
- *Docker and Kubernetes*—You need Docker installed to be able to build and run containers. Furthermore, you need Kubernetes on top of Docker to be able to work with Kubernetes deployments on the localhost.
- *Azure cli*—You need the Azure command-line tool to set up a Kubernetes cluster in Azure.

I'll walk you through installing and getting up and running with the development environment in the following sections.

A.1   Setting up an IDE

There are three IDEs I recommend you use with this book's code. Which one you choose is a matter of taste; all work fine with everything in the book. I, for one, have been switching back and forth among all three while developing the code for the book.

A.1.1 Visual Studio

Visual Studio is the traditional choice for .NET development and has everything you'd expect from an IDE. Of relevance to the code in the book, Visual Studio gives you a good C# editor, code navigation, refactorings, NuGet package management, and launching and debugging of ASP.NET applications.

Visual Studio 2019 comes in a number of different editions. The free edition—Visual Studio 2019 Community—has everything you need to code along with the examples. To get Visual Studio 2019 Community, go to https://visualstudio.micro-soft.com/ and choose Download Visual Studio. Doing so downloads an installer. Run it, follow the instructions, and make sure the ASPNET and Web Development work-load is installed.

A.1.2 Visual Studio Code

Visual Studio Code is a lighter weight, cross-platform alternative to Visual Studio. It doesn't have the breadth of features Visual Studio has, but with the C# extension installed, it works well for the kinds of projects you write in this book: ASP.NET applications. Visual Studio Code provides a good C# editor, code navigation, some refac-torings, NuGet package management, and launching and debugging of ASP.NET applications.

You can get Visual Studio Code from https://code.visualstudio.com; click the Download button to access an installer suitable for your platform. Run the installer and follow the instructions.

You also need the C# and the NuGet Package Manager extensions for Visual Studio Code. To install them, go to the Extensions tab in Visual Studio Code, search for the C# and NuGet Package Manager plug-ins and follow the instructions.

A.1.3 JetBrains Rider

Rider is a full-fledged, cross-platform C# IDE based on the IntelliJ IDE platform and the ReSharper Visual Studio plug-in, both of which are tried-and-true JetBrains products. Rider provides good C# code navigation, refactorings, IntelliSense in csproj files, NuGet package management, and launching and debugging of ASP.NET applications.

You can download a free trial of Rider from https://www.jetbrains.com/rider/ but will need to buy a license to continue using it. To install, click the Download button and follow the instructions.

A.2 Setting up the dotnet command-line interface

You use the `dotnet` command-line tool throughout the book to run microservices, restore NuGet packages, create NuGet packages, and run tests. First, check if you already have the `dotnet` CLI bundled with your IDE by going to Powershell and typing `dotnet`. If the `dotnet` CLI is already installed, you will receive a help text from the CLI; if not, you get an error from Powershell. To install the `dotnet` CLI, go to http://dot.net, click Download, and follow the instructions to install the .NET SDK.

A.3   Setting up REST client in VS Code

REST client is a simple text-oriented extension for VS Code that allows you to make HTTP requests (see figure A.1). You use such requests throughout the book to interact with your microservices. Apart from being simple, REST client has the advantage of working on text files with the extension .http, thus making it easy to share example HTTP requests through version control. You will find such files in the book's code download and its GitHub repository. Moreover, the same files work in Rider in a similar UI.

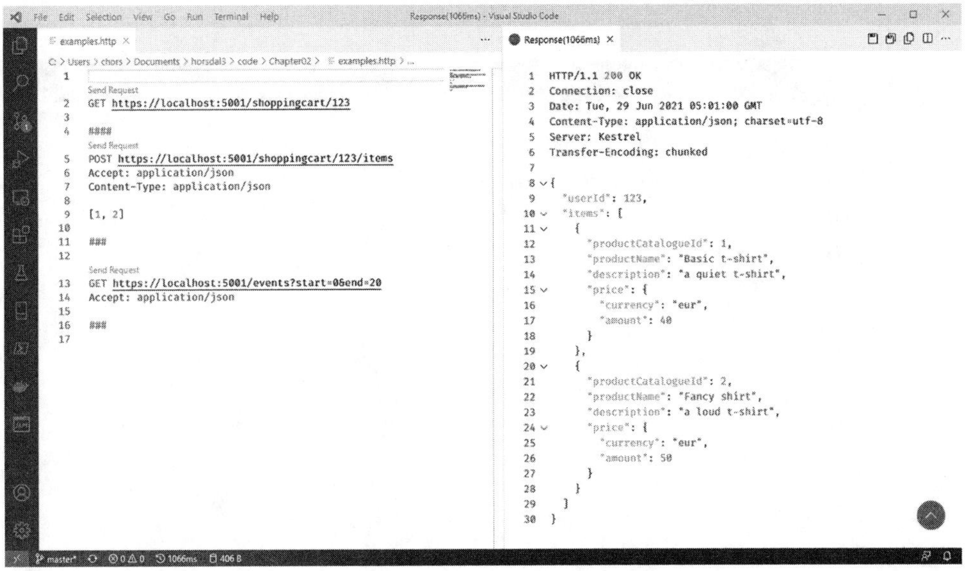

Figure A.1   REST client uses simple .http files. You make requests by clicking Send Request, and the response is shown in the right-hand pane.

To install REST client, go the Extensions tab in VS Code, search for REST client, and click Install.

A.4   Docker and Kubernetes

I use Docker in this book to package microservices as containers ready to deploy to a production environment, and I use Kubernetes on Azure as an example of a production environment. To be able to build Docker images, you will need to install Docker. With Docker installed, you can run and debug your containers, but to be able to run the containers the same as on Azure, you will also need Kubernetes.

If you are on Windows or Mac, you will be using Docker Desktop, and if you are on Linux, you will be using a .deb or .rpm package depending on your Linux distribution.

To install Docker, go to https://docs.docker.com/engine/install/ and follow the instructions for your platform. If you are on Windows, you should choose to use the WSL2 backend with Linux containers while installing Docker Desktop. Once Docker is installed, you should be able to call the `docker` CLI from your shell.

On top of Docker, you will need Kubernetes. If you are on Windows or Mac, you already have Kubernetes bundled with Docker Desktop and all you have to do is enable Kubernetes in the Docker Desktop setting, as shown in figure A.2. This will take a while the first time, since Docker Desktop will download, install, and start Kubernetes.

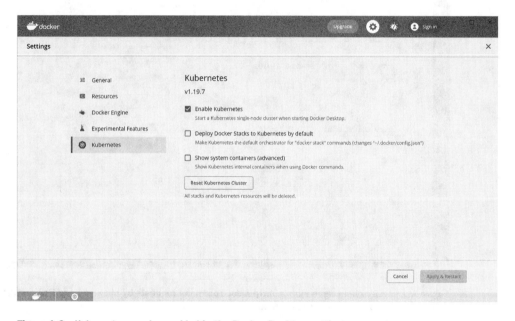

Figure A.2   Kubernetes can be enabled in the Docker Desktop settings.

On Linux, you have to get Kubernetes separately, and there are numerous options. One easy option is MicroK8S, which you can install by following the instructions at https://microk8s.io/. Once you have MicroK8S installed, you may want to add this alias to allow easy access to the Kubernetes command-line tool:

```
> snap alias microk8s.kubectl kubectl
```

Once you have Kubernetes installed, you should be able to call the Kubernetes command-line tool—kubectl—from your shell.

A.5 *Azure CLI*

In this book, I use Azure to set up a small Kubernetes cluster that I can deploy the microservices to as an example of a production environment. To follow along with that, you will need an Azure account and the Azure CLI.

To create an Azure account go to https://azure.microsoft.com/en-us/free/. To get the Azure CLI, head to https://docs.microsoft.com/en-us/cli/azure/install-azure-cli and follow the installation instructions for your platform. When you have installed the Azure CLI, you can log the CLI into your Azure account by running az login in your shell.

Now that you have an IDE, the dotnet command-line tool, a tool for working with HTTP requests, Docker, Kubernetes, and the Azure CLI, you're all set to code along with the examples throughout the book.

further reading

Microservices

Cramon, Jeppe. "Microservices: It's Not (only) the Size That Matters, It's (Also) How You Use Them," parts 1–5. 2014–2015. https://cramonblog.wordpress.com/2014/02/25/micro-services-its-not-only-the-size-that-matters-its-also-how-you-use-them-part-1/.

Fowler, Martin. "MicroservicePrerequisites." August 28, 2014. http://martinfowler.com/bliki/MicroservicePrerequisites.html. "MonolithFirst." June 3, 2015. http://martinfowler.com/bliki/MonolithFirst.html.

Lewis, James and Martin Fowler. "Microservices." March 25,2014. http://martinfowler.com/articles/microservices.html.

Tilkov, Stefan. "`Don't Start with a Monolith.'" June 9, 2015. http://martinfowler.com/articles/dont-start-monolith.html.

Newman, Sam. *Building Microservices: Designing Fine-Grained Systems.* O'Reilly Media, 2015. "Pattern: Backends for Frontends." November 18, 2015. http://samnewman.io/patterns/architectural/bff.

Software design and architecture in general

Beck, Kent. *Test Driven Development: By Example.* Addison-Wesley Professional: 2002.

Conway, Melvin E. "How Do Committees Invent?" *Datamation* (April 1968). www.melconway.com/research/committees.html.

"Defense in Depth" Wikipedia. https://en.wikipedia.org/wiki/Defense_in_depth_(computing).

Evans, Eric. *Domain-Driven Design: Tackling Complexity in the Heart of Software.* Addison-Wesley Professional: 2003.

Forsgren, Nicole, Gene Kim, and Jez Humble. *Accelerate.* IT Revolution Press: 2018.

Forgren, Nicole, Dustin Smith, Jez Humble, and Jessie Frazelle. "Accelerate State of DevOps 2018." https://inthecloud.withgoogle.com/state-of-devops-18/dl-cd.html.

Fowler, Martin. "TestPyramid." May 1, 2012. http://martinfowler.com/bliki/TestPyramid.html.

——————. "IntegrationContractTest." January 12, 2011. http://martinfowler.com/bliki/Integration ContractTest.html.

——————. "Inversion of Control Containers and the Dependency Injection Pattern." https://martinfowler.com/articles/injection.html.

Freeman, Steve and Nat Pryce. *Growing Object-Oriented Software, Guided by Tests.* Addison-Wesley Professional: 2009.

Hohpe, Gregor and Bobby Woolf. *Enterprise Integration Patterns: Designing, Building, and Deploying Messaging Solutions.* Addison-Wesley Professional: 2003.

Humble, Jez and David Farley. *Continuous Delivery: Reliable Software Releases through Build, Test, and Deployment Automation.* Addison-Wesley Professional: 2010.

Martin, Robert C. "The Single Responsibility Principle." May 5, 2014. http://mng.bz/RZgU.

"SRP: The Single Responsibility Principle." http://mng.bz/zQyz.

Nygard, Michael T. *Release It! Second Edition: Design and Deploy Production-Ready Software.* Pragmatic Programmers: 2018.

Vernon, Vaughn. *Implementing Domain-Driven Design.* Addison-Wesley Professional: 2013.

Technologies used

ASP.NET: https://dotnet.microsoft.com/apps/aspnet

Azure: https://azure.microsoft.com

Azure Kubernetes Serivce (AKS): https://azure.microsoft.com/en-us/services/kubernetes-service/

Dapper: http://mng.bz/7LHZ

Elasticsearch: https://info.elastic.co/Getting-Started-ES.html

Event Store: https://www.eventstore.com/

Kibana: www.elastic.co/products/kibana

Kubernetes: https://kubernetes.io/

.NET: https://dotnet.microsoft.com/

NuGet documentation: http://docs.nuget.org

OAuth: http://oauth.net/2

OpenID Connect: http://openid.net/connect

OpenTelemetry: https://opentelemetry.io/

Polly documentation: http://www.thepollyproject.org/

Scrutor: https://github.com/khellang/Scrutor

Serilog: https://serilog.net

xUnit: https://xunit.net/

index